Description of my book.

This is a true story about my struggle living with Bi-Polar disorder and an overview of what it is like to be locked away in a Psychiatric Hospital. The above photograph is of me outside Shelton following three years of freedom. This is my autobiography highlighting the ups and downs of Bi Polar and living an extraordinary life in amongst the ordinary. I am Bi Polar, but I am not crazy and I never was. I'm stark raving sane. I live with my demons every day but I am getting to know them now and some of us are on first name terms. I continually feel at war with myself and I just hope the good guy wins. I don't go crazy I am crazy. I just go normal from time to time.

Yes I am Bi Polar.

I take pills to stop the extreme lows. I take pills to help me sleep.

Junie Pritchard

I take pills for anxiety. I hate taking pills but I enjoy being stable.

I have this happy personality and a sad soul in one body. Having Bi Polar does not mean you are broken it means you are strong and brave for battling with your mind every day. Sometimes even to live is an act of courage. One day at a time sweet Jesus tomorrow may never be mine. People say that it is both a curse and a blessing to feel something so deeply. I only view it as a curse. Time will pass, these moods will pass and I will eventually be myself again. The only person I would like to thank for writing this book is me. Only kidding. You know who are.

FOREWORD

I met June in the summer of 2012 – I can't give an exact date as I had been taken to Shelton by a dear friend when I had got into a manic state. I remember vividly ringing the bell on Stokesay Ward to announce my arrival but after that my memories are extremely patchy as I believe I was given strong sedatives to calm me down – and these have a terrible tendency to blot out your memory. I remember bright sunny days hanging out in the garden at Stokesay Ward feeling very cheerful and June was the most fun person there. I used to roll cigarettes and chat to whoever was outside, often wearing the dressing gown I had been given by my mother when I was young - which I used to wear to fancy dress parties at university. June would often be outside chatting on her expensive looking iPhone – which I was very envious of as my family had taken away my smartphone and given me instead a really basic pay as you go phone with key numbers of family and friends stored on it… they were afraid I would ring a client or other business contact if I was left with my smartphone, much to my irritation. June would often be talking to her friends in a loud voice and roaring with laughter and generally seemed to be having a good time. It felt quite a lot like moments from the 6th form of the boarding school I had been sent to when my parents divorced – rebelling against the teachers and the restrictions of the place whilst at the same time knowing it was a time you would always remember as being significant in some special way.

I really admire June for having written this account of her struggles with bi polar and the people she met going through the whole process – I have tried to write about my experiences and given up as it means being very honest about some stuff of which I feel ashamed and want to keep private. I don't like to think of people knowing about my mental health issues and want to keep up the appearance of being 'normal', whatever that means. I'm now on a very low dose of a mood stabiliser which keeps me level and I haven't been troubled by any major episodes for over three and a half years, since I started on this present medication. Before that I have had some very bad reactions to psychiatric medication which affected my white blood count and meant my immune system was very weak – I was in this state when I arrived at Shelton in 2012 and felt the doctor (who features in June's book, Phillippa Walker) was very uninterested when I tried to tell her how scared I was of being in hospital and potentially exposed to various illnesses and infections. The nurses seemed to be a bit more sympathetic and concerned.

For me one of the most memorable moments in that whole

Junie Pritchard

period in Shelton was a night June mentions but doesn't describe in the kind of detail that I recall vividly. I was outside in the garden when it started and I'm not sure what kicked it off but suddenly someone was smashing plates in the kitchen and someone else was outside in the garden picking up the gravel and hurling it though the open patio doors and into the lounge. The level of violence in the air was very alarming to me as I don't feel able to diffuse anger in other people very effectively and I hurried indoors to get out of the way of it. Another patient, who was very creative and wrote poetry on her bedroom wall together with some amazing sketches, started to get very agitated and grabbed a long scarf and wrapped it round her neck several times and then pulled it hard until she started to go purple in the face and said she was definitely going to kill herself that night and no-one would stop her this time. I was horrified by her outburst as she was a lovely person and was clearly really struggling that night. To my alarm all the staff had disappeared from the scene and had somehow decided we were beyond help and control. I rang my husband and begged him to come and rescue me as I felt so vulnerable and scared but he just quoted me some encouraging words of advice and left me to it. I managed to get down the corridor to my room and so did June and we went in and barricaded the door closed with a chair. June then proceeded to get out her little tin of weed and roll up a cigarette with a bit in and offered it to me. I told her that I couldn't possibly have any because it used to make me very high when I smoked it some years previously – in fact I think it actively affected me so badly that combined with high levels of stress I was going through it brought on the psychosis I had suffered from on a couple of occasions. June was sympathetic but thought it was hilarious that I was so averse to smoking it with her as clearly she didn't get any bad effects from it and it just made her feel relaxed. I don't think she often smoked it and I have no idea how she got this little tin into the hospital… we stayed up chatting until the early hours and I started to feel much more calm after the scary events earlier. Suddenly the door was opened by a nurse who burst in and was horrified to smell the marijuana in the air and find June in my room with me and she angrily ordered June to her own room.

The next morning as I was walking past the door to June's room I saw a couple of official looking people looking at her bags and the little table by her bed and I saw the tin of weed sitting there – I quickly nipped in and picked up the tin and carefully put it into my pocket without them noticing. Later that morning, as soon as I was able, I went into the grounds of Shelton Hospital and hid the little tin in some nettles by a big oak tree, smiling to myself that June wouldn't find it there but neither would anyone else. A little later that same morning I was suddenly summoned by one of the nurses and told I needed to provide a urine sample – what for I demanded to know – and was told it was because they needed to know if I had been smoking dope with June. No, I angrily insisted, I would never touch the stuff because it made me very ill (I had even thought of becoming a drugs advisory person talking to young people about the dangers of soft drugs on susceptible people) and confidently produced for them the required sample. To my horror later that same day I was told the urine sample had come out positive! I knew (and so did they, I think) that it was due to secondary smoking and I didn't hear any more about it and it was all quite funny in hindsight. A year or so after this incident I met the woman who had threatened to hang herself with her scarf – coming out of the Community Mental Health Team offices – and I was hugely relieved to hear from her that she was feeling much better and had moved to another town where she was getting on okay. Oh and June did forgive me for hiding her dope in the bushes...

Several other people stick in my mind from my days in Shelton – mainly the bi polar people who were lively but also some of the depressives who were very beautiful and sensitive and clearly hated being in there. I'm so sad to think that the happy times we had making pottery, gardening and sitting out in the grounds of Shelton – none of those activities are available any more to the residents of Redwoods which is the hospital they have built next door to Shelton Hospital (which has now been redeveloped and turned into luxury flats since closing in autumn 2012) as the staff and facilities are just not there. There is still a wonderful lady who leads singing and other musical activities and there is weekly art therapy and there is a grand piano in the foyer and monthly concerts and a gym so it is not all hopeless. There are also IT sessions, which are hugely challenging when your head is full of the sedatives they give you when you're ill enough to be in The Redwood Centre. Fortunately I've only been in there once and I will do everything I can to avoid going there again. I know June found it to be a terrible place – the mixed wards where you are flung together with people in all states of mental distress is really upsetting – and she managed to get out after a few days there. I wish I had known she was in there as I would definitely have gone to visit her.

I'm looking forward to going to art classes with June soon – she's always such fun to be around. I feel a bit apologetic now though because I feel kind of flat and not a bundle of laughs like I was when we were in Shelton together. I love the way June has interspersed her story with jokes – it's so typical of her approach to life. I really hope this book gets the recognition it deserves. It's not easy to bare your soul to the world and more people – everyone in fact – need to know how painful it is to experience mental health issues. I want to thank the staff at Shelton just like June has done here for the good work they did and thank God that I haven't had to go back into hospital since 2014. Please read this book and recommend it to your friends as a very honest account of one woman's fight for life in the crazy world of bi polar moments.

Jennifer (not my real name) Hughes
September 2018

Chapter	1	Bi Polar Effective Disorder
Chapter	2	My Childhood
Chapter	3	JOEY'S FIGHT NIGHT
Chapter	4	The Ambulance
Chapter	5	JOHN
Chapter	6	BI POLAR
Chapter	7	FEBRUARY 2017

Chapter	8	THE ATTACK
Chapter	9	SUICIDE ATTEMPTS
Chapter	10	DR WASI MOHAMAD
Chapter	11	MY MUM AND ME
Chapter	12	SHELTON
Chapter	13	THE NURSES
Chapter	14	BARBADOS
Chapter	15	ANNIE G
Chapter	16	SOCIAL WORK
Chapter	17	EVEREST
Chapter	18	BRO HAFREN
Chapter	19	SHELTON
Chapter	20	THEFT
Chapter	21	BRISTOL
Chapter	22	MY LIFE NOW
Chapter	23	WASI

CHAPTER 1   BI POLAR EFFECTIVE DISORDER.

My name is June and I have Type 1 Bipolar. It was previously known as Manic Depression. It means I get incredible highs {mania} and desperate lows [severe depression]. One evening, 15 years ago in 2006 my sister and niece came to visit. They were already quite concerned about me because of my recent erratic behaviour. When they arrived and witnessed me self-harming, they called the police. I had no idea. Two very nice policemen arrived, and the Psychiatric Services were called. In some respects, it was quite funny as I was a Social Worker and the female Social Worker who arrived at my home was my colleague. Dr Wasi Mohamad was also present, and I thought we were going to have a party. I thought to myself "wow, who invited him?" as he is extremely aesthetically pleasing. They advised me that I would be going to Shelton, a psychiatric hospital. I had carried out an Assessment previously with a female patient at Shelton and believed that that is what they were asking of me now. However, they then mentioned that I should be admitted as a patient. What??? I hit the roof. I could not believe that this could be happening to me. A patient? F off. I'm afraid my language was very colourful that evening as it all seemed so surreal. In the end I asked my son Joey what he wanted me to do and bless his heart he said "I just want you to get well mum". So that was it. My bags were packed and off I went to Shelton. My niece Donna somehow drew the short straw and came with me the poor little thing and I bet she wishes she hadn't. I was strapped to a bed in the back of an ambulance and pushing my stomach out pretending to be pregnant, asking for gas and air. I think at one point the ambulance man wasn't sure if I was or not and I was going to get some but Dons grassed on me and told him I wasn't. Damn it Dons. I was at the time a smoker and I asked her half way there for a cigarette. Obviously I couldn't have one. She assured me that I could have one when I got there. Bad move bless her heart [when you are on a high you seem to take everything literally]. When I arrived there and was escorted out of the ambulance no one had a cigarette. Oh my god I went ballistic. "You promised me a cigarette". Thankfully the nurses gave me some tobacco and I calmed down a little. Poor Dons.

Before my illness Donna and her boyfriend used to visit every weekend. I was living with my partner at the time named Richard and my sons Joey and Jai. I was so happy. I had gained my Diploma in Social Work and won the European Championships in Kung Fu and Kickboxing and had begun training for the World Championships in Malta. I was on Cloud nine. Everything was going right. The four of us used to play drinking games, chatted and had fun with Joey and Jai. Then BANG. I was like a completely different person and had no idea what was happening to me. It really was so scary as I had no idea why I was feeling this way. I was becoming irritable and angry one minute and the next I would be in floods of tears. I would spend all weekend not being able to get out of bed. I went from being an extremely active person to having no energy at all. I went away with Rich's colleagues for the weekend and could not get up until late in the afternoon. His friends were so nice they bought me a postcard, which I still have saying "I can't understand what I am doing out of bed". That really wasn't like me. I felt exhausted practically all of the time and began getting depressed when I should have been so happy. A short time before I was admitted to Shelton I was in the process of selling my home which I owned jointly with Richard. He was absolutely lovely, but my illness got in the way and we ended our relationship. In fact it was Rich who first alerted my family of my illness. We sold the house and went our separate ways. I bought my new home whilst I was in hospital and this is where I returned to. Wasi could have stopped me purchasing my new home if he chose to. However, as I had begun the process of buying it before I was diagnosed with my illness he allowed the purchase to go ahead. Oh thank the lord for Wasi. Rich was an amazing man but is unfortunately no longer with us, but his memory will certainly live on in his sons. They are the spitting image of him and are really nice people.

SHELTON.

So here I am outside a huge mansion of a building named Shelton, which I knew to be a funny farm and I was escorted in. All that registered with me on the way in was the ward name: Stokesay. Shelton hospital was custom built in 1845 at Bicton Heath, Shrewsbury. The building was designed by George Gilbert Scott. The hospital was opened on the 18th March in 1845 with a capacity of 60 patients. At its peak in 1947 the hospital had 1027 patients. It was then known as a Lunatic Asylum. Oh my god, does this mean I'm a lunatic? Prior to the Community Care Act being brought in, in 1987 by Margaret Thatcher (Love her or hate her) I could have been locked away for the rest of my life. Oh my good god. I cannot think of anything worse. People say she brought in the Act to save money but I really do not care why. I thank the Lord she did. The listed red building and its landscaped grounds are being sold off as luxury flats and it closed as a hospital in September 2012. This is how Shelton looked when I had my mini breaks there.

Junie Pritchard

Isn't it beautiful? At Shelton I had to say goodbye to Donna who luckily forgave my outburst. She was amazing. I was escorted right the way through the ward passing some very scary looking women into the High Dependency Unit known as HDU. When I walked through the ward and saw the other patients I was absolutely terrified. I should imagine it is how it feels to enter a female prison even though I had done absolutely nothing to break the law. Anyhow here I am in HDU where you are watched 24/7. They even wanted me to leave the toilet door wide open in case I tried to harm myself. I thought at the time the nurses were a bit kinky but that really was not the case. Oh my god it was horrible. I was on such a high. I was kicking and punching the walls asking the staff for red wine. Red wine was my favourite drink and boy had I been abusing it recently. Joey's dad had hung himself and my dad died of cancer in the same week 12 months prior to this and I had been using red wine as a crutch. My job as a Social Worker was also extremely stressful. When I say abusing red wine at this point I was only abusing it compared to my standards. I did not drink anywhere near enough to effect my job or my kickboxing training.

HIGH DEPENDANCY UNIT.

People who are placed in hospital are either there on a section, or occasionally patients admit themselves voluntarily. Initially if you are aggressive or your behaviour is erratic you are placed in HDU for assessment. Some of the women were extremely violent and were either kept in there and later allowed out onto the ward or sent to a Secure Unit. I was locked in there for 4 weeks (not for being violent but for punching and kicking the walls) and then allowed out on to the ward. I was so highly medicated I don't remember coming out. My family visited and I did not remember them having been there. I was kept in that zombie like state for quite some time. My family were going to complain and they never complain about anything bless them.

When I was still in this Zombie like state my manager, Claire Turner came to the hospital and asked me to write up assessments of all the clients I had worked with which included half of hers. I could not believe it. I hardly knew what day it was or even what my name was and still she was asking me to work. I wanted to scream but no sound would come out. She really can go and f herself. The nasty uncaring cow . I didn't do it. In fact I couldn't do it

I am so very lucky as I have two wonderful sons, Joe and Jai, a beautiful daughter in law named Hannah and 4 siblings and thankfully we live in the same area and we are all very close.

I know of at least one woman in Shelton who told me she had

committed murder and at one point I was in the four bedded room with her. Really conducive to a good night's sleep. NOT. I believe that to work on a Psychiatric ward you have to be reasonably fit. If a fight broke out or the alarms went off telling them that someone was attempting suicide, you as a nurse have to get there as quickly as possible. Some of the nurses like Craig and Simon were there in seconds. Others dawdled along to the scene of the crime as if it didn't really matter. Oh blimey not another suicide attempt? The fifth this week? Do I really care? seemed to be some of the nurse's attitudes. When I was initially sectioned it was under Sect 2 of the Mental Health Act which means you are being assessed for 28 days. They can then either a) send you home or b) put you on a sect. 3. This means they can section you for up to 6 months. When I was originally put on a section 3 I was horrified. All that registered with me was 6 months. 6 months in this f'ing hell hole? Why? You have got to be having a laugh. But it was true. Oh my god. I was stunned and angry and kept asking myself what I could possibly have done to deserve this? I hadn't hurt anyone. I had hurt myself a little bit but so what? It's my body to do what I want with. I was desolate. Here I found myself living in a strange world that I hardly knew existed. I was really struggling with my faith in god at that time, but they say you are never closer to god than when you are angry with him. I saw Dr M on a weekly basis and he began reducing my medication. YES!! I was back on planet earth. The only downside was I was still in f'ing Shelton. Joey was only 19 when I was first admitted. He visited regularly which was so, so nice. He used to get embarrassed a little as all the girls fancied him. He is very handsome and a couple of the young girls let him know it. But he took it all in his stride love him and I desperately looked forward to his visits. Jai was only 10 when I became ill. God bless my little soldier. His father and I had decided it was best that Jai didn't see me in hospital, so I had to wait an age to get leave to see the little man again. Our mobile phones were a godsend. I used to ask him to look up at the moon. It is the same moon that you and I are both looking at. I also used to imagine that the man in the moon was my father smiling down at me. Oh please just let me go home. Why don't you just meet me in the middle? I am losing my mind just a little. On Stokesay it was a very mixed bag of patients. There were women who were prone to violent outbursts, a couple of drug induced zombie like women. Some of them were as high as kites, and most of us were suicidal. Some of the women (not me) were extremely violent and were either kept in HDU or sent to a secure unit elsewhere. Some violent women stayed on Stokesay as they had nowhere else to go. I told you about the woman there who had supposedly murdered someone and was allowed out onto the ward. That's how bloody violent some women were, and I had to live with them. I was on such a high. I begged the nurses to let me go home. I did not for a second think that there was anything wrong with me and that keeping me here against my will was just one big mistake and the next morning I would be allowed to go home.

As I said when you are in HDU you are constantly watched by two nurses. Depending on the nurses it was reasonably ok in there. When you are let out however it is a completely different story. We were all ill (obviously) and our illnesses affected us in completely different ways. On my release from HDU I was put in a 4 bedded ward as I was still considered to be a high suicide risk. It stands to reason that the other 3 patients were too. What a concoction of people. It was a little like being back in the Army, but this time we were all crazy. One lovely lady stayed for a short while and she used to shout "goodnight fellow nutters" when she went to bed. It really made me laugh. All in all though Stokesay was an acute ward full of people with very unpredictable behaviour and when things kicked off they bloody well did kick off.

As you can imagine, with a ward full of very poorly women there were quite a few fights, (some of them really quite serious) breaking out. Whenever things kicked off alarms were set off and this brought nurses from the male ward running to Stokesay. Fights were normally stopped with no one getting hurt, other times not. I was one of the lucky ones, as even though I had been threatened no one ever hit me and even the times I was threatened still puts a smile on my face now. I will tell you why later.

Our day started off with medication. Everyone was expected to get up at 8.30 when the alarms went off and queue up for our meds. We were like sheep waiting in line to be fed. The nurses watched us take every single tablet but I knew of some women who somehow managed to put them under their tongue and save them up and overdose on them later or even sell them. Goddamn, do you want to get better or what? Some very poorly patients would go back to bed and others stayed up for breakfast. The same cereal, or toast every flipping morning. On the men's ward they were often served up a cooked breakfast but we never were. What kind of a hotel is this? It was so unfair. Our coffee was that horrible cheap powdery stuff so most of us asked our visitors to bring some decent coffee in, in any container other than glass jars, or sharps as I came to know them as. I later found out that our decent coffee was being taken home, along with our biscuits by one of the nurses. Patsy reported her. I was so angry. How could someone steal from very ill and disabled people? How horrible.

On my first admission, bearing in mind it was fifteen years ago, things were very, very different. We were allowed to smoke in a smoking room. (God send). Everyone was much happier in there and some of the non smokers came in there too as we used to have so much fun. Of course there was a camera in there so that the nurses could keep an eye on us. We sometimes used to wind them up and place a cushion over it and the nurses would come running. For some reason we found it hilarious. We had a session on laughter therapy telling us how important laughter was for our mental health and sense of wellbeing. That very same evening we were laughing and Arnie one of the old school nurses told us to shut up as we were upsetting the other patients on the ward. What rubbish. We asked the others on the ward if they minded us laughing and they said no not at all. We began laughing again as soon as he had gone. F them we used to say. Some of the nurses really did think they were god. Others were just bone idle, whilst other nurses ran around like blue bottomed flies. One of the nurses did absolutely jack shit. I did a consensus asking what the lazy cow did all day. One of the doctors told me that it was a bit mean but I really didn't care. I used to ask her to do things every time she was on duty just to wind her up, and she really didn't like it. One day I asked her to unlock the laundry room for me. She told me to come back in half an hour, which I did. She then told me to ask somebody else. I said "no, I'm asking you". She said that she was busy. What? Busy doing nothing? I did lose my head a bit and shouted at her, telling her that "you told me to come back in half an hour and here I am". One of the other nurses who really did work so hard said that she would do it but I was not to be budged. Shift your behind you lazy goddamn woman. And she did with a face like a slapped butt. Ha ha. She reminded me of my manager, Claire Turner at Social Services. Some people really will try and get away with doing absolutely nothing unless they have to. Not this time lady.

We found that if we all stood together we were far more likely to get fair treatment. We asked for better food and more of it. We got it. We asked for lights out to be at 10pm instead of 8.30pm. We got that too. Suddenly we were not treated like animals, but mentally ill patients who needed lots and lots of tender loving care. And many of the nurses gave us that too. I used to say "a hug a day keeps the Psychiatrist away" and some of the nicer nurses did give me a hug if I was crying, and some of the patients did too. Things were not always horrendous. Lunchtimes were spent either on the ward or if you were well enough you could go to the Marches, which was a restaurant on the grounds. We always got fed well there. We needed a ticket to show that we were well enough to go there and this was one of the highlights of my day. It was our little slice of normality. Not only was the food good there but the staff were absolutely lovely. I used to think that they would make a better job of nursing than some of the ones we got. Whenever we had a meal one of us used to say grace. My favourite was little Marriane's, who said "good food, good meat so let's bloody well eat".

Paddy finds a sandwich with two wires sticking out of it. He phones the Police and say's "Bejesus I've just found a sandwich dat looks like a bomb". The operator asks "is it tickin? Paddy says "No I tink it's beef".

I've been doing some serious thinking. A thought has just come into my head. If you don't have a drink when you're living you'll have a hell of a job when you're dead. Do I have a drink problem? Yes I cannot afford the amount I want to drink.

As well as my kickboxing coming in handy in hospital, my experience as a nurse in the Army came in use too. I had nursed on Psychiatric wards myself and knew what should have been done, and some of the staff fell very seriously short. So I started complaining, along with many of the other women and things slowly started to get better. Dinner was the same routine as lunch. We were either fed on the ward or at the Marches. A small slice of escapism. We would also get to eat with those men things, you know, the male patients and whoopee we even got to speak to them too. Again following discussions in the Smoking Room we decided to ask if we could mix with them. This actually happened. We now saw male patients in Occupational Therapy and there was an atrium between the male and female wards where we used to wave to them undetected by the nurses. Some of the girls even pulled their tops up in front of the guys but I wasn't prepared to do that. A smile and a wave was all they were going to get from me. The female patients were allowed out there for an hour a day, we then had to come back onto the ward so that the male patients had their turn. God forbid we actually see them face to face. I found that incredible. We are kept in there against our will and all of the professionals in there tell you that they are helping us to learn how to live in the

"Community again". What were they going to do? Hide all the flipping men in Newtown when I am around? I am convinced that everyone there had spoken to someone of the opposite sex before and now all of a sudden they tried to make us feel as though they were the enemy. Were we the crazy ones or were they? Sometimes we would meet with the guys in the grounds and sit and chat. It felt so normal and not one of the men made me feel uncomfortable in any shape or form. And no to any of the Psychiatrists and nurses who believed we should not speak to those scary men things, we did not have a mass orgy on the lawn. Being in there was meant to prepare you to face the outside world again. Are there any men out there? Yes of course there are. I just so happen not to have found one yet.

Supper time was on the ward. Night time was the worst on Stokesay. We took our meds last thing at night after forming an orderly queue. Again there were women who hid their meds. We hoped to sleep to give us some kind of respite from the place but this was rarely possible. There was a lot of crying and wailing and sometimes it was strange to realise it came from me. Apart from the noises we all made we used to have alarms going off on a regular basis. These alarms used to terrify me. They sounded to me just like Colditz Castle (a prison in an old movie). That particular alarm alerted the nurses to the fact that a fight had broken out on the men's ward and our nurses were called to help deal with them and vice versa. Speaking of prisons; when I was a nanny in the States I went to visit Alcatraz and got out of there with absolutely no problem at all but could I get out of this dump? No

So here I am, still in the 4 bedded room. Several women (some very strange and scary ones) had come and gone so it was about bloody time I left too. A nurse told me that I was kept in there to keep an eye on the other patients. What????? I became very angry about being kept in there. I was not their own private nurse so I kicked off. What about my recovery you bastards? At last I was moved into a room of my own. I felt so much better straight away. When I was a Social Worker I worked in the Leaving Care Team. These are the most vulnerable young people in the County as most of them had spent years in the Care System and had now reached an age to live independently. Many of them had been abused by their parents, or their parents just could not cope to warrant them being put into care. They are then told that complete strangers are going to be their new mummy and daddy. Their education has been disrupted as they often have to change School. This can often happen on more than one occasion. Because of the disruption in their Education Looked After Children rarely obtain the qualifications they are capable of achieving. When they apply for work hardly any employers will entertain you without at least your Maths and English GCSE's, which is so sad as an awful lot of these young people were extremely bright indeed.

I had completed my placement to gain my Diploma in the Leaving care team and had worked there full time for approximately 12 months. Our mobiles are our lifeline to the outside world. Without it I had no way of contacting my children, family and friends. I was over an hour's drive away from home in England when I lived in Wales therefore I had very little contact with them as they all had to work and then my manager Claire Turner had my mobile removed from me. It took 5 nurses to get it off me. I was wriggling about on my bed telling them that I pay the contract for it therefore it remains with me. It was only when I saw that needle coming towards my arse that I gave it to them. I did not hurt any of them and they did not hurt me. I cannot tell you how much I dislike Claire Turner. I am Welsh and proud to be so. When I listen to one of my favourite funny guys, Max Boyce I think the same applies to Psychiatric hospitals as it does for the miners; "Dew it's hard. Cos it's hard. Harder than they will ever know". It is also like Social work; dammed if you do and dammed if you don't. When I feel really happy I get locked up. When I feel really sad I get locked up too.

Trouble in Shelton was seemingly everywhere and was impossible to avoid. Even sitting quietly having a meal, food fights would break out. We had barely enough food to eat so why they wanted to throw it around is beyond me. As I said Joey's dad and my father died in the same week and my job as a Social Worker was extremely stressful, particularly as I was doing half of my manager's work as well. She would refuse to see her clients because she was too f'ing bone idle and I was left to deal with them. She has an arse the size of Australia because she did nothing but sit on it all day.

On one occasion in Shelton, I was returning to the ward from my room when holy crap this absolutely huge woman came walking towards me with such an angry look on her face. That in itself was quite unnerving and then she started swearing at me, "you whore, you slut, you f'ing this and f'ing that". Then she walked straight past me. I don't even think she was talking to me. The relief I felt was immense. She turned out to be a very funny lady and we called her big bird. She had Tourhette's. I got used to her outbursts and she used to make me laugh. She was lovely. I felt a little sorry for visitors though as they looked absolutely terrified of her. Ha ha. Welcome to our world. Most of the patients were really nice and most of the staff too. Being in there was not all bad, but of course it was not where I wanted to be. I wanted to be at home with my beautiful children. It really did feel like I was a prisoner in Cell Block Stokesay.

I was beginning to meet the patients properly now and began going to Occupational Therapy (OT). It was the best thing. On my first stay there I made some tiles in pottery class which are now on my bathroom wall. Occasionally I even clean them. I have never been able to find anything with Jai's name on it so I made a mug and etched his name onto it. It holds exactly a pint of milk and he now drinks from it every day. Go me. I began attending more and more sessions as not only did it get me off the ward I thoroughly enjoyed them, and the staff, were lovely too. I had been told that the more OT sessions you attend the quicker you get to go home. But did it work? No. Eventually I was allowed out in the grounds. What a relief. Cooped up like battery hens and now I had freedom and fresh air. Heaven. I ran, ran and ran some more. However you can never run away from the way you feel. The grounds were beautiful and we had our own cricket pitches which I ran around every morning. Then the nurses started complaining that I was making myself vulnerable because I wore shorts. What?? It was July and it was boiling hot. Vulnerable my ass. But I had to ask Joey to bring me in some joggers otherwise I would not be allowed to train. I think the problem laid in their dirty minds not the male patients. Not one of them made me feel uncomfortable, ever. It seems to me that when you enter those places people in Authority think that we have not had a life before. Did you ever go abroad and see naked flesh, inmates? That is not normal for you nutter's and you will probably never be allowed to do so again. Have you ever been allowed in a Public House in your life before? That will probably never be allowed to happen again either you little freak. When I was eventually allowed my mobile phone back one of my clients Heman stayed in contact with me on it. What is the harm in that? Claire Turner then showed up again and deleted his number from my phone. Little Heman was my refugee client from Iraq who arrived in this country in the back of a lorry. He somehow found out where I was and came to visit me in Shelton. I was too ashamed to tell him where I was so I didn't. I couldn't believe it. He spoke and understood very little English but he did it. He brought me a curry which I shared with a couple of the other patients and we all agreed it was the best we had ever tasted. Bless his little heart. He tells me that he cried every single day I was in there. I found myself crying in there every day too.

I worked for Social Services for a total of fifteen years prior to my breakdown and thought I had made lots of friends. How wrong was I? Only four people from the department came to visit me, apart from Turner my very best friends Annie, Jeanie and a chap called Paul. Jeanie, Annie and I used to call ourselves the three musketeers. Two's company and three are the Musketeers. Unfortunately Annie has since passed away and I no longer have any contact with Jeanie. I guess it was Annie who was the glue that kept the three of us together.

Slowly my leave was increased from days out to overnight stays. I cannot tell you the relief I felt the first time I slept in my own bed, with my snugly quilt, instead of hospital blankets which never seemed to stay on the bed, away from the noise, the patients and the nurses. Oh my goodness. I thought I'd died and gone to heaven, being with my children. I decided there and then that I would do everything possible to get out of that f'ing horrible place. Not even one alcoholic drink. That was my plan at least but I didn't stick to it? Nope's Unfortunately not. What I didn't realise was that one drink of alcohol on my medication would be the equivalent of 4 drinks for everyone else. Two drinks and I was legless. I used to joke with Wasi that I was cheap to take out, but it really wasn't funny. I no longer want to live my life like that. I cannot remember the name of this particular medication but it used to make me appear to be drunk even when I wasn't.

Eventually I was set free. Vintary mintery cuttery corn, Apple seed and apple thorn. Wire, briar, timber lock. Three geese in a flock. One flew East. One flew West and ONE FLEW OVER THE CUCKOO'S NEST. Yay I am going home and home is where my heart is. God knows what my poor neighbours thought, but they are all absolutely lovely to me. Particularly my next door neighbour Eddie. He is so nice and would do anything for me. He also makes me laugh. He said to me today "bloody hell you're looking short. Are you standing in a hole?" Ha ha brilliant. I am slightly vertically challenged but it does not stop me from reaching for the stars. The road that I live on is meant to be the poshest in Newtown. At least it was until I moved in. Oooh not in my back yard. We cannot possibly have a certified nut job on this road. But I am here and this is where I intend to stay for the foreseeable future so suck it up. What I can't comprehend is that when you are crazy and poor you are considered to be nuts. If you are well off and crazy you are known as eccentric. I am not quite sure which category I fall into but quite frankly my dears I do not give a flying f any more, just call me what you want. But NOT a spastic whatever that may be.

It was not long before I was back in Shelton. This time fortunately I avoided HDU and went straight in to the mother and baby unit. I could not eat and I couldn't sleep. The nurses were becoming concerned about my weight loss but there was nothing I could do. I was given Fortisip shakes and I did my best to drink them, but the truth is I really didn't care. I just wanted to stay in bed, begging god to take me. Fair play to the nurses they even brought my meds to me. Eventually the cloud was beginning to lift and I began to eat and drink again. I then realised that there was someone in the room next to me. Her name is Patsy. Patsy is a larger than life character. In her mind she lives with Freddie Mercury. All I used to hear was Queen's music being played constantly. I happen to love Queen so I really didn't mind. It actually helped drown out the screaming and sobbing from the poor girl in the room the other side of me. I was lucky enough to have seen Queen live at Wembley Stadium with Joey's dad. John also took Joey to see Michael Jackson. Music means so much to me and it has rubbed off onto my children. Joey attended the Guitar Institute in London and is an amazing guitarist. Joey went to an Institute and I have been institutionalised. I sincerely hope he had a better time. Jaisee is hardly ever seen without his earphones listening to music either. I used to go next door to visit Pats if I had been invited. When I first met Pats she refused to hug me. I thought stuff it. You know what rhymes with hug. That's fine by me I thought as I probably would not have got my arms around her anyway. We were always in and out of each other's rooms chatting, away from the view of the nurses. One woman came into my room and asked if she could have a pee in my bin??? What??? I don't freaking think so. Bogg off. A woman Pats and I nicknamed Shitzu also visited me and

Pats. She was a very attractive mature woman and could be quite funny but what a snob. She had come from a very wealthy background, blown all of her money and ended up on Stokesay. It must have been very difficult for her to have had so much money and lost it all. I have not had very much money since I finished work so it didn't really bother me too much when I had none. Anyhow we tried our best to include her in the things Patsy and I did but she was such a goddamn snob that I kind of gave up on her. Patsy says "she thinks she's everybody". Patsy has lots of these sayings which really make me laugh. She lives near Telford an

d her accent alone is very funny when she asks me "how am ya Juney?" Her latest one is "smell my rubber bitch". I love it. It is making me smile just writing about it. She tells me she thought that I was a complete airhead when I was first admitted and couldn't believe I was a Social Worker. Well believe it darling as I was and have been told I was a very good one. My clients, Foster carers, everyone who knew me have told me so. I worked so hard and treated everyone with respect and this is how Social Services have treated me. I also had a lot of fun there too. A woman I visited had applied to be a Foster Carer. She asked if it would be acceptable if she smoked. I replied "mmm it would probably be frowned upon but I am aware of foster carer's who do". She then said that smoking had helped saved her son's life. I asked her how so? She said that it was either smoke a cigarette or kill the little bastard. I am pleased to say that they gave her the job.

Have you been injured at home, at work or on the roads? Have you tripped over? Have you hurt yourself? Serves you right you clumsy git. My head was injured at work but I have not received any compensation for that. Pat's has now come up with several nicknames for me ranging from Slutty, Piggy and the latest one Titalot. I wish. Pat's tells me that she likes being Bipolar. She freely admits that she is absolutely crazy and loves it. She tells me she has three brain cells. One to wash, one to wear and one for spare. I, on the other hand hate it with a passion. She likes to be known as Patsy Mercury as in her mind she is married to Freddy. It is quite surreal talking to Pats as one minute she speaks of everyday things and the next she talks about Freddy. This belief has been one of the banes of Patsy's life as many Psychiatrists would not discharge her from hospital all the time she had the delusion of Freddy. However she now has carers coming in twice a day and she lives independently. With Freddy.

Back to Stokesay. I eventually had my mobile returned to me and this was a godsend. I could text and ring Joey and Jai. Oh my goodness, the relief I felt was incredible. Not having access to my mobile phone was complete agony and all due to Claire Turner. Bitch troll from hell. She did not give a damn about me or my sons. I doubt that anything like this will ever happen to her as she never works hard enough to experience stress. I saw her in town only the other day and she looked like shit. I thought to myself, were you weighed or measure for that ensemble? She actually said hello to me. Really? I gave her my very best death stare (which has been known to send irritating little children scarper back to their parents) and walked right on by. This is a text message that will never apply to her looking the way she does; Good looks catch the eye, but a good personality catches hearts. You're blessed with both. Flattered? Well fuck off Claire it was sent to me. I do not wish anything bad to happen to her she just makes me cross.

Illegal drug use is rife in Psychiatric hospitals. In fact I was told that one man posing as a nurse was an undercover cop hoping to do a drug bust. I have never taken hard drugs. I have smoked cannabis occasionally in the past but alcohol was my drug of choice. I thought that I was so clever drinking red wine from pop bottles in front of the nurses. I thought to myself what the eye don't see the heart don't grieve over. But of course I was not being clever at all. It just did not click with me that this was so detrimental to my health whilst taking such heavy-duty medication. Bag search and breathalysed whenever I left the hospital. Almost every time I was guilty of the latter. Must do better

Juney. Some of the other women there accused me of taking their children away once they learned I was a Social Worker. I have never set eyes on you before and you accuse me of something as dispickable as that? We were all in the same boat in there so why try and make anyone feel worse than they already do? They also used to call me a kiddy snatcher. What? I have two beautiful children of my own. What on earth makes you think that I would want to snatch yours? Thankfully I have never had to make the decision to remove a child from their parents. Normally with the right support parents can cope themselves. I have taken children to Foster Carers where other Social Workers have made that decision and it is horrible. Those poor children. They have usually had horrible little lives to warrant them being taken away from their family and are then placed with Foster Parents who are complete strangers to them. They are some of the most vulnerable children of all. I hated working in child protection. And the paperwork involved in placing a child into the care system is horrendous. As I said other Social Workers would make the decision and I was left to do the goddamn paper work. One thing that brightened up my time as a Social Worker was when I visited a woman I was working with who had a drink problem. She had three young children and she was just not coping. On this particular visit a WPC showed up. My client had an open living room and dining area. I stayed in the living room with the children so that they could not see what was happening but I could see and hear what was going on with my client and the WPC. The WPC was absolutely horrible to her and my client socked her in the gob. Ha ha. I couldn't believe it. The poor woman was taken to court and was made to pay a fine. What on earth is the point of fining an already financially struggling mother? All they are doing is taking food out of the children's mouths. Where is their compassion? I wish she had knocked the WPC out now. Not really of course as I guess she thought she was just doing her job. However I believe there is a right way and a wrong way to do your job and she most definitely chose the wrong one. That particular client is now working at the Citizen's

Advice Bureau and has completely changed her life around and all three of her children are fine. A little support and a lot less condemnation goes a long, long, way

Jenny in Shelton was a big old girl and she intimidated most people on the ward, but not me. I knew that one front kick to her fat stomach and she would be on her arse. We just accepted that we would never get on as we were Bi polar poles apart. Jenny's poor mother used to visit her on a regular basis and nine times out of ten the poor woman would leave in tears. I must have been in a bad mood one day because I really did lose it with her. I shouted at her that her mother had carried her for nine months. She did not abort you and she did not put you up for adoption. You treat her like shit and still she visits you. Her face was a picture. She certainly wasn't used to being stood up to. I know that it was none of my business but I had had enough of her cruelty. The rest of the patients were cheering. We had discussed her on several occasions and we all felt the same way. All of a sudden Jenny stood up and began advancing towards me in a karate stance with both palms open. I thought it was hilarious and stood my ground. Ha ha bring it on fatty. However the nurses asked me to move away. Dammit. I did what they asked. The nurses then came and calmed her down. I am glad I didn't hit her as my non violent record remained intact and believe it or not she was a lot nicer to her poor mother after that, but still I couldn't stand her. Why the nurses hadn't put the spoilt cow in her place before now (but maybe not quite as cruelly as I did) was beyond me. I don't think I have ever been that cruel to anyone in my life before but she really was a nasty piece of work. I warned Jenny to stay out of my way in future and she did. Don't hustle with the muscle or you're cruising for a bruising. I had felt like decking her so many times because of her treatment of other patients but I refrained. However a few days later she asked a little girl named Alison if she could borrow her makeup. Alison said "no sorry". Jenny picked up her makeup and began gouging it out with her fingers. Poor Ali was in tears. Again I had had it with the cow. I picked up her belongings and put them all into the bin. See how you like it bitch. Again she went nuts. Ha. She got up to hit me again but again the nurses called me over to them. I did as they asked. AGAIN. I told her if you step on my toes you will get one on the nose. She was the most horrible patient I met in there, and the weirdest. She would stand for what felt like hours with her arms outstretched and all you could see was the whites of her eyes. Scarey. I could never hurt another human being unless I had to, apart from when I was kickboxing. I could no sooner do that than ride a bicycle to the moon. I have been taught to fight to a very high standard and won the European Championships. I am well aware of what I can do to people wearing boxing gloves and know what would happen, fighting bare knuckle. I also believe that without my ability to defend myself I would have been raped. Maybe the police would have done something if I was considered to be normal. "Show me the way to go home. I'm tired and I want to go to bed. I had a lot of medication about an hour ago and it's gone right to my head. No matter where I roam, over land or sea or nut house, you will always hear me singing this song "show me the way to go home". Please, please let me out

Life to me is about having fun. Find the job that you love and you will never have to work again. I loved my time in the Army and I loved working for Social Services and I did have lots of fun. I also worked for the Benefits Agency, two years here in Newtown and five years in Canterbury, Kent. I loved this job too and I had fun. My manager told me that she could not tell the difference between a client's telephone call and a personal one. Treat everyone with respect I feel. Unlike the horrible Benefits Agency staff I have had to deal with since becoming ill.

Even though Shelton is a shit hole as Pats describes it and obviously holds extremely ill patients, I still managed to have fun. Most of the staff had a sense of humour too thank goodness. Some had a face like a slapped arse and were definitely in the wrong job. A couple would have been better off in the Gestapo.

They tried to rule us with a rod of iron. F off. I knew my rights as I had read sections of the Mental Health Act which I believed applied to me and some were definitely mistreating us. Some of the ladies had schizophrenia which I believe is even worse than Bipolar. They sometimes hear voices in their head telling them to hurt themselves or others. It really was not funny at all but on occasion the only way I can handle things so horrible is to make a joke about it. I used to say to them, "I'm a schizophrenic and if you mess with me you mess with the both of us". Bless their hearts though it really is the vilest illness going I think. I would also like to stress for all of you whom I see in Court when this book is published; I have NEVER heard voices in my head. NOR have I ever been delusional. I am purely disillusioned with the system. And that is the truth, the whole truth so help me god.

On my second stay at Shelton they had closed the smoking room and turned it into a tv lounge. We had to go outside to smoke. I had no problem with that at all as I am a bit of a fresh air freak. However it wasn't very pleasant being chucked out in the rain or freezing cold weather. Following the closure of the smoking room they closed my beloved Marches restaurant, obviously to save money. We all had to eat on the ward. What a bloody joke. There weren't even enough tables and chairs for all of the patients. Also if you did not get served first then you may not get served at all. There was just not enough food for us all. My little friend Alison Cowell was practically anorexic and was given a plate of peas as that was all that was left. Little Ali was so thin if you looked hard enough you could practically see every pea going down. How could we not have enough food? We were in hospital for goodness sake, hoping to get better. We weren't going to do that unless we could eat. We all complained like mad and were eventually given sufficient. The food was ok. Nothing to write home about. But adequate. One day we would have Oonozewot. The next, Sum Mat Els, and occasionally OoKan-Gess. However Pats was not happy. She used to write notes to the chef with suggestions of new recipes. His name was David but Patsy used to call him Oberon, king of the fairies as he was gay. David loved it and he did begin to vary the menu. I think he felt much unappreciated as a chef. He was given such a low budget to feed us on it was almost impossible to do so and patients did tend to complain a lot. Then we began to compliment him, whenever we saw him or write him little notes of thanks and he seemed much happier in his work. Good old Oberon. Fair play we did have a patients forum and I made flipping sure I was on it. That's where we got our food budget increased and it's where we got lots of things changed. At least the staff at Shelton listened to us. Unlike another hospital I was sent to later named Bronllys. On the whole the nurses were excellent. They were kind, caring and treated us with respect, but it just takes one bad apple to spoil the bunch and if that bad apple took a dislike to you god help you. I suppose it is only natural that they can't like everyone but they shouldn't show it so blatantly.

Looking back now although Bipolar is one of the most heinous illnesses I have ever known I do not regret my time in Shelton altogether. Sometimes the 3 years I have spent locked away seems like a waste of my life but it is the only interesting thing that I have done in my life that seems worth writing about. I also so want people on the outside to realise that we really are just normal people who get extremely ill and we do very often get better. I really believe that no one is born to be locked away, and all of god's lovely children sometimes lose their way.

I have recently been asked am I ashamed of my illness? For years I felt deeply ashamed and embarrassed. I no longer feel that. I have a critical illness just like diabetes but it can be managed. I don't think that a diabetic feels ashamed (at least I hope not) so why should I? No one with a mental illness should feel ashamed. We certainly would never ask to be ill so why feel ashamed? I used to view myself as purely Bipolar and nothing else, but I no longer do. I am still the same old June I always was but on occasion become extremely ill. Anyone's fault? Yes I believe it to be Social Services. Could they have predicted this? No of course not. Nobody could have. Least of all me.

Fifteen years ago when I very first became ill the stigma towards the mentally ill was extremely strong but I now believe it was due to a lack of understanding and education. Now fifteen years on everybody treats me with respect. Services such as the GP's, the Police, they are all wonderful to me and I would not hesitate to call the Police if I were in trouble. The jury is still out with regards to Social Services. I am really not sure if I can trust them or not, but I guess time will tell.

In the summer months it was lovely having our smoking shelter. We were outside of that place and we gathered together several times a day. We used to tell each other jokes. These are some of my favourites:

You are in a car driving at a constant speed. To your left is a fire engine. In front is a galloping pig you cannot overtake, behind is a helicopter flying at ground level. All are travelling at the same speed as you. What do you do to get out of this situation? Get off the kids Merry Go Round you drunken twat!

Husband always insisted on making love in the dark. After 20 years the wife turns the light on and finds him holding a vibrator. She goes ballistic. "You impotent bastard. How could you lie to me all these years?" Husband looks her straight in the eyes and says calmly, "I'll explain the toy, you explain the kids".

"I keep having my profile rejected on dating web sites. One of the questions is what do you want in a woman? Apparently my cock is not an acceptable answer". Oh please Lord forgive me. And my lovely Vicar.

A convict breaks into a house and ties up the husband and his wife. He jumps on the wife, kisses her ear, then runs to the bathroom. The husband whispers to his wife, "satisfy him or he'll kill us. I saw the way he kissed you, just be strong. I love you". The wife replies "he didn't kiss me; he whispered in my ear he's gay, horny and looking for Vaseline. I told him it's in the bathroom. Let's see who's f'ing strong now". I had better tell you a non smutty joke now in an attempt to make up for the above;

A bear walks into a pub, leans on the bar and looks directly into the eyes of the barman. The barman asks the bear "what would you like to drink?. The bear made no reply, so the barman says "why the big paws?"

We also used to make up silly songs i.e. "Everyone's a fruit and nut case. Psychiatrists take us and they drop us off at Shelton". My favourite was "Wasi says go to rehab and I say no, no, no". He did suggest once that I go to rehab but thankfully I wasn't bad enough. I've heard that you can get your hands on more alcohol in rehab than you can anywhere else. Just as drugs are very easy to obtain in prison. A friend of mine had been imprisoned and he told me that they even trained rats to carry the drugs to each other. I have no idea how true that is but I had no reason to disbelieve him. Blimey. We did nothing like that. In fact there were thankfully very few women on hard drugs and the ones that were, were in a dreadful state when they were coming down from them. Some women even asked me to do the tongue thing and give them my medication to make their come down easier. Not a cat's chance in hell mate. A) The extra meds could kill them and B) I was not prepared to risk my recovery to feed their drug habits. I did feel sorry for them though. I used to wonder what their lives must be like to want to do that to themselves;s..

SHELTON

In low security prisons you have two people to a cell. The inmates may change, but you only have to sort out your differences with one other person. In Shelton I was kept in a four bedded room for months, not knowing who was going to join me. Some of these women had actually committed heinous crimes, and here I was sharing a room with them. Oh be joyful. I spoke with one of the nurses who nursed me there and now works in the community, and he told me that I had been kept there to keep the peace. I was horrified. My nursing days were over and I was ill. I was an extremely ill patient just like them and I was kept there for that reason. How wrong and cruel was that? Oh my goodness the whole thing stinks. What about my mental health? I was slowly going downhill again and they didn't care. They seem to do anything they like to give themselves an easy life. Not all of them just some. Some of them really did care about us.

I worked with a few Psychiatrists when I was nursing in the army and have seen some regarding my own mental health but no one compares to Dr Wasi Mohamad. Some of them were so up themselves and behaved as though they thought they were god, and looked down on us as if we were the lowest form of life.

My son Joey has a sign at his gym which says "leave your ego at the door". And you most certainly have to do that at Shelton. It feels as though you are stripped of whom you are. Even now, fifteen years after my first admission I do not feel that I know who I am any more. I have even been taken from my bed in the middle of the night and been sectioned. Strapped to a bed in the back of a meat wagon (ambulance) for two and a half hours on one occasion. Here we go again. Whoopadydoo. You are strapped down in case of escape or violence and when you get there you are pushed and prodded by the doctors. Look it's my head that is cracked, the rest of me is fine. Leave me alone.

If no one has packed a bag for you, you are given someone else's clothing, which I am very grateful for but you don't even look like you anymore. I could even have been wearing a deceased woman's clothing. I despise those places. No I don't, I just despise being there. When a person loses their sight or hearing their other senses can become heightened. When you lose your mind you lose everything including your identity and it takes so, so long, if ever to put you back together again but the real road to recovery in my opinion begins at home, surrounded by loved ones, not other inmates who act as if they hate your guts.

Bipolar reminds me of having a good first workout you have had in some time. You then discover muscles that hurt where you did not know you had muscles. When you develop Bipolar you have incredible pain in your mind, heart and soul where you had no idea you could hurt before.

Chapter 2 crazy

Jai tells me "you're like a child, Mum" and maybe I am. I have put a lot of thought into this and I don't think being an adult is going to work for me. Maybe because I wasn't nurtured from the age of 14 to 16, when my father threw me out, I am craving it now. But both my parents are dead. My father allowed me back home at the age of 16, but only to care for my mother who had undergone a hysterectomy. It was a huge operation in those days and she needed an awful lot of care. I was taken out of School to look after her. My father really did not care if we went to School or not, and because my elder sister was working in a factory he considered that it would be a much better idea if he took me out of School. I continued with my School work the best that I could at home but left School with only four GCSE's. I now have ten GCSE's, a B tech in Business studies, an A level in Law, my Nursing qualification, Diplomas in both Counselling skills and Social Work but unless I did any physical work my father didn't think I worked at all. AND I am classed as mentally impaired. What? When Joey and I lived at home together we had to live on Income Support for months as Powys social services refused to pay me my pension. We were always broke so Joey used to make me breakfast in bed with a candle in it for my Birthday or Mothers day. He also used to record a cd of him playing the guitar. That was the best present ever. I expect the same kind of treatment from Jai now that he has returned to live with me but I won't hold my breath.

He does on occasion make me a coffee in bed so I won't put him up for sale on e bay just yet. Joey is so laid back he is practically horizontal. He has no sense of timing other than his commitments to his wife Hannah and the gym. He once took the dog for a walk saying he wouldn't be long and came back three hours later. Jai is a stickler for time and I am the same. However he knows exactly which buttons to press to get me going but that is mutual. It makes for a wonderful time. Jai is so funny. He can make a joke out of anything and he has the most wonderful smile to back it all up.

He recently told me a saying which I think is really poignant "An eye for an eye makes the world go blind". I also like the saying "if someone hasn't got a smile on their face give them yours". My suicidal thoughts come mainly in the morning and I have made four attempts to take my life now so I never let my children leave the house or go to bed without me telling them I love them because each time could be the last time I see them. What a way to live. Bipolar really is a heinous illness. There is a very real urge to languish in self pity (and I have done it). Oh why me? Why have I got this illness? What have I done to deserve it? The truth is, shit happens and there is always someone out there who is worse off than you. It is difficult to live with Bipolar or any other mental illness which has required hospitalisation, as I continually ask myself is today the day they will lock me away again. I have not been aware of the highs in the past and have been sectioned every time. However if I were to experience a high again I think I would recognise the signs and nip it in the bud as soon as possible. And the lows - well I will just have to deal with these when they happen.

Crazy.

Why does the word crazy sound so seductive in songs but when it happens to you, you get locked up. It also really, really hurts. I don't want to be crazy any longer. I don't want to go bonkers and end up in hospital. No more highs and no more devastating lows. Please somebody fix me. I used to bang my head against the wall as you have this horrible, horrible pain but it is not the kind that a painkiller would touch. I really hope that none of you reading this book has ever felt that indescribable pain BUT and this is a biggy, 1 in 3 people suffer from some kind of mental illness. 1 in 3. Oh my goodness why? Is it nature or is it nurture? I know that my abusive past has had a profound effect on me, but writing this book has helped me put a lot of things just there where they belong, in the past.

Junie Pritchard

Dave.

I met Dave whilst he was a barman in a pub that I visited. We got chatting and he seemed really nice and he made me laugh. I have a sign in my house that says "Anything that makes you giggle, smile or laugh, buy it or marry it". I wasn't prepared to marry him but I did want to see him again. We exchanged numbers and he invited me to a party at his home. We really hit it off and I ended up staying for a couple of days as he was flying off to Barbados on holiday. I really liked him and we had a lot of fun together. I returned home and Dave went on holiday. That is when I became really ill and got sectioned. I rang him whilst I was in the ambulance to tell him I was being taken to the funny farm and he said "I'd better come and visit you then hadn't I?" And he did. We eventually became more than friends and I was happy. It was almost as if it were meant to be. When I got out of there he came to visit me and it was bliss. I began drinking quite heavily when John (Joey's dad) and my father died less than a week apart. It was the only way I could cope with the pain I felt. My father was my rock and I always turned to him for advice and now he was gone. Who was going to help me now? Joey and Dave got on very well too and after a short period of time Dave moved in. I also got on well with his family and they came to stay. His daughter couldn't really understand what I was doing with Dave because there was quite a large age difference between us, and she warned me how selfish he was. I thought so much of him that I just didn't see it. However I wish I had heeded her warning. I have never met anyone so selfish in all of my life. If everything was not going his way he would walk out and go missing for days on end with no contact at all. What a cruel thing to do.

Dave, the boys and I moved into my lovely stone cottage. This was to be a new beginning. However it turned out to be a very mixed one. I had stupidly thought that the home we were moving to had only needed a lick of paint and the survey had not suggested otherwise. The whole cottage needed gutting. It worked out really well for me though thankfully, as I thought of Dave as being solely a barman but it turned out he was also a master builder and together (mainly Dave) he, Joey and I turned my cottage into something beautiful. He even carried on working on it while I was in hospital. It was so nice to come home after being in that ugly hospital to see my cottage become more and more beautiful every time I returned home. Cheers Rogers. Joey and I carried out 13 mini skips full of rubble out of the cottage. Little Heman helped do that too. We worked hard but we played hard too. We would often sit outside on a sunny afternoon after working all morning, me with a glass of wine and Dave with his lager. It soon became apparent that Dave had had a serious drink problem for many years and at one point it almost killed him. I was steadily heading down that route myself. My Bipolar was spiralling out of control again. Dave and I were burning the candle at both ends and I could not cope with the lack of sleep. I soon found myself back at the Asylum where the lunatics were revolting.

I used to jump over a wall which separated us from a pub. The landlady at the time hated patients going in there. I had been in there several times with different inmates and none of us behaved in an untoward manner whatsoever. We were so nervous about being caught out of the grounds we were very meek and mild. On some occasions I heard her talking about the patients in Shelton in very derogatory terms and I really wanted to tell her what I thought of her. I used to sit there quietly with my glass of red wine. A young man came in and joined me once and we decided to have a go at the kiddies colouring sheets. Who were we hurting? She said that I shouldn't be colouring as they are for children, but she didn't throw the young man out, just me. For some unknown reason (I was ill), I nicked her plastic sign. She chased me to the edge of Shelton grounds then gave up. I didn't even want her stupid sign I had just wanted to annoy her for saying such horrible things about patients. The next time I had leave I arranged to see Dave and his friend Mike.

I warned them that I had had an altercation with the landlady but Mike told me not to worry and that it would all be fine. But of course it wasn't. She saw us arrive and came out straight away to talk to us. This is how I knew she was not aware that I was luxuriating (not) in Shelton because she said that she followed me to the edge of the grounds and asked why the hell I went in there? Hello, because I live there. She told me that she would not serve me unless I returned her banner. The cocky person that I am I pulled a bottle of wine out of my bag and told her to stick it. Mike was lovely and tried to smooth things over but Dave had a face like a slapped behind. I decided I wasn't staying and returned "home" to the nut house. I did have a look for the sign but I could not for the life of me remember where I had put it otherwise I would have returned it to her.

Dave rang me later in a bad mood and told me how embarrassing he found my behaviour. I pointed out to him that he looked dreadfully hung over and looked like a complete and utter pratt because he had his beard dyed green and it was St David's Day. It should have been yellow. I also pointed out that I had run off with a cheap plastic banner and yet I have a genuine metal Silverstone sign in my shed that someone had half inched for him and he was perfectly ok with that. What a dick. I had him on speaker phone and my mates were listening. I thought he had gone and I said to them "f ing men". He shouted "I heard that" so I cut him off. We made up later on but our relationship had become very volatile. So much so that once he shouted at me "I should knock you out", but he knew damn well that I could have knocked him out so he never attempted it, and it was not long afterwards that we ended our relationship for good this time. I realise that it can be extremely difficult to live with someone who has a mental illness as there is very little anyone can do to help. However the way he did it was unforgiveable. He walked out one day and never came back. No text message, no phone call. Nothing. I didn't even know whether he was dead or alive. What a nasty selfish gutless wonder. But am I happier without him? Hell yes. Halleluiah I have seen the light. That was nine years ago and I have been on my own ever since. Maybe that selfish git has put me off men for life. No he hasn't I just haven't met my Mr Right yet. It was not long after Dave walked out before I was re-admitted. On this occasion feeling desperately low. Depression to a Bi polar person is the worst feeling ever. I have been depressed on the odd occasion in my life before but NOTHING can compare to this. It is indescribable. Death is honestly preferable to feeling this way. It's horrendous. If I had a receipt I would take myself back. It is very easy to become institutionalised in Psychiatric hospitals and some people actually want to be there. I can understand it because you are surrounded by people and you have everything done for you. When you return home you have to start cooking and cleaning etc. for yourself and it is a huge culture shock. Particularly, if you live alone. You miss the company so much.

Heather.

I met a lovely lady named Heather on my first admission to Shelton. She was very quiet and obviously very poorly and we hit it off straight away. I used to practically drag her to Occupational Therapy with me and we had a lot of fun. I felt we were really improving together. Her family came to visit and they thanked me for what I had done for her. I had done nothing other than be her friend and I enjoyed her company as much as she seemed to enjoy mine. Then the nurses interfered and told her family that I was ill too and they should not expect me to spend so much time with her. WHAT? We were both female patients, Heather is married and we should be allowed to spend as much time together as we wanted. She went home soon after that and I have never seen her again. That is the difficult thing about hospital. You form really close bonds with most people in there. After all we are all in the same boat, going up the creek without a bloody paddle. Sometimes you would get up in the morning and someone was just not there. Some people were allowed home, others were sent to secure units, some had succeeded in committing suicide and others may have died of natural causes. It was all really very sad. So many times I wanted to go for a long walk off a short cliff. I still remain friends with several people I met in there through really difficult times. What a contrast to the people I worked with for fifteen years, who I believed were my friends but have had absolutely no contact with them for the last fifteen years. I really no longer want their company either. I have not one iota of respect for them and I really would prefer to never see them again.

The Dentist.

The crazy thing is that there is no longer a dentist based at the hospital therefore unless you have leave, you cannot attend unless it is an absolute emergency. I had an abscess on my gum and that side of my face swelled up like a hamster. It was really pretty painful, and I had to be taken about 30 miles to a hospital to get it lanced. Poor old Larry, one of my favourite nurses had to take me. We were there absolutely ages and patients were arriving and sent through before me. This was really beginning to wind me up and I asked the receptionist why this was happening? He stated that because I smiled at him he assumed that I was not in too much pain. What??? I was born with a smile on my face and I am convinced I even smiled through childbirth. Larry was very patient and we sat there for hours. Eventually it was my turn. After the first needle I grabbed Larry's hand and four needles later the dentist lanced it. I will always be grateful to Larry for that as I think I squeezed his hand rather tightly. It felt a little like he was my birthing partner. Bless him he was so nice. On the way back to Colditz Larry told me he thought I was going to kick the dentist. Why do people always think I am going to be violent I wonder? All that way to get an abscess lanced when there was a dentist down the road. I went there when I needed some treatment. I have no idea what he thought of me but I wasn't going to tell him that I was a patient in Shelton. Most people were frightened of us so the last thing I wanted was a terrified dentist in charge of a drill. When he asked me what I did for a living I told him (what a fibber) that I was an Occupational Therapist at the hospital. I don't know if he believed me or not or whether I was just another patient lying about being in there. I have recently been told that the profession with the highest suicide rate is dentistry. Oh I loved that dentist and really hope that nothing bad happens to him. However I really wouldn't miss a couple of GP's at my practise if they happened to croak it. I am joking of course.

CHAPTER 3 JOEY'S FIGHT NIGHT

One weekend I was allowed leave (Section 17 of the Mental Health Act). I went to watch Joey fight. Joey is an awesome cage fighter and he let me tag along. It was amazing. Joey was on first. I was shouting my medium to large mouth off, which just so happens to sound like a foghorn. People told me they heard me several rows back. I do not know whether that was a good thing or not? Yes I think it is as when I made my way back to Hannah people said to me "well done mum". Go Ricey. (Joey's surname is Rice). Oh wow, what an amazing night. I am away from that place, spending the evening with Hannah, Joey's now wife, watching my eldest son fighting in a cage with nowhere to go. At least when I fought they used to run off the mats so that I couldn't get to them. Very sensible as they knew I could have pounded them all. Go Joey. I thought to myself how lucky am I? The guy that Joey fought that night was no slouch either. Joey did not have it easy but he WON. Whoopee. All that preparation, the work, the fitness, stamina, the moves, the awful diet and the mental preparation had paid off. Joey Rice. What an awesome fighter he is. That's my boy. I am as proud as punch of him. He is certainly no quitter. A quitter never wins and a winner never quits. I spent the rest of the evening with Hannah. Poor Han has never known me without this illness. I developed Bipolar before she and Joey got together. How she puts up with me I don't know but she does. I am so proud of both my sons. Joey is so chilled yet works so hard at training and running his gym. Jai is a lad and a half. He is so funny and so clever. Both boys are handsome. Joey with that well hard but compassionate look and Jai is a little romantic with attitude. Hannah is just beautiful inside and out and she always makes me smile. She also buys the best, most thoughtful gifts in the world, and she and Joey have visited me in every hospital I have been in. I hope that one day Jaisee will meet his own little Hannah Banana. When I have to go back to those places I have difficulty dealing with my emotions and I cried my heart out every time Joey and Hannah left. Each time

Joey would say "I wish I could take you home with us mum". I was heartbroken. My children are my world and I would die for them. I can only imagine what I have put them through the last fifteen years. I apologise from the bottom of my heart. Unfortunately I cannot change the past but in future I will do everything in my power to stay well and be the mum that I want to be and one day I hope to make them proud.

Back to f'ing Stokesay.

Fights broke out on the ward almost daily. I was very lucky as I was hardly ever involved. One particular lady however came really, really close. Her name was Audrey and she was in a wheelchair. I and several other patients used to push her wherever she wanted to go. She was quite nice and I joked with her that I would push her off a cliff if she didn't behave. But this lady could turn on a sixpence. She could go from being tolerable to downright nasty. With everyone, but particularly to me when she found out that I had been in the Forces. Apparently her husband was a Captain in the Army and had had affairs with younger women. She seemed to believe that I was one of those women. She called me all the names under the sun. You slut, you whore, tart, etc. etc. Everything derogatory you could think of she called me. I decided to ignore her but never pushed her wheelchair again. I noticed the nurses never pushed her and I found that a bit strange. On another occasion she was parked outside the nurse's station and she threw a cup of coffee over me. I thought to myself "don't hit her Junie, she's ill". So I decided to laugh at her instead. This made her even more angry as I knew it would. Ha Ha. The poor nurses told me later that because of my kickboxing background they thought they were going to witness World War 3. Nah. Not over an old bag like her. But this was the funniest bit. At least I found it funny. She had been verbally abusive yet again telling me that I was the tart who had slept with her husband. I was worried in case some of the women on the ward might think it was true. I had had enough. I did one of the worst things you can do to a person in a wheelchair and kicked it from behind as I walked past. She went ape. She jumped out of her wheelchair and began running towards me. Actually running. Halleluliah. She can run. The nurses asked me to walk away from her but not without seeing how angry she was. Ha ha. Job done. Praise the lord I had performed a pretty major miracle and the old bag could walk. Just call me Jesus. Junie Jesus has quite a ring to it I think. It turned out that the reason the nurses refused to push her in her wheelchair was because they were well aware of the fact that she could walk. She used the wheelchair in order to claim extra mobility benefits. Oh my goodness. Didn't she realise if she sat in that thing for too long she would eventually seize up. The last I heard of her was that she had been moved to a secure unit because she deliberately ran over a nurse in that wheelchair and broke her foot. I really do wish her well though. No one is all bad and I remember being admitted one night and a police officer took me in. I was obviously very reluctant to go in there, then Audrey said "oh I know this lady, she's really nice". The Policeman said "see June? You'll be ok". You bloody go in there then mate. See how you like it. If only he knew. He was one of the nicer police officers however and I really do believe he meant well.

I applied and successfully joined the Police force once but chose the army instead. If I had become a Police Officer I am sure I would have said to myself, this is somebody's daughter, mother, son or brother and would have treated them with respect. Does it happen today? Yes. I like to think that the majority of Police Officers do. The same applies to Social Workers. I have met so, so many bad ones but thankfully there are good ones too. Unfortunately though it is the luck of the draw as to which ones you get. I remember when Joyce Brand, the comedienne Jo Brand's mother came to work with us. She was an excellent manager and absolutely hilarious. There was a problem with an aggressive client downstairs. Joyce rang the police and I heard her say "we need a couple of police officers here at Social Services, could you please send some good looking ones. I don't want any ugly old coppers". If only there were more like her.

We had weekly Christian meeting at Shelton and I don't think I missed one. The Pastor there was so lovely. A Saint really, for having the patience to put up with us. Jennifer and I used to go to church on a Sunday when we were allowed. It was only across the road from the hospital so it was perfect. The Pastor knew that we were from Shelton and he didn't bat an eyelid. He even invited us back to his home for a tea party. It was so lovely. It was a charity event and the children there waited on us. Typical me, I just had to have a go on the kiddies slide. It had been raining earlier on in the day and I slid through quite a large build up of water on the slide. On the journey back to the Asylum I looked as if I had wet myself. Don't worry nurses there is no need for the Tenna pads just yet, it is only a bit of rain. On that afternoon I felt normal for the first time in an age, so thank you Pastor.

This is my little prayer for the future. Dear Lord; so far today, I am doing all right. I have not lost my temper, been greedy, grumpy, nasty or selfish. I have not whined, bitched or eaten any chocolate…However I'm going to get out of bed in a few minutes and will need a lot more help! Amen.   When I got out of the High Dependency Unit I was back in the four bedded room. Life in the four bedded room was the absolute pits. You had no privacy whatsoever. There was a curtain that we could pull around our bed, but patients and staff just used to walk in. It was meant for high suicide risk women. Women would be placed in there after me and be given a single room and I was being left in there. Most of the women were lovely but others not so much. The murderess was there lying in the next bed to me. I really hoped that she didn't take a disliking to me. Some of the women were lesbian which I have nothing against but I did not wish to listen to them together in the night. It is also almost impossible to sleep when women are crying and screaming in the bed next to you. I used to feel sorry for them but think please shut up or go and get a nurse to help you. I was not a high suicide risk at that time so I could not for the life of me think why I was being kept in there. I just wished I could go home to my sons. Whenever I was allowed off the grounds I would go to the shops and buy food. The four of us would have snacks late at night eating delicious food as opposed to the not so delicious food served up to us by the nurses. I think the worst thing for me in there, were the poor mangled bodies of those women who had attempted suicide and self harmed. One poor woman had lost her arm above the elbow when she jumped in front of a train. Another girl's arms were twice the thickness they should have been where she had cut and re-cut them. Another had a scar on her neck where she had attempted to slit her throat. Whenever I felt that kind of anguish I used to bang my head against the wall and after a time wear a thick rubber band on my wrist, pull it and let go so hard it transferred the pain from my head to my wrist and stopped me self harming.

Oh my goodness I hated it in there. When I woke up, opened my eyes and realised where I was I wanted to die. Every single morning. The nights in there were so, so scary. People with Mental Health problems suffer mostly at night, although I feel suicidal usually in the morning. The crying and wailing at night was almost too much to bear. It was terrifying. Often the fire alarms would go off, (not such a bad sound). We were all ushered outside in the freezing cold and had to wait until the fire brigade had attended. When it was deemed safe we were ushered back in and told to go back to bed and sleep. What? Who the hell could sleep after that? I would often sneak in to Jennifer's room (not her real name) for a chat. We were checked upon every hour during the night and had a torch shone on you to make sure you were still alive. That wasn't very conducive to a good night's sleep either. There was also a male nurse who used to shine that torch on me far longer than necessary. I even pretended to cough showing him that I hadn't expired and he still shone his bloody torch. Yuck. Initially it used to wake me up, it was horrible, but I got used to it. Anywhoo what I used to do was lie in bed for a check and then sneak back to Jen's room, then return to my room for the next check. One of the male patients began setting the fire alarm off every night at midnight. This went on for well over a week and of course each time it happened we were put outside in the cold. I thought to myself why don't the nurses stand next to the alarms at that time each night. Drrr. I had been told that it cost the hospital £60 each time the fire brigade were called out so a bit of common sense could have saved them a fortune. I absolutely hated it in there. Goddamn scummy place.

On one occasion I did spy a couple of nurses kissing in one of the side rooms. Oh how lovely. Romance is in the air. One male nurse who worked on Stokesay and also as a prison officer told me that in some respects it was worse than prison. How flipping unfair was that? We had done nothing wrong (well we did have the odd murderess of course) other than becoming poorly and convicted criminals were having a better time than us. Aaaaagh. It makes me so cross. One night an elderly lady was admitted into the 4 bedder. She was extremely ill and upset but very sweet. I eventually got off to sleep that night and woke up with a start to someone leaning over me. I was scared and almost hit out then realised it was the new lady offering me a sweet. Oh thank the lord I didn't hit her.

Eventually after much complaining to the nurses I was moved into a room of my own. Whoopadybloodydoo. I think in the end I had spent some time in every bedroom on Stokesay. Anywhoo this was a positive move. I enjoyed the freedom, peace and privacy of my own room. I had got to know all of the patients and staff and was feeling much more relaxed. I wish that everyone who ever said to me that "you'll be safe in a Psychiatric hospital, they'll take care of you" would spend a week in there and see how bloody safe they feel. I would love to see what effect it had on them and how they came out the other end. I have been fooled so many times, thinking that people are nice when they really are not. I still do it to this day and still become unstuck. My problem is that I trust everyone until they prove me otherwise and they invariably do.

You kind of feel when you have a mental illness that you are not allowed to have fun anymore. These hospitals are full of doom and gloom as almost everyone in there wishes they were dead, but I have always been the type of person to make the best of a bad job so I would have as much fun as I possibly could. And not give a session on the benefits of laughter and the very same evening being told not to do it. Yet again f off.

We used to play games like connect four and snap. Sound's exciting doesn't it but it is the best you can do in the nut house. I also managed to smuggle in a Chinese lantern which we lit and set off in the grounds. The nurses saw it and fair play I didn't get a reprimand this time but a male nurse told me I sure knew how to have a good time. And I do. You just have to make the most of being in that hell hole or you will go under and even though I have been incarcerated for a total of three years I made sure I had fun whenever I felt up to it. I particularly had fun with Jennifer, Pats, Jess and Ginny. I am so lucky that I have kept in touch with these amazing women as it goes a little way to making sense of why I was in there.

I know that every time Wasi sectioned me it was absolutely necessary and he discharged me as soon as I was ready. I also had lots of fun with him. We had Ward Round once a week and got to see our Psychiatrist. I really used to look forward to seeing Wasi. He was so nice. He gave me leave whenever he felt I was ready and discharged me at the earliest possible opportunity. I trust him completely and know that he always has my best interests at heart. There should be more Psychiatrists like him but unfortunately I think they broke the mould when he was born. A so called Psychiatrist named Phillipa Walker who had a face like a slapped arse certainly didn't have my best interests at heart, only the interests of the hospital. The big fat, bleep bleep, bleep. My father would have said "I'd rather keep her for a week than a fortnight" I honestly think that she is the imbecile not me. However the trouble with life's questions is that when you're old enough to know the answers you've forgotten what the questions were and I'm sure that the time will come when I forget all about her. But not before I tell you what she was like later.

I think that trouble is my middle name. I am even fondly known as trouble at my church. I know that he means it fondly as he has a big smile on his face when he says it. I seem to cause it wherever I go. I got into trouble in the army even though I left with "Exemplary Conduct" to my name. "Exemplary Conduct." Me? Are you having a laugh? But I did. I've also almost been kicked out of every Educational Establishment I ever attended and was retired from my job as a Social Worker early. I have never done anyone any harm, I just don't think they like my f you attitude. Life is way too short to be normal. Stay Weird. I had found the job that I loved as a Social Worker in the Leaving Care team, but they took it away from me just because I got ill. However they have done me a huge favour because I am enjoying writing this book much more. So up yours. You nasty creatures. Don't you just love me? Persecution can kill you and that is exactly what Social Services and the Police tried to do to me. Only I'm not dead yet. And the CPS, which I have nicknamed the Criminal Protection Society. They are the body who decides which cases are taken to court and which are not. They sent me to court for supposedly being drunk and disorderly. I do not even believe I was. As Wasi said when he saw the CCTV footage I was ill. The CPS was more interested in prosecuting a severely ill person than prosecuting the criminal who attempted to rape me. (Will tell you about that later also). AND I pay for these people through my taxes.

I believe that I should have the choice who and what I pay for through my taxes and it certainly wouldn't be them. They even sent the bailiffs to my door, and believe you me they are not nice people, saying that I hadn't paid a fine and I hadn't even been to court yet. I wasn't guilty of anything. Here I am, a newly disabled person, single parent of two sons and they send in the bailiffs. There was an electrician working in my home at the time and I feel pretty sure that if he were not there the bailiff would have pushed past me and seized my belongings. Before being charged and found not guilty of anything. They were throwing everything at me from every angle. But I have survived and this book has already been written and this is the truth, the whole truth and nothing but the truth so you can't have me for slander unless you want to take me on? I believe the truth will always prevail. Nothing that is said in the well of the court is considered libel or slanderous anyway so come on, just try it.

Jeremy Patterson, Chief Executive of social services. A kit kat. You complete and utter dipshit. I would love to play a game with Jeremy Patterson (at that time Chief Executive of Social Services) and Amanda Lewis (Iam not sure what her title was at that time but it should have been bitch. I think she was head of Children's Services). It would go like this; "Today we will have a race. The first and the last one back will be shot. Right off you go you two". Having Bipolar has taught me so much. Social Services didn't care when I almost died the first time. I believe they are hoping that I still will, as I can dish up so much dirt on them. I witnessed an awful lot in the fifteen years I worked there and have learned a lot more since.

At one point I had nurses coming in to my home every day and hopefully everything will be fed back to little Jeremy. Suicide threat? I bet he is wringing his hands with glee. Tough shit mate, my book is already written exposing the lot of you. All I am doing now is typing it up. It is here in black and white. I am going to make you all famous darlings, for all the wrong reasons.

Maeve the Rave.

There was a lovely older lady in High Dependency named Maeve. She was so sweet and we named her Maeve the Rave. Whenever someone was put into High Dependency I used to wave to them through a little glass window in the door. They must have thought what a flaming nut job she is but they used to wave back. I just wanted them to know that they were not alone. I had no idea who they were, I just used to feel sorry for them as

I know how alone I felt when I was in there therefore I used to do it. Anywhoo, Larry the nurse brought her onto the ward and sat with her so that she had some company. I thought to myself "why is this sweet little old lady in HDU?" But then…. All hell let loose. She began punching and kicking poor Larry for no reason at all. I thought "so that's why she's in there". I have to admit I found it hilarious watching a little old lady punch hell out of him. Sorry Larry. He was very good about it love him and gently guided her back to HDU. You never know about people do you? You just never know. I have seen so many seemingly placid people erupt like a bloody volcano. And I have also met people in there who have looked at me as if they wanted to kick my head in but are really, really nice. There is a saying that I quite like; "the harder you are on the outside, the softer you are on the inside". (I am just soft in the head). Is it true? I have no f'ing idea but I will always be ultra wary of people in future, and I just hope and pray my future is at home. I'm sure the day will come when I just don't want a drink as I am well aware of the devastating effect it had on my life and those around me. My extended family would ring me and ask if I needed anything. When I asked for a bottle of wine they always refused. You don't give someone with an alcohol problem a bunch of bloody grapes do you? They have to be fermented first. It really was a pointless thing for them to do as I would then walk half way across town to buy some making myself even more vulnerable. But they meant well. When I had the money I would order a takeaway meal which also consisted of a bottle of red wine. I would drink the wine and the food would be left in the fridge. I really was a disgrace and never, ever want to go back there.

It really is true that nobody wants to know you when you are down and out, but I was down but not quite out. I also believe that sometimes you have to hit rock bottom before you decide which direction to go in. The only people who wanted to know me at that time were my children and my little jail bird friend Alfy. We used to get drunk together and talk about everything, including his stints in prison and mine in the nut house. We really encouraged each other not to drink and neither of us does anymore. I went to a couple of sessions at my local drugs and alcohol centre and surprise, surprise they had neither. Trading Standards should be called methinks. It really was not for me. They suggested I go litter picking. Excuse me? I want help to quit drinking. I am not on f'ing Community service. Next they suggested I go and work on people's gardens. I have enough of a garden of my own, which I struggle to cope with when I'm not well, I really cannot do other peoples. Ooooh no. Not for me. I am sure it has helped a lot of other people it just didn't suit me.

I remember one evening watching a so called comedian named Frankie Boyle on TV. He spoke of a Psychiatric hospital filled with patients saying "I wanna go ome". And yes it is like that. Of course we want to go home. I thought how dare he take the piss out of severely ill people. I really like people who make jokes about my illness but he was just downright cruel.

I have hit the point now that I wanted to. I have not had an alcoholic drink for eight years and would no sooner drink a glass of red wine than I would a bottle of bleach. Actually one poor woman in Shelton did drink from a bottle of bleach in an attempt to kill herself. Oh my goodness that poor desperate lady. Still at least she was clean. On a lighter note; Paddy meets Mick in the street and says "I wish you would close your curtains when making love to your wife. All the neighbours were laughing at you yesterday". Well says Mick, "the laugh is on them as I wasn't home yesterday".

Paddy says "Mick I'm thinking of buying a Labrador". "Feck me" says Mick. "Have you seen how many of the owners go blind?

CHAPTER 4 The Ambulance

I met a chap called Johnny when we were both locked up in Shelton. We got along with each other famously. We were sitting on a bench chatting when an ambulance drove in. The medics were taking a poor victim into the hospital. Johnny was a mechanic and seemed to know everything there is to know about engines. I thought about the film "One flew over the cuckoo's nest" and dared him to start it. When the Ambulance guys had taken the poor shmuck they had brought inside, Johnny and I checked it out. The doors were open. YES!! Johnny did the necessary and away we went. Oh my god I've never had so much fun. We didn't in fact make a run for it we just drove it around the grounds. We returned it in one piece and he parked it just so and the whole thing went undetected. OH MY GOD!! What fun. We laughed and laughed till the cows came home. I think I had a grin on my face for about a week and still laugh when I tell the tale now. Rules and regulations have it! Johnny got moved soon after to a high security unit as he was a danger to himself. He self harmed an awful lot but at least we had some fun before he went. I never saw him again and I really miss him. I also did that in the army, but this time with a tank. Three of us, driving around the compound inebriated. If we had been caught we would have been on jankers (punishment) for a month, but we weren't.

The Olympics.

We have a tv room in Shelton which we are allowed access to at weekends until 11pm. and until lights out at 10.00pm on weekdays. A few of us had followed the Olympics avidly, and others had dipped in and out. We were sitting peacefully on a Saturday evening watching our country do amazingly well when a female nurse (and I use the term lightly) who I had never seen before opened the door and told us very abruptly to go to bed. It was 8 o'clock. The others were getting ready to go. I don't f ing think so. The nurses loved it when we went to bed early so that they had jack to do, but they never insisted on it. I politely told her that it was only 8pm and we are allowed to watch tv until 11pm.

She had such an arrogant look on her face which made me want to slap her. A row ensued between us and a couple of the other nurses came in to witness the goings on. They knew me well and had never seen me get angry before. I even surprised myself. She looked at me as if I were a piece of dirt on her shoe. I then told her to choose an f;ing window as I was going to put her through it. She then ran out of the room. The other nurses bless their hearts just asked me if I was alright. I felt a bit bad about behaving that way in front of the other patients as even though I know I can look after myself I did not want them to be scared of me. I wouldn't really have put her through a window. At least I don't think so AND we got to watch the rest of the Olympics. That particular nurse was then transferred to the men's ward and subsequently got the sack. Hoo bloody ray. I have no idea why she got the sack but she really was a horrible woman. Most of the nurses in there really are wonderful.

My release date.

At last. At long, long last. Five flipping months of my life spent in there and I was going home. Yay f'ing yay. If you have been locked away from Society for 5 long, long months everything seems strange at first. Believe it or not everything seems so much faster, cars, people walking in the street, everything. It is bizarre. It was not all bad, and there were times when I enjoyed myself in there. All of my best friends have Bipolar. I think they are the funniest people in the world. Dave moved in from day one and when I returned home he and Joey had done amazing things with my cottage.

It was decided that I needed a holiday so Dave and I went away for a couple of weeks. It wasn't the best holiday I had ever been on as Dave was grumpy from day one. I felt that he wanted to control me. We had to do whatever he wanted to do which was drink, drink and drink some more otherwise he would sulk, and he could sulk for Britain. Anywhoo I hadn't thrown him over the balcony as I was so tempted to do and we arrived home to my darling Joey. When I got home Joey told me that the Police had been to my home and said that I was to be placed under arrest. What??? They didn't tell Joey what for and he was visibly shaken up. As if that boy hadn't been through enough. The town which I live in is so small and the police were well aware that I had been sectioned for five months. They were even present when it happened. I rang the station immediately and the Police came and arrested me. When they informed me of what I had been arrested for I was gobsmacked. It transpired that I had been accused of stealing a kit kat. You bastards. A flipping Kit kat. I know full well that I would not have stolen a Kit kat as I was training for the World championships at kickboxing and would not allow myself to eat chocolate. A bottle of wine maybe but not a Kit kat. Get lost PC Plod I am joking. I do not go out stealing anything.

At one point in the Police station I reached over to see what a PC had written about me. I accidently tore the page of his notebook. They were then going to do me for criminal damage. Oh my life. Thankfully my solicitor made that young officer look like the idiot he is. They had put Joey and I through all of that for nothing. The manageress of Spar, a Denise Morgan who just so happened to be my ex Rich's sister in law and knew full well what had happened to me had had me arrested over a chocolate bar. She told the Police that I had picked it up and taken it to the checkout where Dave was paying for other goods but the choccy bar was not paid for. Why wasn't he arrested then? The police took my finger prints, mug shot the lot and yet when they showed me the CCTV footage from I couldn't even see a Kit kat. I wonder how much that whole procedure cost compared to the price of a Kit kat anyway. God I dislike that woman so much. I see her in the street occasionally and I really would like to have it out with her. I really don't care what she did to me, but for what she put my children through I will never forget that. Poor little Jaisee thought that I was going to prison. It couldn't be much worse than Shelton though, if not a little better. The next time I see her in the town I might tell her that I am writing a book and that she is one of the main characters in it. But no, I really cannot be bothered.

I was walking through the precinct one day in town and passed Denise and one of her daughters. I have no idea what Denise had said to her daughter but she gave me a really filthy look. Bring it on little girl as I am not one teensy little bit afraid of you either. The charges were dropped, but not before the Police broke my right to confidentiality and informed my employers. They jumped all over me. I was interviewed by yet another bitch troll from hell named Amanda Lewis. She threatened me with the sack and asked why I had not informed them about the incident? Because I didn't f ing do it you arsehole. Of course I didn't say that but I dislike that creature so much. What did she expect me to do roll up for work and say "oh by the way I didn't steal a Kit kat today, nor yesterday but I'll sure as hell let you know if I do tomorrow" You idiot.

I saw her in the town recently and it was all that I could do to stop myself from shouting at her. Social Services a caring profession? My dear aunt Fanny.

I have been told that she and Jessa have left Powys now. Good flipping riddance. They really are horrible people and it's quite frightening to think that they were and still may be in positions of power. The thought of them possibly moving to another authority scares me. God help anyone who employs them. I wonder as outsiders how they view the human race. I spoke to Amanda on the telephone one day before she left Powys and I used the term abuse. She went on to say that if I had been abused in hospital that I should put in a complaint. I had not been abused by anyone in hospital at that point (only later when I was under Phillipa Walker's so called care). My complaint is about you Amanda. Bang. She put the phone down.

Shame and Scandal in the family.

One evening I was out with an ex-client of mine, a young man named Heman who visited me in hospital. We went to a local pub for a drink. I immediately sensed that they didn't like Hem or the fact that I was with him. We were going to leave and then we were told to. We put on our coats and left but 3 men followed us outside. One man was named Howard Johnston, another called Jim Mc Bride and a third man I didn't know. They began hitting Heman and Jim held his arms behind his back and Howard kicked him between his legs. When I tried to help Heman Howard threw me to the ground and began punching and kicking me. This is a photograph of how I looked when they had finished with me.

This however hurt me far more than the beating did when Howard shouted to me that I was a disgrace to my family. I think everyone will find that I am not a disgrace to my family and in fact they are rather proud of me for withstanding 3 years in the nuthouse and finding the strength to quit drinking, so f you Howard. I don't beat up women and children. I wonder how your family feel about you? The police were called and they took me home. I felt extremely disorientated and went straight to bed. When I rang the police the following day to find out what was happening they told me that I was lucky not to have been arrested myself. What for? Lying on the ground while somebody kicked me? When I told them what they had done to Heman all they said was "we know Heman and he can take care of himself". A nineteen year old boy up against three grown men? Oh my god. Someone who lived nearby also told me that people were regularly beaten up outside that pub.

When my father ran his pub it was self policing. It was five miles outside Newtown and normally only locals visited it. On the odd occasion that strangers came to the pub and started to cause trouble the locals just threw them out. But nobody took them outside and beat them up. The Police called very rarely and when they did they were lovely. They all seemed to know my father well and would ask him if everything was alright and when my dad assured them that it was they left.

Anyway back to little Heman. What I find unbelievable is that most of us Brits strive to obtain a sun tan, but a person like Heman who is born with one, has to cope with the most insufferable abuse. Horrible.

When I first developed Bipolar a person's mental health was something not to be mentioned. I don't think my family told anyone thankfully. One evening after being discharged from my first admission I went out with my sister Annie. I felt very self conscious and didn't know if anyone knew I was a certified nutter. We walked past a pub where people were queuing to go in and a young man shouted to me, "Hi Junie, remember me from Shelton?" The young man was so nice I stopped to chat with him and thought, well if they didn't know before they sure as eggs do now. Shit!!!

I was very embarrassed and ashamed of my illness for several years, as Bipolar is so unbelievably horrendous but I now consider myself to be a survivor. Annie was absolutely brilliant and has let me stay at her home on several occasions when the powers that be felt I could not look after myself at home but was allowed out of hospital. I have no idea how she put up with me but she did. Other times though she would visit me and Joey when I was extremely manic and left the house saying to Joey "good luck" and left the poor boy to it. But at least she visited, love her

My four pence.

Another problem with Bipolar is that when you have a manic episode you spend, spend, and spend some more. IF you have any money. My children both say "we know when you're on a high mum because we get lots of presents". And they do. You feel so happy inside you want them to feel that happiness too. However I was getting myself into all kinds of pickles financially and had no idea how to get out of it. I must mention one particular firm Bang and Olufsen in Shrewsbury. What a firm. The members of staff there are so so lovely. I got it into my head that I could afford one of their amazing cd players. It would have looked and sounded amazing in my musical dining room. I soon discovered when standing orders were being returned to me due to insufficient funds that this was just not going to happen. I wrote to them and explained my situation, fully expecting to lose my deposit. Straight away they sent me a cheque for the £600 I had paid. They were excellent. A million bucks says I will own one of their players in the future. What a difference between them and Sky and Everest. Just wait and see.

A girl I know has now been diagnosed with this horrendous illness. Bless her. When she is on a high, or stable she calls us crazy fuckers. But of course she suffers with the lows too. She says that her head feels like a jigsaw puzzle and she can't put the pieces back together. She also says that she would like to take her brain out, give it a good wash and pop it back in. If only.

My Family.

Since my last very serious overdose my family have been amazing. They are really supportive. I know that if I needed them I would only have to pick up the phone and they would be here. Initially they didn't understand my illness at all and just thought I was being a bigger pain in the arse than usual. I didn't understand my illness so I couldn't expect them to. However, I have felt all my life that I am different from my brothers and sisters. I had dark hair and they were all fair. I was a risk taker, they were not. When I was a child I used to think that maybe I was the milkman's or perhaps had been left by a stork. But I know full well that my mother would never have cheated on my father. He acted as if he didn't like me very much, to the point that most other people felt that way too. But I know he loved me, and I am too much like him not to be his. Maybe that was the problem. I'm not sure about my brothers but I know my poor sisters were frightened of him but I really didn't give a damn what he did or said to me.

My siblings used to hate school, and never sat a single exam, but I loved it. I just so much wanted to learn. No one ever picked on me either. My elder sister Annie was a bully in High School so when I started School the bullies used to say "that's Ann Pritchard's sister, don't touch her". Cool. My siblings went into manual work whereas I was just a pen pusher in my father's eyes and felt I hadn't done a day's work in my life, but I didn't give a toss what he thought. I was doing what I wanted to do.

Once I was diagnosed with Bipolar I researched it like crazy. Oops. Bad choice of word huh, but I did. Any little bit of information I could find I read. I went away on a weekend Bi polar course. It was great. Twelve nutters, in one hotel. I learnt an awful lot. I often wondered what the staff thought when they found out we were all basket cases but they were all lovely. I have attended seminars and went to a talk on Bi Polar by Ruby Wax who has this illness and is absolutely lovely. I did everything I could to learn how to cope with this illness. Am I any further forward in learning how to deal with it? Yes I like to think so.

Accepting this illness is the major battle. When you have lived your life as a normal person until the age of 44 and then out of no-where you suddenly develop such a critical illness it is difficult to accept.

Prior to this illness my life was great. I have two wonderful sons, a beautiful home, and a nice partner. I had gained my Diploma in Social Work and had a good job and a bright future. My hobby was kickboxing and I had just won the European Championships.

European Champion

A member of staff from social care is celebrating after winning the women's European Kickboxing Championship.

Post Care Worker June Pritchard shone in the freestyle category. A former Welsh Open Champion, June now qualifies to compete at the 2006 World Championships which take place in Malta later this year. It has been a rapid rise for June who only took up the sport three years ago. She was introduced to kickboxing by her son. After attending several sessions as a parent observer decided to give it a try. "It's very much a discipline sport and far from the aggressive activity many people assume," explains June.

Kickboxing is currently an amateur sport so competitors rely on their spare time for training and competition. To keep on top of her game June has to train six times a week. She is a member of the Powys freestyle kung fu and kickboxing club where she recently won 'fighter of the year'.

June has worked for Powys County Council for 15 years, initially as an administration assistant and then a Community Support Officer. After completing a diploma in social work through the Open University which was funded by the council, June has taken up a new position of Post Care Worker in the 'leaving care' unit – a small team which helps young people leaving foster care into the transition of independent living.

Junie Pritchard

Here is a photograph of me just after winning the Europeans.

See how happy I looked? Then bam!! I lost Joey's dad, my father, I lost my partner, my home, my career as a Social Worker had ended and certainly not through choice, and I lost the opportunity to fight in the World Championships kickboxing. All of that, in a matter of a few months. None of that really matters to me now as I am extremely grateful I still have my children. They truly are amazing. They have put up with fifteen years of Bipolar and eight years of me drinking. I really am one very lucky Bi polar bear.

Life before Bipolar was pretty normal. I was brought up until the age of 13 in a pub and on a small farm. I used to love spending time in both. My nan and granddad lived a couple of fields away and I loved going to stay with them too. I had so much fun there. I normally stayed there with my lovely cousin Ivor. My nan used to get a mop and stand outside our bedroom window at night and tap it pretending that she was a ghost. My grandpa would sometimes pick me up and put me on top of a calf and I would try to ride it. He milked the cows and sometimes squirted the milk in my face. He would also tie my hat onto a sheep and I would have to run after it to retrieve it. My childhood was practically idyllic. Unfortunately my grandpa passed away when I was 13 and my nan lived alone for many years. I loved my nan so much. She could be a little bit strict and a little scary but that did not stop me thinking the world of her. Towards the end of her life perhaps she didn't take as many baths as she might have. My siblings would hardly go near her, but I didn't give a monkey's about any of that and I used to regularly hug her. She told me that I was the only person that ever gave her a hug. So what if she smelt a little like "eau de la cabbage" instead of Brut? I certainly didn't.

I find it so sad to know that some elderly people do not experience the feelings brought on by a hug for months on end. The motto that I had in Shelton still applies now that I have my freedom. "A hug a day keeps the Psychiatrist away". People hug trees for goodness sake. Why not hug a person instead? I don't think the trees would particularly miss you.

The only bad thing I remember was my father's use of his belt. I have no idea how many times he used it but use it he did. He would also say to me if I said I didn't want to do something that I would be the death of my mother. I was very young at the time and I really believed that she might die, so I did everything he told me to do. My mum was diagnosed as a Paranoid Schizophrenic at a very young age so I assume my Bipolar may be hereditary, but I believe that my job being extremely stressful and the way my managers treated me when Joeys father and my father passed away within a week of each other were to blame for bringing it on. Otherwise why haven't my siblings got it? And how come I got to the age of 44 with no problems at all? Most people develop this absolutely horrible illness in their twenties. I honestly believe that Social Services, particularly

Junie Pritchard

Claire Turner and her managers, Amanda Lewis and Clive Bartley are to blame.

I left School at the age of 15, enrolled in the army as a nurse, but couldn't join up until I was seventeen and a half. So I went to College and did a B tech course in Business Studies and lived and worked in a pub in the evenings and weekends to support myself.

For some reason I smile a lot. I think it is probably laziness as it takes fewer muscles to smile than it does to frown. My father used to sometimes hate it, my superiors in the Army did and my kickboxing coach did too. The amount of times I was told by all of them that they wanted to knock that smile off my face was in the hundreds. Bollucks to them I thought. Why don't you try and make me?

This is a poem written by Spike Milligan and I believe it could have been written with people like me in mind; SMILE Smiling is infectious You catch it like the flu. When someone smiled at me today I started smiling too. I walked around the corner and someone saw me grin When he smiled I realised I had passed it on to him. I thought about the smile and then realised its worth. A single smile like mine could travel round the earth. So if you feel a smile begin don't leave it undetected, start an epidemic and get the world infected. God Bless Spike as he had Bi Polar too. My smile also used to get me out of a lot of trouble. I was caught smoking in the toilets at School by a lovely teacher named Dr Leighton. I thought I was really in for it this time. I said I was sorry and smiled at him. He said "get out of here smiler and don't do it again". Phew, that was a close one. At College I was in trouble yet again for going on a trip to London to the stock exchange as part of my Business Studies course. I thought to myself while I'm down here I might as well visit my friends in Kent for a couple of days. I informed my tutor and as it was the weekend I could go. He asked if I had informed my parents and with my fingers crossed behind my back I told him that I had, and off I went. One of my class mates grassed me up and told him that my parents weren't on the phone. I rang my mum on the Saturday morning at work and she was fine about it. As I said they just knew that I would be alright. I think that my parents saw me as the capable one and would be alright wherever I went. I remember going to the seaside on our Annual Sunday School trip and all the kids ran into the arcades except for me who bought myself a beef burger. The seller said to my parents "she will never go hungry". And I was still as skinny as a rake. When I returned to College I was hauled in front of the Principal. He said to me "June you are above average intelligence and you are wasting it". I apologised and smiled at him. He said "you can't get through life with only that smile of yours you know" He then said "but on this occasion you can but get out of my office and don't come back here". I said "if it's any consolation Sir I had a rotten time". "Did you June?" "No". Why can't I just quit while I am behind? I thought I was really looking at expulsion this time, but I carried on with the course and passed with flying colours. Phew again!!

At the age of sixteen I joined the Army. I could not join fully until the age of seventeen and a half. I was eventually allowed to go to Aldershot to do my basic training in the army as a nurse in the "Queen Alexander's Royal Army Nursing Core". I really was a nightmare. I think because my father used to shout at me so much their shouting used to go straight over my head. I believe that the reason for Basic Training in the Army is an attempt to break you. And boy did they try hard to do it. They used to shout obscenities at us and do their level best to belittle us and break us. Some poor women they did.

Because I am Welsh they called me a sheep shagger, but as my friend Alfy says "we shag them, you eat them, enjoy your lunch". But I can't stop smiling. I am happy for the first time in an age, and I was happy in the Army too. On one occasion I wanted to grow my hair. They had a ridiculous rule that you either had to wear your hair up or it had to be so short it had to be above your collar. My hair was too short to put up so I just let it grow. One day on parade my hair was touching my collar. My Regimental Sgt Major bellowed at me "get your fucking hair cut Private Pritchard". (They swore at us a lot which I thought was really rather rude. My father hadn't sworn at me once.) So I thought ok you really horrible specimen I will. I got a set of clippers and buzzed my hair so short I was almost bald. You should have seen her face the next time I was on parade. It was priceless. Ha Ha. F ing have it. You were the one who told me to get my hair cut sarge so I have. I am only following orders. On another occasion they had set up a mock bombing incident. It looked very true to life and there was carnage everywhere. One woman had a bandage around her head covered in fake blood. As I walked past she said "I ain't half got a bloody headache". I found this hilarious and couldn't help but laugh. My Regimental Sergeant major, who really wasn't a particularly pleasant woman at all shouted at me "this is no laughing matter Private Pritchard wipe that grin off your face". I continued to smile as I looked directly at her as I walked past and thought to myself "where's your sense of humour woman?"

I loved the Army. Initially when I joined up at the age of 17 I was very homesick. My father would not allow us to have a phone in our new home as he was used to it ringing late in to the night at the pub, normally from women asking were their husbands still there? This meant I could only speak to my mum on a Saturday morning when she was at work. We were not allowed to go home for what felt like an age in case we didn't go back. In the army all of us stuck together. I also got on well with all of the guys in the force.

For some reason everyone had it in for the Paratroopers. I had no idea why. You could spot them a mile off because they wore maroon berets. The remarks that were made about them were horrid. However, whenever I treated any of them in hospital they were perfectly lovely. I was not prepared to get involved in any of that pettiness. Speak as you find I feel. After all is said and done, more is said than done.

We were issued with the biggest grey bloomers I had ever seen. They were worse than Bridget Jones's. We even had to iron them. Who they thought was going to see my neatly pressed knickers I just do not know. I was also made to wear a grey beret which really didn't suit me. It made me look like Frank Spencer, for those of you are old enough to remember him. Here I am in Aldershot with a whole bunch of women I barely knew (just like Shelton only this time we were not all crazy) and we had lots of fun together. I eventually got over my homesickness and loved every minute of it. Well almost every minute. On one occasion whilst I was nursing we had to deal with a terrible road traffic accident. A Military Policeman said to me. "I have spent all day looking for a shoe". When I asked him why? He said "because there was a foot in it".

We used to use a lot of black humour to get us through incidents like this in the Army. However it would have been frowned upon at Social Services. I find Political correctness utterly dull and boring. I believe that the Army also prepared me for Shelton. I have no idea of the figures but there seemed like hundreds of women of all ages and backgrounds and we all had to learn to get on. Lots of women had to leave because they failed the fitness tests. Others were thrown out because they were deemed not suitable and some just couldn't hack it. They used to shout such horrendous obscenities at us and do their best to belittle us. Many women left very quickly.

One of their favourite verbal barbs towards me was "you think that life is just one big joke don't you Private Pritchard". I used to reply "no ma'am" but all that I used to think to myself was "no I think you're one f ing big joke ma'am". I passed the fitness test with flying colours, I believe because of my 3 mile walk that my mother and I went on everyday and my general hyperactivity. Why we had to be absolutely super fit to become a nurse baffles me somewhat but we did. They certainly were not in the Psychiatric hospitals I had been in.

Those of us who got through the basic training then had a passing out parade. I can see why they called it a passing out parade. Women were passing out left right and centre. Luckily I had been told that when you are standing to attention for a very long period of time to twiddle your toes and this would stop you passing out. I gave all of my friends this piece of advice but I could not tell everyone. They were just dropping like flies. But luckily I didn't.

My parents actually came to this parade and I think that that was the only time in my life my father was actually proud of me. He asked me to come with him to Chapel wearing my uniform when I was home on leave. I did and this time it was him who was smiling. It saddens me that he never got to watch me play football or kickboxing.

Anywhoo here I am back at Aldershot with a whole bunch of women I barely knew (just like Shelton only this time we were not all crazy). We had lots of fun together when we were off duty and drank copious amounts of alcohol at weekends normally in the NAFFI or the Army and Navy club. In the Army and Navy club I met the first lesbians (that I know of) in my life. One was a Captain in the Air Force and another, a Captain in the Army. They asked me if I would go back to their room with them and I just knew they didn't mean for a cup of coffee. I was terrified and went straight back to my friends. One of the guys I was drinking with had heard what they had asked me and said that he was going to hit them? "What? You can't hit a woman". He said "I know them and they are not women they are dykes" (another word I hate). I begged him not to and thank goodness he didn't. It was all very disturbing and I didn't go near them again. Back then gay men and lesbian women were not allowed in the forces so they were taking a huge risk asking me.

We had to be awake at 5.30 every morning to get ready for room inspections and everything had to be spotless. These days

5.30am is still the middle of the night for me. We weren't even allowed a drop of water in our sinks. We had to catch a bus to the hospital at 7am. Every day one particular girl was late and that would make us all late. In the Army if one person messes up we were all in trouble. How unfair is that? But that is the way it was. So we hatched a plan to get the lazy so and so out of bed. About ten of us all set our alarms for 5.30am and placed them outside her door. It was hilarious watching her panic and try to turn them all off. She wasn't late again.

Our punishments for insubordination in the forces was usually peel a mountain of potatoes, clean the toilets with a toothbrush or do press-ups in the exercise yard with our back packs on. I have had to do all of them on more than one occasion. All I ever seemed to hear was "jankers Private Pritchard" and thought "here we go again". Jankers is what they called our punishments. When I left I almost fell through the floor as I had in my mitts on my discharge papers stating that my conduct had been exemplary. Who me? I couldn't believe it. I almost wanted to stay in, but not quite.

Apparently Sgt Bullock was in the army. Lord preserve us. I said to one of the police officers that Sgt Bullock should be pepper sprayed so that he knew what it felt like. He informed me that he had. So he knew exactly how much pain he was prepared to inflict on a vulnerable adult for being "difficult". It makes me feel sick to think that men like him were in the Armed Forces and he is now a sadistic police sergeant. Sgt Bullock epitomises bullying.

I honestly believe that there is something wrong with the man and would benefit from a mental health assessment of his own.

Another thing that is pertinent to my story is that even following all of my complaints, and other Police officers have told me that they are not impressed by his tactics he is still in post. See? The nastier you are in the Police force the higher in rank you seem to go. In my view he is a complete and utter waste of space and had such a detrimental effect on my mental health. And yet again following a night in the with him in charge I found myself back in Shelton.

As I said in the Army we were like one big family and watched each other's backs. In Shelton you could seemingly get on with people like a house on fire then bang, they would turn on you like a sixpence. There were very few women I trusted in there. In the Army all of us nurses stuck together. I loved the army. I thoroughly enjoyed the basic training and feel that it gives you a very good grasp of how to take care of yourself. When I joined up I didn't even know how to write a cheque or change a plug but I soon learnt. One of the things I did not enjoy was the gas chamber. I don't know if the Army still does this but it was horrible. We were given gas masks to wear and made to walk around the chamber a few times. We were then told to remove the canister at the side of the gas mask which kept the air in and the gas out. Next we had to recite our name rank and number before they would let us out. Luckily I remembered mine and do to this day; (Private Pritchard Q1013629.) Other poor women didn't. They had blisters all around the outside and inside of their mouths. What on earth is the point of doing that to us? I thought that was just cruel, and I would have loved to have shoved the officers who did it to us in there too, with no gas mask available to them at all. Take nice big breaths you nasty people. Luckily I learnt from that experience not to put water into your eyes when you are pepper sprayed as this begins the whole burning sensation again and could lead to permanent scarring or even blindness. Sgt Bollocks you are a complete and utter arsehole.

Then I began my Nursing training and loved it. Sometimes, since my diagnosis of Bipolar, people ask if I am suffering from Post Traumatic Stress due to the Army, and although I saw some sights that maybe a 17 year old shouldn't see I am convinced that this is not the case. The Army took very good care of me. I used to socialise with the officers in my time off. Some of them were so nice and apologised to us for what they had to put us through, but explained that they had all gone through it themselves. Others had the Sgt Bollocks syndrome and they were really f,ing enjoying putting us through it. But, people were always there who would help me through it in the Army. You soon find out who is nice and who isn't and I would only spend times with the ones I liked.

The ward I hated working on the most was the Children's ward. I will never forget one little girl who had pulled at the chord of a kettle and had scalded herself all down the right side of her body. Her parents and nurses had to wear cotton gloves because as soon as you touched her without them it would cause her to bleed. I honestly had nightmares about that poor little tot. She was kept away from the other children in a little glass room. I thank heaven that I was not the nurse responsible for her but I used to tap the glass and wave at her and visit her whenever I could. One day I went to see her and she said in her tiny little voice "I love you Junie". Oh my god I so wanted to hold her but I couldn't. I begged them not to put me on the children's ward again but that was just not possible. That went a long way to making me want to leave. I just did not have the stomach for it at the age of seventeen. I left the Army after 3 years a) because of situations I have just mentioned and b) as the main reason I joined was to travel but I didn't. I certainly wasn't going to join up for another six years to be needed here.

As I mentioned I applied to join the Police Force, and was accepted but am so glad I didn't go through with it. I now know I could not fit in there in a million years. I am way too honest to begin with.

CHAPTER 5. JOHN

When I left the Army I secured a job in the Benefit's Agency, both here in my home town and in Canterbury, Kent. I lived in Kent for seven years. That is where I met Joey's dad, John. When I first saw him he was a doorman at a nightclub. He was standing at the top of the steps on the way in, wearing a tuxedo and I thought Wow. He looked just like Henry Cooper. He held the Light Heavyweight boxing title for the whole of Thanet. He looked so fit and handsome, I thought, definitely my kind of man. John was most definitely the love of my life. I guess with John's boxing background and my kick boxing it was inevitable that Joey became a cage fighter. I believe it is in his blood. Joey was born in 1987 and John and my relationship were already floundering before he was born. We both loved Joey with a passion but in the end we split up when Joey was four. He continued to be an excellent father travelling from Kent (where he returned to when we split up) to Wales to see Joey right up until his death. Joey was born out of wedlock so what I find really frightening was that up until 1962 (the year I was born) women who were not married and gave birth to a child would be locked up in a Psychiatric hospital while the men got away scot free. What a cruel world we live in.

When Joey was four I started work for Social Services. I worked in administration for four years and one of my bosses suggested that I apply for a job in the Children and Families team. Admin was fine but there were no challenges in the job, therefore I applied for the post and got it. Annie G and I did a job share. It is a known fact that part time workers work way and above their contracted hours and Annie and I sure did. We were never able to take time off in lieu as the Social Workers did as we just did not have the time. I also worked with Out of County Placements and two of my clients were in foster care in the Cotswolds which meant I worked late into the evening with that family and many others. The foster carers in the Cotswolds' Social Worker was on long term sick which meant I had to work with them as well as the children. Talk about being used and abused. I worked my ass off for that team and even more so for the Leaving Care team, and when I got ill where were they? Plotting to get rid of me. I was an embarrassment to them. And they knew that I knew way too much about them.

Jeremy Patterson was the Chief Executive of Social Services at that time and he has a lot to answer for. And so do Amanda Lewis and Claire Turner, and Clive Bartley. In my mind the four of them are oxygen thieves and complete wastes of space. According to my friend Glyn they are wankers and it's a shame that their fathers hadn't been too at the time of their conception. The world would have been a much happier place without them. I am not being rude, they are just insignificant. I believe that Jeremy Patterson would be out of his depth in a car park puddle. Now he has left Powys I believe he is not so much of a has been as a definitely won't be. You are not being paranoid Jessa everyone does hate you, but nobody more than me. I have just heard that Jeremy Patterson left Powys with a whopping £170 thousand pounds pay out. He was TOLD to leave Powys for failing to protect children. I did not fail to protect a single child and left with jack shit.

Clive Bartley and I were friends. He came to my home on a couple of occasions and even met my son Joey. However the moment (if not before) I became ill he was nowhere to be seen. He did not visit me in hospital or even send me a get well card. AND he was hugely instrumental in ending my career.

In Shelton I tried to get on with everyone but some people made it practically impossible. There was always someone who was prepared to grass you up to the nurses. I used to be a beautician for the Body Shop and I took lots of products in to the smoking room to do my beautifying. Pat's took a disliking to this and in her words "twitted on me" to the nurses. The nurses came in and saw that what I was doing was harmless and didn't say a word. I don't know what her problem was but "up yours Pats". I loved working for the Body Shop and got to meet Anita Roddick who was the founder of the company. She was the first person to refuse to use animals to test make up on. She began her company by mixing products in her bath. Wow what a long long, way her company has come. And she did it without being so completely and utterly nasty as Sky and Everest. Sometimes I have to admit I was a bit mean as some of the women I had to make up I really did think to myself "what on earth am I going to do to make you look good". Others I really wish I could have worn gloves. But I did my best to make them all look good and I think I succeeded.

When I told Pats that I was a Social Worker she didn't believe me. She had an image in her mind of a harsh looking woman wearing a tweed suit, and that certainly wasn't me. She was bang on the mark with a lot of them though. In hospital I had tirades of abuse thrown at me for absolutely no reason. But I decided to rise above it and told myself they were ill, and although that is not how I chose to behave, they obviously did. There were too many freaks and not enough circuses in there.

The stigma towards mental health sufferers still exists, but it has thankfully improved greatly over the last fifteen years that I have been ill. One day in the Park offices in Newtown when I worked in the Leaving Care Team, I was coming up the stairs and heard some commotion going on at the front of the building. A lovely girl I will call K, who had had a horrible little life, in and out of children's homes and back and forth to foster carers, had understandably, I feel, developed a drink problem. K was passed out on the floor, lying in her own vomit. There was a balcony upstairs looking down towards the front entrance where she lay. I could not believe what I was seeing. Her social worker was looking over the balcony laughing at her. Oh my god. I and a lovely lady from administration put her into the recovery position, cleared her airways and called an Ambulance whilst her own social worker found the whole thing hilarious. That poor girl could have choked on her own vomit and died. How these vile Social Workers keep their jobs, or even get their jobs in the first place is beyond me. She is definitely a candidate for management. In the short period of time I had the privilege of working with K she gave up the booze and then I went into hospital. Sadly the young girl has now passed away due to alcohol related illnesses bless her.

We did have one lovely Area Care manager. She came into my office one day with a little boy who was going to be adopted. He came in with his shoulders slouched and his head down. She said to him that when couples who have their own children they have no choice at all, they get what they have been given. She then went on to tell him that he was special as his adoptive parents had chosen him. His head raised and he puffed his little chest out. What a beautiful thing to say. I will never forget it. I can see exactly why she went into Social Work as opposed to thousands of others who so obviously don't give a damn.

The Police.

One evening the police arrested me as they believed I was drunk and disorderly. I wasn't. I was going through a manic stage of my illness. They literally threw me into a cell, denied me my life saving medication, refused to let me telephone Joey to let him know where I was. I showed them a Crisis card which was given to me by Social Worker clearly stating that I had Bipolar and that if I were to behave out of character my Social Worker, Lauraine Hamer should be called immediately. Not that the useless cow would have done much anyway. They were obviously too thick to read. They ignored it and my right to contact a solicitor was also ignored. I was locked in the cells overnight on three occasions and they thought it was fun. Three, times. Ha Boris Johnson got into trouble for calling the police plebs. I wonder how this is going to sit with them. You complete and utter tossers.

Here I found myself in the Police cells on the third occasion. I was very, very poorly. Yet again I had been refused all of my rights. The stupid idiots learn fast don't they? Sgt Bullock called me to the door and pepper sprayed me directly into my eyes. The pain was excruciating and it is a very effective disabling device if the poor little babies are ever under threat. I think you can guess what I have nicknamed him. I was approximately three inches away. And yes I am talking about the distance between us and not his nether region. I think three inches would probably be a bit of an exaggeration there. The little needle dick. Here is a copy of a solicitors report stating that the spray should not be used less than 3 FEET away unless life is at risk.

'Rambo' cop slated for CS attack on mother and son

By Charles Yates / Published 21st March 2010

AN innocent mum won police compensation after being CS sprayed by a "Rambo" officer.

Angela Parmenter, 46, was driving her son Daniel home from a party when they were pulled over by an unmarked police car. But Daniel, 15, who had been drinking, became abusive to the police – PC Damien Lowe and colleague Brian Gibbs – and they warned him they would arrest him for swearing. Daniel, who was upset that they'd been stopped, continued shouting at the officers despite his mother trying to calm him down. When he refused to leave the car, in the centre of Evesham, Worcs, PC Lowe fired CS spray into it, blinding the pair. Now Angela, a hairdresser, has sued the Chief Constable of West Mercia for damages in the first successful case of its kind. She was awarded almost £6,000 and costs of around £30,000 at Birmingham County Court. At a one-day trial, Judge Martin McKenna called the use of CS spray an "excessive response" because Daniel offered "no physical threat" to the officers. Worcester-based PC Lowe, who joined the force in 1996, admitted that firing the spray into Daniel's face from just two feet away had been "an error on my part". QC Mark Lynne, representing Angela, pointed out that West Mercia guidelines say it shouldn't be used at "less than three feet unless life is at risk" and it should not be used in confined spaces. The Chief Constable's guidelines also stated CS spray should only be used on violent people and Daniel had offered "no physical violence". Outside court Angela said: 'It was horrific. As soon as he strode up like Rambo and sprayed into the car, we were blinded and the stinging was horrendous. "At the time Daniel was a skinny schoolboy. He was swearing as he'd been drinking. Harm "They were two burly policemen and should have physically removed him from the car without the CS spray. "I still can't believe it happened. But I'm glad justice has been done." Her solicitor Nick Turner said: "It sends a clear message police officers mustn't harm innocent bystanders as they perform their duties."

When you are in those cells there is absolutely nothing in there to harm yourself with, unless they think I'm going to strangle myself with toilet paper. There was a camera in there so they could have been watching me go to the toilet. Oh my god it was horrible. On the same night of the pepper spraying I had my period and asked for some sanitary products. They wouldn't even give me that. What did they think I would do? Shove a tampon up my nose and die of toxic shock poisoning?

The following morning a female DI spoke to me at the desk and she was quite apologetic about the lack of feminine products but not worried about the pepper spraying at all. What an idiot. This all happened very soon after my diagnosis and I wanted to see what my behaviour was like when I am really ill as I am not fully aware of it. I went to see Sgt Bullock and asked him for the CCTV footage. He refused. I asked what my behaviour had been like and he replied "you weren't that bad you were just difficult.

Difficult? If that is what you do to difficult members of the public what on earth do they do to hardened criminals? I have since heard that a young man in Newtown was being arrested and a police officer pepper sprayed him. It was windy that day and some of the pepper spray had blown into the officers eyes. The young man was then charged with assaulting a police officer???? Who was the one with the pepper spray?

On my second arrest good old Sgt Flanaghan told me I was ugly the second I came through the door. Exf'ingscuse me? Is that really the best you can do? He was obviously trying to antagonise me. He is no flipping oil painting himself. However he has not given me a complex and I do not feel the need to leave the house with a paper bag over my head. I believe that beauty comes from within so that nasty little bleep has no chance.

I obtained the CCTV footage of my arrests from my solicitor and it was clear that they left me in handcuffs for an age, far longer than necessary and they hurt like a bugger. I begged them to take them off and was eventually let loose from the handcuffs. I am not proud of my language or behaviour in there but Dr Wasi Mohamad has also viewed the footage and it was clear that I was extremely ill and becoming more so.

One of the young Police Officers who brought me in told Sgt Flanaghan that I had Bipolar and had been to my home to section me on a previous occasion. Sgt F took no notice and continued to antagonise me. I was on a high and he obviously found my behaviour funny. Again my rights to my medication and to contact someone were ignored. Again I was kept awake all night. Sleep deprivation is a form of torture particularly to someone who suffers from Bipolar and I believe I was tortured in those cells in this sleepy little town of Newtown, on not one but on three separate occasions. Yet again I was literally thrown into a cell by a young police officer. I could not believe it. What the hell had I done wrong? Absolutely nothing other than get ill and this time I was being locked in a police cell as opposed to the nut house.

Whilst I was in the cell I was raging. I could not believe they were taking my liberty away from me yet again. I have to admit that my behaviour was not all that pleasant either. I was shouting and swearing, calling Sgt Flanaghan Hitler, (Apparently Hitler had Bipolar too). Not my bestest claim to fame) but in my view that is exactly how Flanaghan behaved. I am not proud of my behaviour but I felt completely ridiculed by the police. They laughed and made jokes about me and I really felt that I was a sport to them. Ooh we've got the town nutter here for the night so let's have some fun. The later in the night it was getting I was becoming increasingly out of control. They were despicable. I used to have such a healthy respect for the police but now I have none. Actually I am gradually changing my mind about them as recently I have met some very nice officer's and now that they are getting to know me they really do seem to wish me well.

When I made a complaint about SGT Bullocks use of pepper spraying a DI Oliver from the Independent???? Police Commission asked me if I had any permanent scarring. When I said no, he replied that's ok then we're dropping the case. Are you for real? What about the pain and suffering one of your officer's deliberately caused a known disabled person? If I had not known what to do from my nursing days I would probably have had permanent scarring and quite possibly lost my eye sight. DI CK Oliver. When they took me to court good old Sgt Flanaghan swore on oath that he had no idea I had Bipolar. My solicitor showed the court CCTV footage showing clearly that he had been told by another officer that I had. The smug bastard walked out of court without even a reprimand. Why aren't the police done for contempt of court when they so blatantly lie? The whole system stinks. I must stress though that whenever the Police have come to my home to help section me they have always been excellent and treated me with respect. One gorgeous young Police Officer even put up with me pinching his bottom. Some of them would have had me for sexual assault. I WAS ON A HIGH OK? But don't worry Sgt Bullock and Sgt Flanaghan I wouldn't go near you two with a barge pole as I do not view you two as men, you are just excuses for them.

Ha ha I am going to be hated by the whole of Powys when this book is published. It gives me a little warm glow when I think about it. My friend has just told me a joke by Jethro. It goes a little like this: One night he had been stopped by the Police. The officer asked how much he had had to drink. Jethro said "I've had six double vodka's, three whiskies, and a double gin". The police officer asked Jethro to blow into this bag, so Jethro said "don't you bastards believe anything?" I also like these; 23 people have been found glued to the ceiling and walls of a train in Dublin. Police believe Irish Muslims have set off the first "No Nails bomb". Mmmm. I think I will take some to the Police station.

BBC News reports a wild, mentally retarded, ugly fucker is on the loose. There is a £100,000 reward. You know I need the money so where are you Junie? One of the traits of a Bipolar person is that you do become overly familiar with members of the opposite sex. No man is spared. (Flanaghan and Bullock are excluded again). I even flirted with the top bod in Shelton. I asked him out to dinner in front of everyone else on the ward. Later I apologised for any embarrassment I may have caused him. He was absolutely lovely and said "don't worry Junie I was born embarrassed". Gosh the difference in men hey.

CHAPTER 6 Bipolar

Bipolar is not all bad. It has enabled me to retire early and have the time to write this book, which is something I have always wanted to do. My teachers always told me I should become a writer even in Primary School and Bipolar has given me something to write about. I guess the Bi bit means two and the Polar means Poles apart. You have the incredible highs where you feel euphoric, but can also put you in danger and you become extremely vulnerable, and the devastating lows where you feel like ending your own life. Sometimes the thought of death is preferable to the way you are feeling. As the Robbie Williams song goes "I don't want to die, but I ain't keen on living either". Sometimes I talk to God and ask him why I have got Bipolar? But there are no answers, I just have. And it is not God's wish. It was the wish of Social Services. I now realise of course it was not the wish of Social Services, for however abhorrently they treated me they could not have predicted Bi polar. Nobody could have, least of all me. I now forgive the people from Social Services who caused my illness. I am trying my best to forget them, but when they do creep into my thoughts I use them as a reminder NEVER to treat others the way that they treated me.
Sleep.

I think that the most important thing to a Bi polar person is their sleep. I once slept through a fire engine with the sirens on arriving next door in the middle of the night. And that's how soundly I used to sleep. Before I was sectioned for the first time I can't remember how long it had been since I had slept. Bipolar sufferers can go without sleep for an age and it is hell. You can imagine how ill we become. I believe it was the hurt and frustration of the bereavements which had occurred within a very short period of time, and most definitely the way Social Services used and abused me during this time.

Joey's dad had hung himself on the Thursday and the following day Joey wanted to be with his friends, so I went into work hoping to take my mind off things. I knew that we had a day planned at a local outward bound centre with the young people who are so much fun I thought it would do me good. I explained what had happened the day before to my manager Claire Turner and her manager Amanda Lewis and they put me in a room with two of the young people's babies to take care of. I couldn't believe it. I qualified as a Social Worker not a Child Minder. They were in another room having all the fun and I was stuck in a room on my own with two little people who were too young to speak. All I could think about was Joey. The following Tuesday my father died of cancer. Oh my god. I didn't know what had hit me. Poor Joey, he had lost his father and his grandfather in the space of a week. When I told him about his grandfather, bless his heart, he said "I'm sorry mum". I was given two weeks compassionate leave. On the Wednesday Joey and I drove to Kent to attend his father's funeral on the Thursday. We returned home on the Friday and that evening was the only time I could have seen my father in the Chapel of Rest. So that's what I did. I was absolutely devastated. My whole world had fallen apart. Even though we had had our differences like most families do I guess, I loved my father so very much.

I returned to work following my two weeks leave. As I said I had not slept in so long and my colleagues knew damn well how ill I was becoming. I fell asleep in supervision for goodness sake, how exhausted do I have to be? My boss found this hilarious and made fun of me. Still she continued to pile more and more work onto me. Another colleague named Carolyn who I thought was a friend at the time, was also a friend of my sister's and she visited us at my sister's home. I was extremely ill, banging my head against the wall and crying my heart out. She said to me that I was lucky not to have been sectioned that day. I didn't even know what sectioning meant. Whilst she was there I told her something in complete confidence, and do you know what she did? She blabbed to my manager. I will never trust any of those people again. Also pot calling the kettle black Carolyn.

When Social Services decided that I should have a graduated return, working mornings only and then building up to full time again, they shoved me down to Welshpool which was a further 15 miles away from where I used to work. I had not driven a foot in the five months that I had been locked away and was full of anxiety driving again. I was terrified. I knew not one of my colleagues so did not have the luxury of seeing any familiar faces. I was meant to shadow an experienced Social Worker to give me the feel of things again. This did not happen. The crappy manager told me that I should smarten myself up as I was no longer working with young people. Why? You look like shit, is that the new style now? What an idiot. Do you really think it matters? But my trousers were put away and out came my dresses. I really don't think my clients gave a flying f how I dressed (and I was never scruffy). What mattered was how I treated them. It was not a fashion parade. That woman is so insignificant to me I don't even remember her name, but I do remember what a complete and utter arsehole she was. I cannot contain my indifference to her. I did not sweat blood and tears to qualify as a Social Worker to spend my day making my clients feel that I was the have and they were have not's. I now know the name of that manager. It is Jane Jones. Next she asked me to make everyone there a drink as soon as I arrived into the office each morning. Are you for freakin real? There were four offices with three or four Social Workers in each. I used to have a little pad of paper taking their orders. When I was 13 I had a Saturday job at the Lion Café here in Newtown. I did exactly the same thing there but I didn't need an f'ing Diploma to do it when I waited on people then. THEN she wrote to Human Resources stating that by the time it took me to make MYSELF a drink in the morning I had no time left to do any work and she was unable to manage me. Even though I couldn't remember her name, I remember her face. Both of them you two faced cow Jane.

Sometimes I really wonder why people go into Social Work, and just like the police the higher up the ladder they go the nastier they seem to become. They show no care or compassion towards their clients or their staff, so why do they do the job?

On one occasion whilst I was in Shelton, my Social Worker Lauraine Hamer visited me. She stated that another Social Worker was going to ring me. She did. She told me that Social Services had received a report that I had left Jai in the house alone until 3am. God forbid I stay out that long. Are the nutters no longer allowed to party? Jai was 14 and Child Care law clearly states that a 14 year old is at an age when he can be left alone anyway, but I wouldn't do that. I knew that both boys were home together. At the age of 14 a youngster is deemed fit to babysit another child so I wonder which of my sons was babysitting who. They even interviewed Jai (poor little thing) and he confirmed that Joey was home with him. So what the f is your problem?

That should have been the end of it. But no. Because it was me they contacted me and told me all. I am in a Psychiatric hospital, already extremely worried about my children and they make a phone call like that. She even wanted to come to Shelton to interview me. And Laurraine Hamer (my wonderful Social Worker NOT) sat there throughout the whole phone call without saying a goddamn word. Whose flaming side was she on? She is honestly the worst Social Worker I have ever met and I was foolish enough to trust her. Oh my gosh it makes me so angry when I think of her. My poor, sensitive Jai being interviewed about his mother when she is miles away in a Psychiatric hospital. How could they?

I never had a single complaint made against me in the whole time I worked for Social Services. Other members of staff treated complaints like trophies. They even had star charts for every complaint they had. I swear to god. Unbelievable. And I'm the one who gets treated appallingly because I became ill. They really came at me from every angle. The police were arresting me at the drop of a hat and Social Services were investigating bogus reports, even when they knew they were unfounded they made damn sure I knew about it. They didn't care one iota that

I was in Shelton feeling like a bag of crap. They just went ahead and did it. I really despise Jeremy Patterson and I have never even met the creature. I'm sure I will though when I take them to the European Court of Human Rights. IF they allow him in though as I am pretty sure you have to be human in the first place to be allowed in and he just isn't.

I threatened to kill him once. Ha ha. I was really hacked off with the way he had treated me. He didn't even respond to the kind and encouraging words I had written to him. I was talking to my nurse and was just sounding off and told him I was going to kill him. That is exactly what your Psychiatric nurse is for, to be able to sound off about anything. I didn't mean it of course and I think I have enough restraint not to go near him, butt rat tat tat the police were at my door. PC Plod said "this could be seen as harassment June. We know about your kickboxing skills therefore we are concerned". Me? Harassing him? What about all that he had done to my children and I? I assured them that I was not going to going to go near him and they left. Phew!! Ha Ha. I wonder how it feels for Jeremy knowing that the local nutter is now allowed out without a nurse and I am gunning for him. I really hope he feels just a fraction of the fear that I have. I realise how harsh that sounds but where my children are concerned I really will do anything to protect them. The pen is mightier than the sword; therefore I am going to get my own back by writing this book. I'm going to make you famous Jeremy and for all the wrong reasons. I want the world to know what nasty people Powys Social Services are. Especially, when it is one of their own members of staff and I truly believe that I had never knowingly put a foot wrong. I really hope that he still thinks of me because I think a lot about him. And not fondly either. I will not let madness take its toll because it was you who drove me insane Jeremy.

CHAPTER 7 February 2017

My nurse came to visit me today. His name is Neil and his experience in mental health is vast. He is so interesting I could talk to him for hours. He has done a lot of work with forensic psychiatry and out of county placements. He made a very interesting point in that when criminals go to prison they have a release date. The mentally ill do not. We can be locked away against our will for indefinite periods of time, even for the rest of our lives. Oh bejesus. Escape is futile as the Police would just bring us back. Living with the thought of ever being sectioned again is almost unbearable. These places are the pits. I'd love to lock up a few of the people who have authority over these places for a week, be given the horrible medication we are forced to take, or maybe an injection in their behind and see how they like it. A lot of people who have been in charge of my life are complete and utter idiots and couldn't run a piss up in a brewery. I could though as I have had so much practice. I would love to be in charge of Jeremy Patterson, Clive Bartle, Amanda Lewis and Claire Turner even for just a day. I really would show no mercy. When I look back over the fifteen years of my life I think about the people in Authority who refused to help me. Social Services were by far the worst. I believe that they are solely responsible for my illness. If they had treated me properly from the word go I would not have become ill at all. Even after that very first episode if my graduated return to work had been handled properly I would not have developed Bi Polar. People ask me if I am glad to be out of Social Services. The answer is a big fat yes. I would never work for those people again. I would rather stick pins in my eyes. I will rebuild my life in time and I hope I will be happy again.

Unreasonable force.

Unreasonable force has been applied to so many people with mental health problems it is beyond belief. Both my friends Pats and Jennifer and I have suffered severe mistreatment from the Police. Pat's was being sectioned and she swears she was cooperating with the authorities and was not violent in the slightest. Three burly policemen brought her to the floor and lay on her. When she got to Shelton she was peeing blood. Those excuses for men could have killed her. When Jennifer was being sectioned, and this is outrageous, a Policeman cut her finger with a razor blade. An f'ing razor blade. I have seen the scar. Since when have the police been issued with razor blades? Talk about a Police state. Just who do they think they are? Neither of these incidents occurred in Powys.

As I have said every Police officer who has been to my home to section me has been amazing. I am not an easy person to deal with when I am ill and they treated me with the utmost respect. I don't know their names but maybe they will read this book one day so thank you. But then we have officers like Sgt Bullock who pepper sprayed me. I think that that was way past reasonable force when I am already locked in a cell. If you read this Sgt Bollocks, you can fuck off and piss off as well.

Some nurse's used to use unreasonable force too. You would see women with fingerprint bruises on their bodies when the nurses went over the top. I can only remember being restrained on a couple of occasions. One was when Claire Turner had told them to take my mobile phone away. I was struggling like crazy.

I probably weighed about 7 and a half stone at that time and there were five nurses restraining me and not one of them hurt me. Another was when they tried to stop me going down to the shop to transfer some money for Joey. I had three hours leave a day which I hadn't used up and got a text from Joey about six pm stating that he had no money. I told them I needed to go the shop and they refused. I explained what I needed to do and one of the agency nurses lied (I hate liars) and said that the shop was shut. It stayed open until 10 every night. It makes no difference anyway as the cash point is on the outside of the shop. Honestly, some of the nurses thought we were thick, not ill. They wanted me to stay in the hospital as it makes their life easier. I was not going to leave my son with no money so I kicked off. Five of them carried me into high dependency.

What? HDU? For exercising my rights? We had a huge argument in there and I told them that I have 3 hours leave a day and I have the section 17 papers to prove it. Sect 17 is leave. They had no choice other than to let me go. I went straight to the cash point and did what I had to do and Joey got to eat that night. I really felt like buying some alcohol (sometimes they bloody drove you to drink) but I thought better of it. I was gone for about 20 minutes. All that drama THEY created for nothing. No one used unreasonable force on me the horrible agency nurse just lied. God forbid if you or anyone you know gets admitted in to one of those places get to know your rights, because if it is easier for them no one will tell you them. Only Wasi.

Bi polar is one of the most heinous illnesses I know. Even when you don't have too many worries suicide is still somewhat appealing, and death seems preferable to life. Bipolar is a burden and not a choice. I would give anything to get rid of it but there is no cure. It is just rounds and rounds of illness with in my case limited periods of stability in between. Even when I am stable I continually ask myself if I am behaving normally, can people tell I have Bipolar just by looking at me. Am I going to be locked up today? When you have spent a total of three years in the last fifteen locked away against your will you end up with zero confidence which is something I am trying to address right now. And at this moment in time I am allowed out without a nurse. YES!!!! Bipolar brings with it an awful lot of guilt. Guilt for how my illness may have affected my children. Guilt for ever having being rude to anyone. I know that guilt is a wasted emotion but it is so difficult to shake off. I even feel guilty sometimes for being born.

I really do hope you enjoy this book. I hope that Social Services are scared of it because they should be. But hay ho. You can't please all of the people all of the time, only some of the people some of the time. I can only please one person per day. Today is not their day and tomorrow doesn't look too good either.

I tend to avoid most people now particularly my ex colleagues. Most people will tell me about their ailments and how bad they are feeling. I know it sounds harsh but I just cannot afford to care. I have a disorder that means tomorrow may never come for me for all I know. I may not get to tell Joey, Jai and Hannah how much I love them ever again. So your bad back or your ingrowing toenail pales into insignificance. All I want to hear about is who's knocking off who, sex drugs and rock and roll. Again I am joking. I am well aware that I now have a very dark sense of humour and often feel too scared to speak in case I offend someone. BUT, it is the only way that I can cope with this illness. I honestly do not wish anyone any harm but as I said it helps me cope.

Joey and Jai.

I know I've written about them before but they really are worth mentioning twice. Joey is so laid back and kind. He has a way of making me feel that everything is going to be alright. He is awesome. He is a cage fighter and runs a gym named Empire. When I go to watch Joey fight he walks into the cage and looks so scary he doesn't even look like my extremely handsome, gentle son. Jai on the other hand is my little barrel of laughs and a true romantic and looks beautiful. He has this way of cheering everyone up. He has moved back in with me now and I couldn't be happier. He has been very funny from day one. On one occasion when Jai was about four years old I was in the kitchen and the boys were playing the piano in the living room. Jai came running in to me saying that Joey had shouted at him. This was very out of character for Joe. Joey then explained that Jai had bitten him. I asked him "did you bite your brother Jai?" and he replied "no mummy I was just feeling his arm with my teeth". I cannot believe they are both so well adjusted considering what I have put them through.

Jai works at Laura Ashley customer services. It sounds easy sitting down all day answering the telephone, but honestly some of the customers he has to put up with are such snobs. One lady

Junie Pritchard

asked Jai to have her furniture taken back and redelivered in a Laura Ashley van as it had been delivered in a white van and her neighbours would not have known it had come from Laura Ashley. I could not do that job. I would have told her to get a life. Jai can on occasion be a little grumpy, so sometimes I wake up grumpy and other times I leave him in bed.

CHAPTER 8. THE ATTACK.

One evening in 2010 about 8.30 I took my dog for a walk as usual. We walked to my local park and a man jumped out at me. He tried to touch my breasts and put his hand down my trousers. It was quite dark, he wore a hood and I could not see his face. Luckily I had a large torch with me which was shaped like a truncheon and as he tried to push me to the ground I hit him hard on the head with it and he fell to the ground. My dog Sox and I ran to the police station and gave them a statement. I was not offered a cup of tea or coffee or even a lift home. They kept my torch for forensics and I have never seen it again. I had to walk home the long way home to avoid the park. I was distraught. When I got home I was so upset my son called the Mental Health Services. I was immediately sectioned again that night. I was on a very, very deep low. My sister Annie and I contacted the Police and we were told that a Sgt. Davies was in charge of the case. We could not speak to him or her as they were on a training course. A lot of bloody good that did them as they did absolutely Jack shit. It is incredulous to me that they tried to prosecute me over a KitKat yet did absolutely nothing over a potential rape case. Neither Sgt Bullock nor Sgt Davies has any integrity or ethics at all. They make me feel physically sick when I think of them. Hey ho. Time to move on. I wonder how Sgt Davies would have felt if it was their daughter, partner or mother who had been attacked, if anyone is stupid enough to marry them. It would be a bit different then wouldn't it?

In hospital I was getting lower still. It felt as though the police couldn't care less if the town nutter got raped. I hate Sgt Davies and I've never knowingly set eyes on the man or woman. They completely ignored a very serious sexual attack on me, which resulted in me having ECT. Why? Do they think that I deserved it because I have Bipolar? The f'ing word NO applies to me just as it does to any other female. Obviously they think differently. I pay for the Police through my Council tax to protect us, however I have never needed them to protect me more than I did then.

As I said I am gradually changing my mind about them now. I think that we have called a truce. They now realise that I am ill and I know realise that they are doing their jobs. Or not in Sgt. Davies' case.

One particular CSO named Graham has always been nice to me and told me that if I ever needed him to call the station and he would call me back. I did just that one day and waited for him to return my call which never came. I rang the station again and the lying toad on the end of the phone said that Graham was not on duty that day. I told him that I had seen Graham in the town less than half an hour ago and unless he is going to a fancy dress party he is working. He then put the phone down on me. I do think Graham is a lovely guy but he did not receive my message asking him to call me. There are of course exceptions as all of the officers who have ever been involved in sectioning me have treated me really well. Some of them even had a sense of humour, so a big, thank you, to those particular officers. These days I walk home the long way round and make sure I am home by dark o'clock.

My beautiful mother was a Paranoid Schizophrenic. She was hospitalised in her teens and given 12 sessions of ECT just like me. She believed that she saw monkeys on her back and that has always stayed with me. I hate monkeys almost as much as I hate Social Services. There is a huge likeness there too and who can you educate? YES!!! A monkey. Following the attack I fell deeper and deeper into depression. I found it so difficult to cope with this onslaught of thoughts. I felt as if my head was going to explode. Nothing was working to get me out of this low and as I mentioned before that this is when Dr M suggested I have ECT. Oh my god. But at this point I really didn't care what happened to me and I agreed. It was explained to me that I would have 12 sessions of 1.4 volts of electricity into my brain. Each session would bring on a fit. Holy crap was I scared, but as I said I felt so low they could have given me a lobotomy and I wouldn't have cared. AND I trust Wasi completely. There was an ECT suite in the hospital itself and I was taken into there in a wheelchair. I was then asked to lie on the bed. Once again I was strapped down. Luckily one of my favourite nurses was present and she held my hand. The person who was to carry out this procedure was tall and wore a white coat. He looked a lot like Peter Cushing in a horror movie. Oh crap. I was given general anaesthetic that thankfully acted quickly, but not soon enough to prevent me seeing him moving towards me with two electrodes coming towards my head, unless I imagined this. 54321 out. Sgt Davies I despise the ground you walk on. I underwent this procedure twelve times. Aren't I the lucky little git. My beautiful mother passed away at this time and I was allowed home on leave to attend her funeral. I do not even remember being there. I keep wracking my brain and hopefully one day that memory will return.

According to my family, following the ECT I was like a zombie for weeks in there, but I do not remember it. I was eventually allowed out to stay with my sister Annie. How she coped with me I do not know. I know from experience that if you spend time with someone who is depressed it can drag you down too so it really was very sweet of her to put up with me. I did make sure that I went to bed at 6.30 every evening so that she could spend time alone with her husband but I still think she worried about me when I was in bed bless her,

I was very out of it there too but was eventually allowed home. However this is when the nightmares began. I dreamt of rats and spiders crawling over me, gargoyles, fire and what I perceive the devil to look like, and like my mom I dreamt of monkeys on my back. I honestly thought I was in hell. This went on for weeks and I dreaded going to sleep at night. I have never been so scared in all my life. I also had really bad problems with my memory and concentration. I could barely remember my own name. I could not concentrate enough to read, I couldn't bear the noise of the tv or even my normal lifeline, music. I just used to lie in the dark in silence. My poor children. It must have been so hard for them to see me in that state. I now try to think of it as me being both physically and mentally worn out like a battery, and ECT were the jump leads giving me a jump start. I was watching one of my favourite tv programmes the other evening called Absolutely Fabulous. One of the characters said "ECT is addictive. I can't walk past an electrical socket these days without wanting to push my finger into it", which I found hilarious. Luckily it has not had that effect on me.

I now take a drug called lithium which they actually put into batteries. I am now going to change my name to Fully Charged Ever Ready or maybe Duracell as I go on and on.

People often say that suicide is the coward's way out. I do not believe that for a second. It takes an awful lot of guts to kill you'rself. Trust me I know. Some people think it is easy. It most certainly is not so if you have never felt that way please don't judge others who have. Both my sons have got through it bless them. All of it. My Bi polar, my drinking, ECT everything. I really don't know how they have managed it but thank the Lord they have. They just seem to accept that mummy just isn't wrapped up too tight any more.

Pontypool One evening I cannot remember who came out to section me but it wasn't Wasi. I was told I was being sent to Pontypool. I was strapped down in the back of an ambulance for two and a half hours. I didn't even dare ask them to stop to let me have a pee as I'm sure they would have insisted that they accompany me in case I hung myself with the light pull or drown myself down the toilet. When I finally got to the Psychiatric hospital they had no idea I was coming so I spent the night in an armchair in the corridor. Hours later I was interviewed by a Psychiatrist who told me that I was more sane than he was. Why aren't you sitting on this fucking side of the desk then? I did say that out loud to him and got the whole zero tolerance to abuse spiel, but how would he feel in my situation?

Strapped down for two and a half hours. Trying to sleep in a chair all night then being told to go home. What a wimp anyway. Poor Wasi has put up with way more than that from me bless him. Sorry Wasi. They then sent me all the way home in a taxi. Situations like that obviously make you feel worse and again SSD really should get their act together. That taxi ride alone cost Powys £250. What idiots. I thought the poor taxi driver might be wary of me being picked up from a Psychiatric hospital, but we chatted throughout the 80 mile journey home. He probably did me more good than the wimpy Psychiatrist anyway. There are so many costly mistakes made in this Local Authority. That is just one example. What could they have done with that £250 alone? They just can't be bothered to learn from their mistakes.

I feel that I am getting a little depressing now so I hope this cheers us all up: Jim and Edna are patients in a psychiatric hospital. One day Jim jumps in the pool and stays at the bottom. Edna dives in to save him. The manager calls Edna into his office and says "I've got some good news and some bad news. The good news is you are sane enough to save another's life therefore we are discharging you. The bad news is, Jim hanged himself in the bathroom". "No!!! cried Edna, that's where I hung him up to dry".

Down but not out. And just so you know on the way to the bottom you make a lot of stops. In the past I have alienated my family, (not my children). And I really do not blame them. On one occasion I was in Shelton for two months and my siblings did not contact me at all. I would ask the nursing staff every morning if there had been any phone calls and there had not. Other people had lots of visitors, particularly if they lived locally, but some patients had no visitors at all. Once more I was one of the forgotten few. Some patients had hour long visits from their Social Workers. I only ever saw my useless social worker very occasionally at ward round and when that was over she would disappear again. I have been known as the Social Worker who went nuts, not right in the head, a cretin and other derogatory remarks. I was drinking a lot to help me deal with what I was feeling, to help me sleep, and to forget for those few hours that I had Bipolar. I am certainly not proud of that fact and have not drank for eight years now, and mistakenly thought and hoped that I would have no further episodes but I have been sectioned on two occasions since. On both occasions on a low and the Bipolar is still here. When I was down and out (but as I said sometimes I feel you have to hit rock bottom to realise which direction you want to go in) no one wanted to know me but now it seems as if everyone wants to be my friend. It is so wrong. I am still the same person I always was but am extremely poorly. And those of you who did turn your back on me please don't ever attempt to speak to me again. And just remember the saying "there but for the grace of god go I".

Social Services.

I discussed what Powys had done to me with my ex husband who had also worked for Powys for twenty years in the Highways department and he believes it was a Powys hatchet job. They wanted rid of me a) because I was an embarrassment. The Social Worker who went nuts and b) they knew that I knew way too many bad things about them.

SOCIAL WORK ASSISTANT.

When I first began working as a Social Work Assistant in the Children and Families team, I did not have a clue what I was doing. We were given SWA training but it was generic and we only had one days training in child care. And that was the extent of it. F'ing hell. A job carrying that much responsibility after one days training. How ridiculous. But that is honestly the way it was. I remember being asked to go to the Police Station as an Appropriate Adult not even knowing what it meant. We had training on that the following month. Too little too late, mate. The Children and Families team in Powys are now at Special Measures which means they are failing children badly. How more and more children are not getting hurt is beyond me, but maybe they are as Powys does a very good job of covering things up. When you are a Social Worker you obviously cannot tell anyone about your cases, and I have seen some sights I can assure you. Therefore you end up kind of internalising it all and it is so hard to deal with. Sometimes I would go home on a Friday night after visiting a child, just hoping and praying that that child is alive on Monday morning. As I said no one can be there 24/7. My ex husband used to come home and tell me where he had spotted a pothole in the road or a hedge that had not been cut. I did my best to look interested but I really was not. I was dying to tell him how I had visited a young mother who had left her twins upstairs, naked apart from their nappies in their cot, who did not even cry because they knew that their cries would not be answered because their mother and her boyfriend were working their way through a crate of cider. I used to think I do not care about your pothole or even if you'd witnessed a UFO landing in a nearby field. I DO NOT CARE. Take a seat, take the weight off your feet and fall asleep. And he did. Every evening.

When I was first retired on ill health grounds it felt like yet another bereavement. I felt that no one would employ me with my sick record. They probably still won't. My career was officially over at the age of 45. But now? Would I ever work for anyone else again? Would I heck. I have been asked to become a mental health advocate, and I was tempted. But the answer is no. My Mental Health Advocate no longer returns my calls, so I am not impressed by that service anyway. I do not wish to spend my days with depressed people and I know that sounds harsh but it would undoubtedly have an adverse effect on my own mental health and I am not prepared to do that to myself. I have a diploma in counselling skills and have been asked to do that too. Sorry but I no longer like people enough to counsel them. I am only going to work for myself in future.

This book is going to take another 3 or 4 months to type up and when this is finished I will find another way of working just for me. I am going to be the nicest boss. I will never pile too much work onto myself, take regular coffee breaks (without having to make the whole of Social Services a coffee) and I will never get the sack. Every Friday will be POETS day. Piss off early tomorrow's Saturday. I might even throw the odd sicky. They say hard work never killed anyone but why risk it? I would also like to earn some money as opposed to living on a pittance of a pension and benefits. People say that money doesn't make you happy. I believe that this is only said by rich people to make the poor feel better. And as Joey say's "I would rather cry in my Ferrari mum". Also, if you think that your millions don't make you happy why don't you give some to the poor. Not bloody likely I'm sure they would say.

I was a nanny to twin boys in California for twelve months prior to taking the job at Social Services and Joey was five years old. And that was the extent of my knowledge in Child Care. How I was meant to relate to a damaged little person I don't know. When I used to attend meetings I used to be very quiet 1) because I didn't really know what the heck I was talking about, I just had to wing it and 2) you learn an awful lot more by listening than you do talking. I had brilliant colleagues in Annie G and Jeanie R and if ever I had a case that I wasn't sure about they would give me the best advice. I really looked up to them both and wanted to emulate them. Annie and I were the little lowlife social work assistants. To say we were taken for granted was an understatement. Now that I am qualified, I realise that we did exactly the same work of a Social Worker with absolutely no respect shown to us and for a fraction of the pay. I even had to write a court report before I was qualified. I was bricking it. One wrong word from me and those children could have been returned to their abusers. I rang the legal dept. at County Hall before it was submitted to court and they gave me a nine out of ten and stated they never gave a ten. Oh thank heavens. At one point my manager in the Children and Families team asked me to carry out an assessment with a patient in Shelton. What? I knew absolutely zero about mental health. I believe it should have been carried out by a worker in the mental health team, but as I said I was a willing horse and off I went. Prior to my leaving I asked my manager what was wrong with her. She stated that she was depressed and that she goes into Shelton for a few weeks now and again and she is fine again. What???? You ignoramous. If only it were that simple. When I visited the hospital, I must admit I was a little wary. The nurses let me in and showed me in to an office where the woman sat and left us to it. The poor woman was desolate. She, like me when I was there, only cared about her children. Bless her heart. I did my best to reassure her that her children were fine. I knew this as I had visited them at a foster carers home before I visited her. I asked her if she would like me to bring them to the hospital and she declined. She told me that she did not want them to see her this way. Gosh if only I knew then what I know now. I asked if there was anything else I could do for her and she said no. I gave her a hug and took her back to the ward. I assured her that I would make damn sure that her children were cared for. That poor poorly woman. My manager had made it sound like a bloody holiday camp in there

The more and more I think about Social Services the more and more I dislike them. They completely and utterly used and abused me and when I suffered a nervous breakdown due to all the pressure they put me under they hung me out to dry. (Not in quite the way that Edna hung Jim out but they might as well have). Big style. I have written this book partly to get my own back on Social Services and to show everyone who and what brought on this critical illness so that hopefully everyone reading it can avoid the same thing happening to them. Do I respect the Police anymore? Yes. Almost all of them. Do I trust them? Yes most of them. Before I got ill I had never once been in trouble with the Police, not even any points on my driving license. Zero. But this counted for absolutely nothing. They even sent me to Probation. I used to work closely with these women and they couldn't believe that this time I was the one in trouble. They wrote me a glowing report but the Police still took me to court. Again and again. I even had to drive to Welshpool court one day as I was told by the Police that I had to attend and was told that I would not even be seen that day. I felt so worn down by it all I just could not cope.

HOSPITAL.

Some women actually liked being in hospital. I think they enjoyed the company and felt safe there. I hated it. Every second in there was a second away from my children, and all those seconds added up to three years. Three long, long years of my life. It really is like being in prison. My friend Alfy told me all about prison and us mental defectives had the poorer deal. At least they always got fed. Bipolar is a very severe disability but people expect me to behave normally or they won't accept me. I do not have this condition through choice. It was not something that I had put on my Christmas wish list. I would not wish it on my worst enemy. I try my best to behave normally and people get cross with me when I don't. I am disabled. You wouldn't shout at a paraplegic to get out of a wheelchair and walk would you? Unless you're named Sgt Bullock of course. I think he would.

My friends at All Saints accept me the way I am, even though I explained to them right from the get go that I am different to other people, they just don't seem to mind. My beautiful great niece Ebony has just visited me and left me a little note. She is only five years old and it goes like this…" I love you June even though you are crazy, love Ebony". How does she know? Maybe I am nicely nuts after all. I have been told that 200 people in the town I live in have this disorder with a small population of 12,500. Only 20 of the most serious cases are seen by the mental health services. Bipolar is now becoming known as one of the most serious illnesses in the world. Gosh. I just have to do everything I can, that I know of to stay well. Hopefully a cure will be found and we can all live happily and normally in society.

My friend has told me another couple of jokes. They go like this; a man visiting someone in a Psychiatric hospital asked, "is that clock right?" The patient replied, "well if it is it is the only thing that is right in here"

A man hates his wife's cat, so one day he drives to the next town and dumps it. By the time he gets home the cat is already back. The next day he drives 50 miles and dumps it again but when he gets home the cat is back again. Finally he drives to the other side of the country and dumps it. Hours later he rings his wife and asks "is the cat there?" "Yes" she replies. He says "put him on the phone I'm lost". I really do not view myself as not "right" in the head. I view it as just regular people becoming seriously ill because their lives are so stressful and we all know that stress can be a killer.

Shelton.

Life in Shelton could become very mundane. People came and went. We got to know if they were lucky enough to go home and we would give them a big cheer and wish them luck. Others would just disappear in the night and we had no idea where they had gone, or even if they were still alive. I was still drinking the demon alcohol and me, an ex nurse what a prat!! I think it is true that doctors and nurses make the worst patients. I have to admit the most part of me hated it when a fight broke out between patients, as women can be pretty darn vicious. But as long as no one got hurt, I used to think to myself "well at least that broke up the day". I never used to get involved with fights as luckily the alarms would go off and nurses from the women's and men's ward were there like a shot. Even though I could have stopped the fight, it felt kind of like when your child falls out with another. If the parents get involved we could enter into a feud that lasts forever, whilst the kids are back playing with each other again as if nothing had happened. That type of dirty fighting is not my kind of fighting anyway. Even though I know how to do it I never ever would. If you are determined to fight me stand up and fight me face to face, I am not prepared to roll around the floor pulling hair or trying to gouge your eyes out. Even better why don't we talk things over with a cup of coffee.

CHAPTER 9 Suicide Attempts

Suicidal thoughts with Bi-Polar are extremely hard to control. The temptation and need is so great. I have now made four serious attempts to take my own life, and the next person who says to me, "next time think of your children" really will get the biggest mouthful of their life. Do you really think that I don't? I love my sons more than life itself but when you have that incredible urge nothing or no one else can stop it. People have said to me "if you ever feel like that again just ring me". What for? So that you can stop me? I really do believe that they care about me but it just doesn't work like that. The pain is so incredible it is unbearable and the last thing you want is to be stopped. You just so much want to die. I now have my sons photographs placed strategically in front of my medication and I just hope and pray that this will be enough to keep me alive. So far, it has worked. Following my last suicide attempt my ex-husband called the Home treatment team and the police came and broke my door down and I was taken to hospital. He later said to me that he had saved my life. For months and months afterwards I felt that it is not your life to save, and wish that he had left me there. I even asked Wasi if I could just kill myself. He told me that he could not let me do that. It must be very difficult being a Psychiatrist (a good one like Wasi that is) as they must see some extremely ill patients. As I have said if I had a dog in that much pain I would definitely have it put down and maybe some Psychiatrists really think to themselves "well it really would be the kindest thing to do", however they are bound by law to do their best to save your life. Three years on though I am glad to be alive. Once, again thank you Wasi.

Recently I have been honoured to work with a wonderful Psychologist I will call Dr. M. I sent him a message telling him that Jai and I watched a tv series named "After Life". It was written and directed by Ricky Gervace. He also stars in it. It made me laugh when one chap went to see a Psychologist. The Psychologist says "I don't know whether to psychoanalyse you or take you to a fucking good vet and have you put down". Luckily Dr M has not had me put down.

I have always made sure in hospital that I have a suicide plan in case life gets too much for me. In Shelton I had smuggled in a razor, in Bristol I broke a glass inside a carrier bag and hid it in my drawer. I cannot tell you the amount of times I put that blade and glass to my wrists but I just did not have the courage. In Brecon the nurses had failed to take my dressing gown cord away and had planned to hang myself. But as I said it takes a whole lot of guts to do it and I just didn't have it, even though I wanted it so badly. Whilst in hospital you have to hand in your mobile phone charger. I completely understand that as one patient managed to hang herself with the cord. However, what used to annoy me in Bronllys hospital was that when I asked them to charge my phone for me my charger was never in my locker. It would always be in the bloody nurse's office because they used it every night to charge their phones. What a flaming cheek. They didn't even ask my permission. How about if I help myself to your belongings? How would you feel? I hated it there. When you feel that you just want to die, there is an absolute compulsion to do it. You beg God to let you die. And when you witness a woman who feels so badly about herself she attempts to smother herself by putting a carrier bag over her head and tying it, it has a profound effect on you. That poor woman must have gone through such emotional pain and torture and I think everyone with Bipolar Type 1 has felt that way. Over and over again. This particular woman did this 3 times and the trauma of witnessing this caused us other patients was horrific. I certainly won't be trying to emulate that one. I apologise if any of this sounds disturbing, but you must want to know what Bipolar and/or what Psychiatric hospitals are really like or you wouldn't be reading this book and unfortunately they are both disturbing.

Today is National "Holy Shit You're Hot day". Send this to someone gorgeous, but not to me, I've been getting this f'ing text all day.

Coffee.

I am absolutely and utterly addicted to coffee. I cannot get enough of the stuff. However in Bronllys hospital they viewed us as being incapable of making one due to the possibility of hurting yourself or others with boiling hot water. So we had break times and the nurses or auxiliary staff would make us a drink. These breaks were hours apart. We used to have weekly meetings there, to give us the misapprehension that our opinions mattered. Every week I would ask for a drinks machine or have access to a kettle. We did in Shelton and The Priory in Bristol and no one got hurt. If you asked for a hot drink without milk you had yourself a cup of boiling hot water anyway so what is the flipping difference? Drrr. They really are thick. Or they think that we are. Again, I have a mental illness, I am not stupid. Following our many requests they stated that they would put it to management yet again. The answer was always no, in fact it was no to practically everything we asked for so what was the point of the meetings anyway. Another patient told me that the patients had been left thousands of pounds in an ex patient's will. Everything was a no no so how about tv's in our rooms so that we could watch what we wanted to watch instead of them. The nurses there would choose the channel they wanted to watch and then take the remote control into the office and sit down all day and watch it. The tv was there for the patients and they controlled it completely. Do you think that this is fair because I certainly do not. Anyhow, I ended up telling them to stick their meetings as we got our requests turned down every time, and they held on to that money gathering interest, which I would put even more money on the fact that management use it for their own ends. Occasionally I get indigestion and took some Rennie into the hospital due to that fact. They even confiscated that. Did they really think that I would overdose on that? One evening I had indigestion and went to the nurse's station to ask for the Rennie. They said that they would have to call a doctor to visit in order to have it prescribed for me. How flipping costly would that be? I hated Bronllys hospital. It was like something out of the dark ages and the nurses were the ones with only two brain cells to rub together not the patients. We are the forgotten few, shoved in the nut house only to be wondered about occasionally as to how we're doing. The Authorities obviously don't care about us as you should see some of the places I have been in. The general public only gets to see the nice bits about them. The nurses making coffee as soon as my visitors arrived no matter what time of day it was. When they had gone the same nurse would tell you that you have to wait until teatime to get a drink. The room that my visitors and I were allowed to sit in was very plush and clean. When you go back to the rest of the hospital it is scummy and dirty. (Not Shelton). I spent an awful lot of time in my bedroom as I felt safe there. That is where I am now. In my bedroom, typing away.

In Bristol that was frowned upon. "You have to come and mix with the other patients". When you feel so incredibly low and your thoughts are so disturbing all that you want to do is sleep and hope that those thoughts don't manifest into nightmares but the nurses didn't like it at all.

That only happened in hospitals other than Shelton. I viewed Shelton as the best hospital I had been in. I think that the staff and even the management really cared about us and did everything they could to help us get well, whereas others really couldn't care less. It was just a job to them and it showed.

Anyhow the powers that be say I am allowed "back into the Community" and have been for almost five years now. I don't like that statement "some illnesses you just can't see", when they refer to mental illness. I know it is true but I am glad as I just don't want anyone to see it. These days I would rather blend in rather than stand out. When you have been locked up for long periods of time you lose most if not all of your confidence. I often walk into town thinking "Oh my gosh, can people tell I am Bipolar?" I absolutely hate it and would give anything to get rid of it, but I have it. I now accept that and I don't mind people knowing I'm a nut job, otherwise I would not be writing this book. I just don't want to look like one. When people come to my cottage now they think it is quirky, it used to be called the nutter's house. I am now considered to be eccentric rather than a nut job. Why? I am the same person that I was then so why now? Why have, Everest and Sky been so horrible to me as soon as they find out I have a mental illness? Why have all my friends and colleagues from Social Services had nothing to do with me since I became ill?

Prison.

I have asked a lot of people I know who have spent time either working in or as an in-mate in prison, and I believe the low security prisoners who have committed crimes get treated better than the people in Psychiatric hospitals where most of us have committed no crime at all. There is a saying "if you can't do the time, don't do the crime". What crime? I had never hurt anyone but myself, and it's my body to hurt so why was I banged up in a place worse than prison? Prisoners are allowed to smoke and watch tv in their cosy two bedded rooms. They only have one other person to sort out their differences with. I was kept in a four bedded room with different women coming and going for months. Also us crazies now have to go outside in all weathers to have a cigarette.

Not that I really minded but it is so unfair. They are served better food than us, have exercise periods out in the fresh air. If we are on a constant, which means a nurse has to be with you at all times if you are a suicide risk we had to exercise sitting on our chairs. And again the most important thing to me is that discharge date. Something to cling onto. Being able to think only x amount of time to go. We were in there indefinitely. We could be kept there for the rest of our lives. God I'd rather end it all now. Definitely a fate worse than death. When we were allowed

Junie Pritchard

outside for a cigarette, there was a tree planted there with a little brass sign saying something along the lines of "in memory of Reggie. A patient here from the age of 12 until he died aged 78". What??? A) what could a 12 year old possibly have done to be put in this hell hole, and B) he was there all of his life. Bless that poor man's heart. How insensitive to put it there also. That in itself depressed the hell out of me. It really was a question of suicide or escape.

I have also been told that in the early 1900's if parents didn't want their children they would put them into Shelton when it was a work house. Oh my life. Quite possibly that is what happened to poor Reggie.

Escape from those places is always possible (unless you were in the dangerous person's section where you were surrounded by an electric fence, or so I was told. I certainly wasn't going to touch it to check it out. Staying escaped however is very difficult. It always reminds me of the Only Fools and Horses sketch where Del boy and Rodney pick up an escapee from the local funny farm. They had a police helicopter out looking for him and when the escapee panicked Del said "don't worry it's only Barrats". I thought it was hilarious but when I think that that is what would have happened to me I find it incredulous. The Police would obviously look for me at home first. The Police (understandably) had to batter my door down once when I took an overdose. (they don't flipping put it right though. It even costs a lot of money to commit harrie carrie these days) and I don't think that they would hesitate to do it again if they suspected I was in there. Alerts would be put out on every exit from the country. As soon as I withdrew any money out from a bank I would be traced. So there really was no point in trying. I am sitting at home now with a cup of coffee that I made for myself, whooo. I am about to cook dinner for Jai when he finishes work and am thinking to myself "gosh I really didn't think that I was that important". Some people did however. The fence would have been so easy for me to get over. My slightly older friend

Annie climbed over it and broke her ankle. She told me that it was well worth it being out there for twenty minutes until the nurse found her, even though she was in pain. Ha she really was a star. The youngsters would escape to go out at night (it didn't appeal to me even though they asked me, bless them). The police brought them back. They looked very poorly as they had not had their medication and I think they may have taken some other kind of substances. I'm glad I stayed put.

When I left the Police cells I felt traumatised from the pepper spraying. However, nothing compared to when I was in the Redwoods so called "Therapeutic Centre". That place was worse than I have ever known or imagined it could be. It made the film "one flew over the cuckoo's nest" seem like a Holiday camp.

Normal.

Do you know what? When I am stable, I am the most normal person I know. I don't have any weird fetishes or fantasies, and I don't break the law. When I used to go shopping with Joey's father he used to eat the grapes before buying any and called it "quality control". He was so funny. I do admit to stealing some sweeties from Woolworths pick and mix when I was a child. However that is the extent of my criminal activity. And if you would like to chop my hands off for committing such a terrible crime feel free but could you please leave me with my two fingers. I am nice to people if they are nice to me. I stand at my door with a vacant look on my face when the Jehovah Witnesses call by, but I am never rude.

I heard about a chap who had Love and Hat tattooed on his hands. Unfortunately he had lost one of his fingers.

Since I have been diagnosed several people have not been nice to me. Not only have they not been nice to me they have been downright abhorrent. One thing I have learnt since I have developed this horrific illness is that people in authority think that they can do absolutely anything they like to me and get away with it. And the sad fact is they can.

Mania.

Mania or being high is incredible. It is not always incredible in a good way but it feels so, so much better than the lows. Personally I think the health professionals (not Wasi) would prefer us to be low than high as we are much easier to manage that way. When you are on a high it does all kinds of strange things to your mind. The feeling of sheer happiness is amazing. See? It is not all bad. As I've mentioned Bipolar sufferers are prone to spending money they haven't got when they are high. I know one woman who bought two cars on HP with no way of paying for them. As I mentioned my sons get lots of presents when I am high. The feeling of elation is so great that you want to pass it on and you become extremely generous and this can be taken advantage of by some unscrupulous people. It can also make you prone to taking inappropriate sexual partners. Thank goodness this has never happened to me. My last relationship was nine years ago and I have not had an intimate relationship since. Mind you he was so horrible he could have put me off men for life. I am only joking and still believe that I will meet someone to fall in love with when the time is right. I have male friends, and that is a major feat in itself. It takes them months to realise that sex just aint gonna happen.

Jaisee is my little love guru, but his idea of a new step daddy is Kane Dingle from Emmerdale Farm or Phil Mitchell from Eastenders. God help me. Jai thinks I am too picky but as the song says "it's got to be perfect". I cannot and will not pretend to be attracted to someone that I really am not. I have been asked out on quite a few occasions recently, but usually by men who are young enough to be my sons or old enough to be my father. If I had wanted another child I would have given birth to one, and although I loved my dad so very much I am not looking for a father figure either.

I have now been promoted from being the anti Christ in Jai's eyes to Mummy Bear. Only joking. Right now he calls me trouble. Has he only just noticed? Yay. He now sends me texts telling me he loves me more than life itself. Aaaaah. The girl who happens to win Jai's heart will be a very lucky one.

My parents really lucked out with me. My family goes like this; boy girl, me girl boy. I think they really wanted me to be a boy. Anyone's fault? I don't think so. I wouldn't have minded being a boy at all because back then they got treated way better than us mere females. I could also be living with middle child syndrome. I don't really know what that is but if it is any kind of syndrome I've probably got it. I had a real passion for football and played it in every Primary School breaks and in my spare time at home. I remember one of my father's friends saying to him "she should've been born a boy Pers". See dad I am trying. If you didn't get the boy you wanted you will have to make do with a tom boy. (My father's name was Percy and my mother's was Elsie). When I hit High School, girls were not allowed to play football. We were allowed to play hockey and sissy netball. In my so called "grown up" years I was captain of my local town's football team. When I played football we had some of the most amazing women's footballers I had ever seen. Our goalkeeper whose name was Jane (she was the best goalkeeper in the league in my opinion) played in a match on the Saturday, and got smacked in the face by the football which broke her nose. I couldn't believe it when she turned up and played for us on the Sunday. I think that the premadonna professional footballers we have now would have not made an appearance for weeks. What made me laugh when I played, was at the end of every match the guys would not ask what the score was they just wanted to know what happened in the showers. "You will never know darlings." We used to have so much fun and arranged a dinner for the players every year. I was the only player in Powys to get a yellow card and was given a certificate saying "To June, for her kind and encouraging words to the referees". I am so proud. I still have it hidden away somewhere. When I was a child I seemed to have so much energy that my kind, placid mother used to send me out for a run whenever I became anxious or agitated. She always seemed to know just how to handle me and I miss her so very much. I was very active as a child and was extremely skinny despite being better fed than any other family I knew. I was so thin that when I started High School at the age of 11, my skirt was meant for an 8 year old, and I remember my dad saying to me "you will never get any fat on your legs girl, as you never sit still long enough for any fat to stick to them". These days I'm surprised I don't have bed sores.

When I was in Shelton one day I took two plastic flowers from the front entrance and used them to decorate my room. The next time I went there the lovely guy on reception joked with me about it. I felt really bad and returned them straight away. He laughed and said "I bet your dad had his work cut out with you". How right he was. I think I've already mentioned that my parents were extremely religious. I wouldn't dare swear in front of my father. I used to tease him and say bloody. When he told me off I told him "bloody's in the bible, bloody's in the book, if you don't bloody believe me have a bloody look". My poor dad despaired with me but we had so much fun together and now I am as religious as he was. But I obviously don't have a problem with swearing. My English teacher told my class that words that are considered swear words today are not really swear words at all. They are words which man has made up to be insulting. He believed that swear words were terms like "go to hell", when people really meant it. I wonder, if you are in hell where do you tell people to go. I don't think the odd f word is going to hurt anybody, otherwise I would have been hurt so many times.

A lovely lady I will call L was in HDU. It seemed like an age that she was kept in there but was eventually allowed out. She seemed quite hard but I believe that mostly if you are hard on the outside chances are you are soft on the inside. I used to go to her room for chats and her walls were covered in beautiful poetry that she had written and pictures that she had drawn. She was extremely poorly, love her. She spoke a lot about death.

She went home on leave for the weekend and when she got back her walls had been painted over. She was so upset. She ran out into the kitchen and began breaking plates and tried to slice her wrists and neck with them. The nurses managed to restrain her and the alarms went off. A nurse from the men's ward came running down the corridor and punched L straight in the stomach. Hard. She then ran back to the men's ward. We all went nuts (good word for us). I couldn't believe what I had just witnessed. Thankfully that nurse was sacked. I still have a little man made out of pebbles which L made for me and I intend to keep it forever.. She was beautiful.

Back to decorating, our rooms. Poor L writing poetry on her wall and me putting flowers in mine, one of the nurses commented "my god, what people do to their rooms". What she failed to notice was that we had to live in those rooms. Has she never hung a picture up in her bedroom or put flowers into a vase? Get lost!! I would also like to point out that this book was printed on recycled paper. Re-cycled mainly from trees that have been hacked down in the rain forest. There is a special limited edition available completely inked in human blood and scrawled on pages of human flesh. This is available by mail order, direct from Cell no 8, The Redwoods.

Eventually I was allowed home. One Saturday night I was extremely drunk and manic. Joey rang the emergency services and he was told to take me to Accident and Emergency at our local hospital. We saw good old Doc Porter. He told me "I can't assess you June because you've been drinking". And that was it. A) There was hardly ever a time when I hadn't been drinking and B) I know of hundreds of people who turn up drunk at A and E on a Friday and Saturday night and they are not refused treatment. That man really is a tosser. Tosser of the caber of course as he is Scottish. Nah I think I was right the first time.

When I am extremely manic (as I was then) it takes two highly trained nurses to deal with me and that useless idiot sent me home with my 19-year-old son to take care of me. I don't know whether the man is thick, bone idle or quite possibly both. I was sectioned later on that evening and put straight into High Dependency. I have no faith in that doctor whatsoever. I wish he would go back to Scotland or to whatever planet he came from. And if we can put man on the moon why can't we put him there?

Oh my goodness I have just looked at my past writing and I can hardly understand a word. It is so scruffy. I think that that is how I felt though. Scruffy inside and out. I have read a text message which someone sent me and it goes like this; white husband in a delivery room. Midwife hands him a black baby. "Is this yours Sir?" "Probably" he replied "she's always f'ing burning things". It also says that the height of laziness for me was when a young child asked me "am I going to do that or is somebody else?" Ha ha brilliant.

Another joke I have recently heard is; a man goes to a fancy dress party with his arms painted green carrying a woman on his back. When he was asked what he had come as he said "I'm a turtle". "And why have you got a woman on your back?" He replied "this is Michelle".

I also remember being asked to dress up for Halloween at the nightclub John and I worked at. This is a photograph of how we looked. John, Joey's dad is the one with his arm around me.

Talk

about the gruesome twosome. Another guy showed up who seemingly made no effort at all but kept his jacket on. The manager was a little annoyed and asked what he had come as? He explained "I'm a jacket potato".

The Police.

I am reading some information on Bi polar. It's called "the secret life of a manic depressive". It says, and I quote "studies have shown that one of the fastest ways to tip people with bi polar disorder into mania is to deprive them of sleep". That is exactly what the police did to me on not one, not two but three separate occasions by denying me my medication. If I had taken them I would have slept all night and caused them no problem at all. As it was I was becoming more and more manic, and they knew that, and they really did not care. Following every night I stayed in those cells I was sectioned on my release. I wonder if they will care now. Sleep deprivation is also a form of torture, particularly to someone with Bi polar. That along with the pepper spraying means that I was tortured by them on three separate occasions in a sleepy little town called Newtown.

As I have said that all happened at the beginning of my illness and I really do not think it would happen today. However I am certainly not going to get myself arrested to check it out. Those cells are a very lonely, scary place to be. All of that happened when I very first became ill. The Police that I have had contact since then have been way more understanding of my illness and treat me with respect. I have regained my respect for them too and once more they make me feel safe.

Oh my goodness I have just read something that I'd written in April 2010 stating that it was on my bucket list to get arrested. I thought it would be for knocking a policeman's helmet off like Nanna Moon in Eastender's or something else really trivial but oh my god little did I know. Oh well at least I can cross that one off my list and mark it down as something never to be repeated.

I have never trusted SSD. In the umpteen years I was there I saw an awful lot of goings on that were a) not legal or above board, and b) things that were so serious that we were warned not to speak to the press about, but I really didn't think that they would stoop as low as they did.

Stir Crazy.

After a time you go stir crazy in these hospitals and get a real sense of cabin fever. You were either in a room the size of a box, or your little area in the four bedder which was even smaller. You see the same myriad of crazy faces every day, including when

I looked in the mirror. You eat with them and you sleep with them. Most of them looked like they hated my guts. But they looked at everyone like that. Sometimes I think that Bi polar sufferers are scathed by their abusive pasts. Almost everyone I spoke with had been through so much abuse it was unreal. I do have difficulty dealing with my emotions but in retrospect I have been abused by men all of my life. My father was very handy with his belt and an ex partner was violent towards me. I do not blame my father one bit for using his belt on me. At that time it was considered a normal thing to do and after talking to him about his childhood it was only a fraction of what had been done to him. The attacker in the park was another. Oh thank god for kickboxing.

I was mentally abused by Social Services and both mentally and physically by the Police. Following the attack in the park they asked me to go to Victim Support. I had to go to the police station to meet with one of them. The chap invited me to sit down, which I did. I had taken with me all of the paperwork I had regarding the attack and had written some notes on it. The only input I got from him was "you shouldn't write on official documents". Is that it? Is that the extent of support you can give me over a potential rape case? Please don't tell me that I am paying for that absolute idiot through my Council Tax too. Quite possibly. I think I am going to be hated by the whole of Powys when this book goes to print. Doc Porter hates me. I think the whole of Social Services hates me also. Does this face look bothered? Not an f'ing bit. The people holding positions of power in this County need a really good shake up. And please don't show me any concern because I dislike you lot as much as you dislike me.

People ask me following the attack do I trust men? The answer is yes I do until they prove me otherwise, and I am so lucky I had my kickboxing skills (and still do) to protect me, and they would come in to play again if anyone did anything untoward to me again. I also think of my sons and realise there really are some nice guys out there. No they really don't frighten me anymore.

And I now feel that if someone were to harm me the Police would offer me their full protection.

Thankfully suicide in Shelton was rare. However once you have witnessed it, it stays with you always. I thought of suicide almost constantly but now I am stable I thank my lucky stars my attempts didn't work, most of the time. I remember attending a training course at Social Services ran by a chap named Mike Brown, who was rather gorgeous by the way. He said that a child will be abused in some shape or form at any given time. We cannot be there as Social Workers 24/7, and nurses cannot watch over us 24/7. There is an hour between checks every night and you can do an awful lot of damage to yourself in an hour. My friend Derek once told me that he felt as though he was bleeding inside. Robbie Williams sings in one of his songs that he bleeds internally. I can relate to that fully. But no-one can see it. No one who has not got this illness can possibly understand the desperate, desolation we feel. James Blunt sings "find comfort in pain". I don't believe there is comfort in pain. It hurts so much there are no words to describe it. It's just tears and pain. That's all we feel on a low. I also believe that I have cried a river over the past few years. However I believe that crying is a sign that you are getting better. When you are really feeling desolate you cannot even experience the relief of sobbing your heart out. When I saw Derek it was like looking into a mirror. The eyes are the window to your soul. His soul was broken just like mine. Aaagh, the pain. Please make the pain go away. I don't want to die but I never wish to experience pain like that again either.

When my thoughts race they come rushing in and I just cannot cope with them. This onslaught of thoughts feels as if your head is going to explode or even spin around and around. On those occasions I really do want to die. At one point I believed that my hair was falling out due to the medication I was taking. Joey came along with me to see Wasi. I told Wasi what I believed and Joey said "Mum you are tearing your own hair out". I have heard people saying "it makes me feel like tearing my hair out" but I thought that it was just an expression. I did not think that anyone would do it. But I was. I won't tell you about all the methods of suicide I have seen or heard of in case it gives anyone ideas but there are lots. A far better option is not to do it. Life can get better and it will. Every time I get low I think to myself what goes down must come up. So far I have managed to convince myself of that fact.

The problem with highs when mixed with alcohol are that you are so far out of it you don't always remember everything you have said or done. (The same as any other drinker I suppose).

You also get delusions of grandeur. I once told Wasi I was a barrister. A barrister? (Wishful thinking on my part) Yeah right. I struggled like mad to get my A level in law. I have absolutely no idea where that came from. But before I see you people in Court and you try to use that against me that is the ONLY time that it has happened. Obviously Wasi knew that I wasn't a barrister but he said "June you can be so convincing". Maybe I should take up acting. Bipolar people in my experience may be a little bit crazy, but they are also an awful lot kind, caring, generous and most importantly to me they are so funny. They are also very creative.

Just a reminder that tomorrow is "Hug a Retard day". So I won't freak out like I did last year. Nobody is trying to hurt me.

When I was in Shelton I went to Occupational Therapy and one of the guys had drawn the most amazing picture. It was incredibly detailed. When we began chatting he explained that he had learnt to draw like that by forging bank notes. He showed me a note of his. It was amazing. Where the signature should be he had written Joe Bloggs. He made me laugh so much. And yes I know it was wrong-ish. My grandfather went to prison for something he didn't do. He didn't wear gloves.

CHAPTER 10 KICKBOXING.

Kick boxing is absolutely amazing. It is not about attacking it is all about self-defence. I love it so much I have converted my shed into a gym. I am so glad I took it up. Particularly against my attacker in the park. If I could not take care of myself god knows (I think I can guess) what he would have done to me. It also helped in Shelton. I was extremely relieved that no one in there frightened me. I was a little unnerved by some people but not afraid. The nurses even commented that I was not scared of anyone and I am not. I don't want anyone to be scared of me either as I will never hurt another living soul. I never fought to hurt people on the kickboxing mats. Sometimes people would shout to me "finish her off". I didn't. That just isn't me. I think that a lot of the young fighters thought they would have an easy time with me because I was normally twice their age. But I lulled them into a false sense of security and beat them all. I was the only female fighter in my category in the club, so I mainly ended up fighting the men at training. It was tough but it made me stronger, and some of the women I fought were big old beasts and even looked like men. I am convinced that a couple of them had undergone a sex change. I have to admit that sometimes, when I first started fighting I was a bit scared. When I was told that I was to fight a black belt when I had not even gained a belt yet I did think to myself holy crap. But the feeling I got when I beat them was amazing, but the more fights I had (and won) I did not feel scared at all. As Mohamad Ali said, "throw a punch and walk away, then you will live to fight another day". I was lucky because I am small, I was fast and I could land a punch and move out of the way of theirs. They occasionally landed a big haymaker but again I am lucky because I can take a punch too. So many women I fought believed that they were really hard. And they could throw a good punch or kick, BUT they couldn't take a punch. Easy pickings. After I had won the European Championships and spent days and days fighting in the Welsh, English and British open series Social Services then told me that I could have had time off work to fight for my country. AFTER the event. No wonder I became ill.

This was my week. Four mornings a week I was up at 5.30am. I went for a two mile run, followed by 40 minutes bag work then press-ups and sit-ups. The boys and I would get ready for School and work and off we went. Jai and I stayed at my mum's on a Monday night as she missed my dad being there so much bless her. I cannot imagine being married to someone for over forty happy years to then suddenly find they are not there anymore. Tuesday evening I took Jaisee to football practise. Wednesday Jai was with his father so I had to go to college to study my European Computing Driving license which would have given me a degree rather than a Diploma in Social Work which I held. Claire Turner insisted I did that as I sometimes finished work half an hour earlier to pick up Jai from School. I became ill though and only completed half of the course. Joey was at the Guitar Institute in London. Thursday evenings I trained at Kung Fu and Kickboxing but I had to take three clients with me and invariably took them home which meant I got home even later. The same thing happened on a Saturday afternoon. Kickboxing was the only thing that I did for myself and Claire Turner is telling me to take clients along with me. I had to find twelve hours a week study time to gain my Diploma through the Open University. Sundays were housework and gardening. And I cracked, and at the age of forty four I found myself on the unemployment scrapheap. I was devastated. What do I do now I thought? No job, no prospects and very little money. My Police check would not look too healthy either. The theft of a whole bar of kit kat, and grabbing some little paedophile who was really very rude to me by the collar and two suspected drunk and disorder lies. Wasi even attended court with me as an expert witness and luckily the magistrates realised how ill I was and was not drunk at all and I was found not guilty on every count. I believe if Fran Foster attended court with me she would have convinced them to put me in prison and thrown away the key. Bitch troll from hell. Actually, I have just remembered that all of those years ago I was on a certain medication which I cannot remember the name of made me appear to be drunk even when I had not consumed any alcohol at all. All of this led me to another sectioning.

Hello Shelton yet again. This time on a low and believe you me I was at rock bottom. As I mentioned before, no one from Social Services visited me apart from Annie G and Jeanie R. and Karen A and Paul. Annie brought me the most beautiful china mug which was confiscated in case I harmed myself with it. I never saw it again. And Jeanie brought me a gorgeous little teddy bear which someone stole from my room.

I hate Social Services with a passion. Losing my post in the Leaving Care team felt horrible. I had such plans for my future career and these were all dashed just because I became ill and I really believe the fault lay with them for piling more and more work onto me in the first place. My manager Claire Turner would refuse to see her clients, therefore I had to work with them also. She told me that she knew I was getting ill because of my erratic behaviour and still she piled more and more work onto me. I fell asleep in supervision for goodness sake and all she did was make fun of me. How bloody knackered did I have to be? I'm sure that if ever I have to speak with her again I would fall asleep through boredom.

When I was sectioned into Shelton my colleagues were warned not to tell anyone where I was and definitely not speak to the press. Again, the embarrassment. I had been working full time as a Social Worker, and was training for the World championships Kick boxing. I had won the Europeans and I just knew I could have won the Worlds. I was so happy. Then Bang. My whole world fell apart. Section 2 of the Mental Health Act equalling 28 days Assessment, followed by Section 3, up to 6 months, completely against my will. Six months in this shit whole. Why? I just couldn't understand it. And this was the weirdest thing. I honestly did not know why I was there. I believed it was some huge mistake and the following morning I would be allowed to go home. I even refused to unpack the bag that Joey had packed for me thinking there is no point as I will be

The Forgotten Few

going home tomorrow. Right? Wrong.

Looking back though, I can appreciate why. I was punching and kicking the walls and smashing my hands onto anything I could. I could have done some serious damage to my hands and feet but luckily I didn't.

I want the whole of Social Services to leave me alone now. Some of them now try to speak to me in the street but I really don't want to know. As Marilyn Munroe said "if you didn't want to know me at my worst then I do not want to know you at my best. One Social worker who was well aware of what had happened to me I just could not avoid as she was heading straight towards me proceeded to tell me that she had had two months off work with stress but had now returned to work. Aaah diddums. Try fifteen years Bi Polar see how that grabs you. I worked for Social Services for fifteen years and could expose them for all kinds of misdemeanours. I am not sure if I should or not. What do you think? Hell yes. Well some of them anyway.

One of our male Area Care managers was accused of sexually harassing his staff. He was asked to leave the department with a whopping great pay out. We were warned not to speak to the press otherwise we would lose our jobs. They wanted it all hushed up and it was. I will not mention his name as I do not believe he harassed anyone. He was a lot flirtatious but so was I. He always treated me with the utmost respect. BUT the point I wish to make is that those are the lengths Powys Social Services will go to, to avoid any scandal. They tried to get rid of me without paying my pension which I had paid into from the very first day I started work there. Human Resources and Unison were as much use as a chocolate tea pot. God I was angry. A male social worker was accused and found guilty of domestic violence and still kept his job. One female Social Worker had an intimate relationship with one of my 16-year-old clients. She is still in post. What is wrong with them? There is a whole lot more I could tell you about but I will keep that for another day. I don't know why they victimised me other than the fact that I was a huge embarrassment to them and I knew way too much. And they would have saved my measly monthly pension.

SHELTON.

It was such a strange existence in there. We were completely cut off from the outside world. If we were lucky enough to be allowed out or someone visited us we were searched for anything that we may harm ourselves or others with. We were regularly breathalysed too. The nurses on the whole were amazing. I did not like the feeling of being responsible for any patient with a mental health problem. When I was a nurse in the Army the psychiatric ward was the largest in the hospital. It was impossible not to get attached to some patients as some of them were just so loveable. Other's not so much. And that unpredictability of behaviour could at times be very frightening. Most of the nurses in Shelton though would have done anything for us. One of the nurses even gave me her pasta bake for my lunch when I had that abscess as it was the only thing soft enough for me to eat. Bless her heart. It is things like that that you never ever forget. We had nicknames for all of the nurses, some of them rude, some not. I think I had run in's with all of the nurses when I first arrived as I viewed them as my jailors and could not understand why they would not just let me go home. I gradually changed my mind about them. They really did work so hard and did a marvellous job. I like to think that I made a bit of an impact while I was there. I think I did. Wasi told me that I had all of the nurses running around after me. I hope he meant it in a good way.

Whenever I used to work with my clients as a Social worker, and I also use it in my day to day life, whenever you have contact with someone they are always somebody's mother, daughter, father or son and should be treated with respect and I felt privileged to be invited into my client's home. I used to remind myself that we are all unique, just like everyone else. That is another reason why I would not wish this illness even on my worst enemies as everyone has someone who loves them and it just would not be fair on them.

School Party.

My School reunion was due any day now and I was desperate to go. I was really very high, but Dr M agreed that I could have leave from the hospital to attend if my ex-husband Mike would take me. The poor man. What a wally I made of myself. I was dancing on the tables (going back to my footballing days only this time I was the only one). I am really quite embarrassed looking back at that evening, but fair play when I bump into my old School friends they all treat me so nicely and even talk about the next reunion. If they weren't aware of my illness before that evening I feel sure that they are now, but they treat me as if I hadn't got it bless them. BUT I DO!!

CHAPTER 10 DR WASI MOHAMAD

Wasi is my super hero. He recognised the fact that I had Bipolar on my second visit to Shelton and the best way to deal with any illness is an early, accurate diagnosis but accepting it is the difficult part. I have done a lot of research into Bipolar since my diagnosis and there is no doubt in my mind/minds that I have it. Wasi has helped me re-gain control of my life again, whereas fifteen years ago I was completely out of control (although I didn't realise it) and was spiralling more and more out of reality. I had absolutely no idea what was happening to me. The feelings I got. The sheer strangeness of it all terrified me and I just did not know what to do. Thankfully Wasi did. I have certainly not been a model patient either. I have definitely put him through his paces, with reports for my employers, the courts, and he even attended court with me bless him. He has saved my life umpteen times now, even though I have not always been happy for him to do so. I don't know where I would have been without him. Quite possibly in the gutter.

When I was first sectioned in 2006 people's perception of people with Mental Health problems was completely different. People were afraid of me. People I had known all of my life would cross to the other side of the street to avoid me. It got back to me that people were being rude, using horrible words to describe me such as a nutter and she is not right in the head. One man asked me to marry him. When I refused that is when he called me not right in the head. Oh and you are? Asking a woman who is thirty odd years younger than you are to marry you? I think it is you who is not right in the head mate. What a lucky escape I had.

An almost exact same situation happened to me again. A much older man asked me to marry me and when he declined he asked me why not? I said well there is the small matter of the age difference between us. He replied "well id doesn't bother me". Well it bloody wouldn't would it. Again I had him telling others that I am nor right in the head. If I'm not right in the head then I must be wrong. I really wish that people would keep their nasty comments to themselves. I have gained two Diplomas in my life and I will show them who is right in the head when I have finished writing this book. I did not wish or ask for this illness and it is bad enough trying to deal with it without people being so horrid. Not right in the head. I just never thought that that term would be used referring to me. I am Bipolar. I may be wrong in the head, but if they are right I don't want to be. I get extreme highs and devastating lows but for the most part I am normal. At this precise moment I am at home on my own without having to ask some miserable nurse (not the nurses in Shelton) what I am and what I am not allowed to do. Yay. I am free. I watched the Stephen Fry documentary on "The secret life of a manic depressive" and very few people want their condition known. Every person with Bipolar who appeared on the show, bar one said they were glad they have got it. What???? They said they had danced with Angels. I feel as if I had danced with the devil following my ECT and would give my right arm to be rid of Bi Polar. Sometimes I feel like moving away. Somewhere that no one knows of my condition, however I would miss my sons way too much. There is no running away from it anyway. I have this for the rest of my life and it will rear its ugly head again wherever I choose to live. The medication we have to take too has side effects. I have put on a little weight since being on it, but please god, if you can't make me thin…please make everyone else fat. Others can bring you out in a rash which could potentially kill you. Oh be joyful.

It was Wasi who first encouraged me to write this book so if no one likes it I am going to blame him. Only joking Wasi, I am enjoying writing it. I bet he wishes he hadn't asked me when he reads it. Wasi is a Consultant Psychiatrist with more initials after his name than I have in my surname. He is a very down to earth, personable man and I have been lucky enough to have had him as my Psychiatrist for the past thirteen years, bless him. I have put him through so much and he has forgiven me everything. Please forgive me for this book too Wasi. Wasi seems to see only the good in everyone. Even Fran Foster, as opposed to me who absolutely abhors her. I would also like to beg the question that Wasi has sectioned me on many occasions and has even arranged for me to have ECT. If I were going to complain about anyone it would be him.

Fran Foster saw me for a very short time thankfully and she did not section me or arrange ECT. What possible motive would I have to accuse her of such a serious crime knowing all of the above, when I went to Cuba. It makes no sense at all for me to do so.

I believe that I see the world differently to other people. In Juneyland all I care about is love, happiness freedom and having fun. I wish there was a love bank where we all have big accounts. We'd pay for things with kisses and give snogs for large amounts. When I go out I realise it is not a perfect world and want to go home again where I feel safe. However I have even been sectioned whilst lying in my bed.

I mostly feel anxious when I leave the house. The most frequently asked questions by my nurses are a) do you feel like harming yourself? No. b) Do you want to harm anyone? No. Not even Jeremy Patterson, Clive Bartley Amanda Lewis, Claire Turner, Sgt Bullock and Sgt Davies, Fran Foster, Phillipa Walker and Laurraine Hamer. I have never, and will never harm another living soul. Only with the might of my pen. C) Do I feel as if anyone wants to harm me? Yes. Social Services.

Anxiety is different. It is not exactly fear but it can make me feel and become on occasion physically sick. I can become anxious about anything. At the moment I feel anxious in case people I don't know can see that I have Bipolar, but I am getting used to it. I take medication for anxiety which really helps but the most effective method I have found is going down to my gym. Today I have spent half an hour knocking Claire Turner's head off on my punch bag. It really is a great release. I don't think most people realise that I have this illness as I often have to show people proof of my disability.

Home Treatment Team

We are lucky in my area as we have a home treatment team. They have kept me out of hospital on more than one occasion. I feel very privileged that one of the nurses who worked in Shelton hospital on several of my admissions is now working in the Community. It is so nice to reminisce with him and gain his point of view of how I behaved whilst on a high. He said "well you certainly had a voice June, you were very vocal". I was very relieved that that was the worst he could come up with. The other nurses are great too. I am lucky enough that when I am ill they can visit me daily and taper off the visits when I am well. I am now discharged from the Home Treatment team and I must admit I kind of miss them, although I am well aware that the idea of the team is to visit me in times of crisis but not allow the danger of dependency to occur. They always seem to know when that time comes, and I am stable once more.

Oh my days. I have now been told that Fran Foster has been promoted to being the manager of the Home Treatment Team. Promoted? Her? She is honestly the worst Psychiatrist I have ever come across in my life and I have met so many. It really makes me wonder what she did to obtain that promotion also. Quite prepared to snuff out a client's life perhaps?

Music.

When I became very ill music was extremely important to me. It went a small way to help block out my racing thoughts. When your thoughts race at one hundred miles an hour it can be extremely scary. It feels as though your head is spinning. I could not concentrate on reading or watching tv. I played music practically 24/7. I listened to James Blunt over and over again. He was a Captain in the Army, and as I was in the Army I felt that I could relate to his music. When I was in Shelton I played music constantly there too. I listened with my headphones on at night as it was a good way of drowning out all of the screaming and wailing. Oh please god, don't ever let me go back to one of those places.

When you are depressed you feel as though you are living in a dark room and unable to see, but at least I could hear my music.

CHAPTER 11 my mum

My mum was beautiful. She was sweet, kind and loving. She was an amazing mother and grandmother. (My father was a wonderful grandfather too). She insisted that whoever visited our home needed feeding. She was an amazing cook and had five children to look after. Oh my goodness. Five kids, (and one of them was me), a farm and a pub to run. I don't know how she did it.
When I was just a little girl I asked my mother what I will be. "Will I be pretty? "Will I be rich?" Here's what she said to me "kay Sera Sera, whatever will be will be, the futures not ours to see Kay Sera Sera, what will be will be". She never once told me that I would be a nut job.

My father used to say to people "never leave this house feeling hungry". But it wasn't him who fed them it was my mother. I think I have my mum's smile too and I like to think I have inherited my dad's wit, but I guess only other people can be the judge of that. One Christmas my uncle visited and asked my dad if he could cut some holly from the hedge at the bottom field. My father said yes. When my uncle returned with the holly he thanked my father. Dad in his broad Radnorshire accent said "that's alright boy it inna my hedge". I also remember going into one of our fields and we found a dead sheep. I asked "what did she die of dad?" He replied "probably short of breath". Oh please god let me die from short of breath and not suicide. On occasion I would ask him where he was going. He would reply "there and back to see how far it is". He really was incredibly funny. My mum was a Paranoid Schizophrenic but I can honestly say I never saw any signs of it. She was just so sweet. Joey and Jai loved their grandparents very much.

When I moved a few hundred yards down the road from them with the boys they were amazing. My dad would pick them up from the local School in his land rover (the same Primary School that I attended) and kept them amused until I finished work. Both boys would occasionally stay the night too which gave me the opportunity either to study or to go out. Life was perfect.

Junie Pritchard

My mother developed Parkinson's disease, which I believe was brought on by the amount of heavy duty Psychiatric medication she had to take. When my mum passed away I never felt anger towards her the way I did my father. It always felt that my mum needed protecting. Not from my father, he idolised my mum and rightly so, she was just so nice to be around but always seemed very fragile. The anger I felt towards my father was just a normal part of the grieving process I guess. I loved them both very much just in different ways. I didn't really feel too much guilt when my mum passed away either as I used to take her to all of her Parkinson's outpatient appointments. It was horrible seeing people with different degrees of the illness. One lady was completely bent over in a wheelchair and bless her she couldn't even manage a drink on her own. I could almost feel my mum looking at her and thinking "that could be me one day". She had tears in her eyes and I just wanted to hug her, so I did.

When we went in to see her specialist he asked what medication she was on. When I told him he said she can't be. I produced the bottle of medication she took and the dosage. He said that that was enough to knock out an elephant and she had been left on that medication for years. None of the family had even met with her psychiatrist. They had obviously prescribed it and as she wasn't posing a problem they just left her to it. Oh my goodness these things make me so cross. My poor mother.

Wasi and I have already discussed me cutting down my meds when the time is right. See how good he is? That is if Doc Porter learns how to count by then and gives me my correct medication I need to stay alive. I have to stop running the GP's down as he no longer works at my local surgery. It was only really Dr Porter I had a problem with. And I have to say that whenever I go there to have my blood taken or whatever the whole atmosphere there is so much better now that he has retired. Possibly if he was horrible to patients (and I know I am not the only one) he was horrible to staff members too.

My mum was great. As I mentioned we would go for walks every day, even when I had to put her shoes on for her because of her Parkinsons we had such fun. She thought that every man we bumped into liked me and thought I could get any man on earth. I couldn't of course, but that's what good mums do I guess.

My Father and I.

My father was an amazing man. However, he and I had quite a strange relationship. He was extremely religious and expected his children to follow in his footsteps. If ever he wanted something done he would ask me to do it, even though there were five of us. June do this, June do that. I used to think to myself "f off and do it yourself" but I would never have dared swear at him. I just used to go ahead and do it. The rest of my family knew that he treated me differently, but they somehow got it into their heads that I was his favourite. Favourite? I really didn't think so. He treated me as if he hated me. He and I used to have great debates but he couldn't bear to be proven wrong. He used to use his belt on us quite a lot too. He used to say "this will hurt me far more than it hurts you". Whack. "I don't bloody think so". I was always the cocky one who used to say "that didn't hurt" and then we'd get yet another belting. I don't know why I said it. There was just something inside me that had to do it. My sisters were none too happy with me but I always bore the brunt of it anyway because I slept on the side of the bed nearest to the door. It really did not bother me at the time as I didn't even realise it was wrong until many years later. However the thought of taking a belt to my sons little bodies absolutely sickens me. I could never ever do that.

I believe that abuse goes in cycles. If a son witnesses his father hit his mother then the chances are he will go on to do the same thing. These cycles have to be stopped. Abuse of any kind whether mental or physical has to be stopped. Mothers should leave their abusive partners and so should men as it may carry on via their children. Stop it now. Neither sex should have to put up with an abusive partner. There are hundreds more out there who won't abuse you. Honestly

My father was very funny though, he had such a dry sense of humour. Sometimes I would ask what he was doing when he was relaxing and he would reply "keeping the dust off the chair". If I asked him how he had slept he would say "with my eyes shut". I loved his humour. On occasion he would ask "had I done this or had I done that" I would reply "yes can't you see?" He would then say "I can see more than I can have gel". On occasion I would go with him for a drive in his land rover. He was in my view a typical Sunday afternoon driver. He never drove over 30 mph. I would sometimes say "come on Dad can't you go a little bit faster". He would say, "you know where the door is gel lets see how fast you can walk if you want to". He was lovely. A friend of mine came to stay over and we were going to our works party. We took forever to get ready and actually looked quite good. She was originally from Birmingham and knew nothing about country life. I told her that we were having a lift with my father. We waited outside and he turned up in his land rover. My friends face was a picture. She could not believe that we were going to a party in a slightly smelly land rover. He told her "it is this or walk girl. Newtown is 5 miles that way". She even insisted that we were dropped off quite a long way away from the venue. My friend was incredibly funny too. She used to eat lots of banana's and would always ask us girls if anyone would like to use it before she eats it.

Living with my father though was like living in the dark ages. I know it was a long time ago as I am pretty ancient now but good grief. When he and my brothers had their weekly farmer's union meeting, the girls were told to leave the room. What? Why? When we didn't have housework to do, we also helped out on the farm, feeding the cows, bottle feeding the lambs etc but he thought we were incapable of making any decisions. He also used to be in complete control of the television too. Normally some kind of sport. When we thought that he had fallen asleep in his armchair we would change the channel. As soon as we did that he would wake up and say "I was watching that". Oh flipping heck bloody sport again. The whole family used to get together every Christmas night. The females did all of the cooking and waited on the men while they ate their meals first. We ate after them and also did the washing up. I felt like tipping my brothers meals on their laps or making them wear it on their faces, but I had to be a good little girl and do as I was told. Sorry bro,s but I did. The thing that got me most was when my father called me a wench. It made me so angry, as if I were some kind of servant. I could not wait to join the Army and get away from there. Now though I would give anything just to spend one more Christmas night with him.

My dad died of cancer and luckily he had his faith in God to help him through it. He was so, so brave and stayed at home with my mum right until the end. I believe that he knew that the night the ambulance came for him and he refused to allow anyone to go with him that he was going to die and he passed away that night.

I feel I have been through all the normal feelings of grief. Anger, missing him, and guilt. I was angry with him because he would no longer be able to give me advice, especially regarding Joey, as Joey's father died only five days before him. I felt guilt, because I had argued with him so many times more than my brothers and sisters had. And I still miss him to this day. I did love my father very, very much and deep down I know he loved me too. We were just too much alike. I feel that I do have a clear conscience regarding my parents however a clear conscience is usually the sign of a bad memory. Actually, I do have a bad memory. I have just thought of a reason I did let him down. Big style. He always used to ask me not to go out and get drunk and make a fool of myself. I apologise Dad as I have done just that on more than enough occasions. I am so sorry dad. Joey and I had been on our own since he was 4 years old. John was a very good dad but lived in Kent therefore it was very difficult to see Joe, but he used to make the trip at least four or five times a year. The rest of the time it was just Joey and I. When you are a single parent it is down to you to make every decision. I could never respond to any of his questions with "ask your dad". I would often question what his dad would do in this situation? Or what would my dad have done. But neither of them was there to ask and I felt angry with them for leaving me. Every single question they have is directed at you and you cannot use the threat of "wait until you father gets home" as my mum used to because he wasn't.

Joey's dad and I had so much fun together. Every Christmas we would make mince pies together and throw flour at each other. We both looked like flour graders. We also had water fights and I once ran and put the tuxedo jacket on that he would be wearing that night as a bouncer and could no longer squirt me as his jacket would get wet. But he got absolutely soaked. I really, really miss John and my parents and I am sure I always will.

The Bevvy Squad.

I am now a fully-fledged member of Jaisee's bevy squad, even though I don't drink. It consists of Jai and several of his friends and they meet at my house at weekends. I am proud of the fact that Jai's and Joey's friends are well aware of the fact that I have Bipolar and none of them bat an eyelid. It's great. When I was in hospital one of the nicer nurses said to me "always be yourself June". I know that she meant well however I thought to myself "when I am being myself you lot always lock me up, so just what is a girl to do? " Oh gosh I have to tell you this. My friend Patsy has a new nickname for me. It is Sluttykins. How cool is that? Sluttykins. Even though, I haven't had a partner for nine years. A little bit better than June Prickhard as some people have called me all of my life.

Pats told me that on one occasion she was sectioned and brought into Shelton by the Police. She was waiting quietly outside the doctor's office when 6 nurses used excessive force to drag her from there to the High Dependency Unit. She was then thrown onto a dirty bed, injected and left there for two whole days. How disgusting. She could have picked up an infection being injected on a dirty bed. How can this stuff be allowed to happen? Two days? She has no idea what she was injected with, but to knock out a large lady like Pats for that length of time would have to have been some pretty heavy duty stuff.

I have spent months when I cannot get out of bed, wishing that God would take me instead of other people who want to live. Joey has had to run a bath for me, make me put some clothes on and walk a few yards up my lane with him. I cannot eat and dread going to sleep because I know I have to wake up and may feel suicidal again. At one point I could not eat a thing. I had lost an awfully lot of weight. My Social Worker contacted the GP and requested Fortisip shakes which are used for exactly the situation I found myself in. Dr Margaret advised my Social Worker that I should try diet. My, they are good. If it was that bloody easy doesn't she think I would have done exactly that? These days I fear I may be expecting twins as I eat enough for three. But, I am no longer there now and I am not going to dwell on it. I am actually munching on a biscuit, with no goddam excuse for a nurse taking them home in between spurts of typing right now. Mmmm. I used to go to Joey's gym and thoroughly enjoyed it, but now I have converted my shed into a gym and work out there practically every day. I am a great believer in a healthy body is a healthy mind. I am obviously not as fit as I was when I was fighting but I like to think that if I continue to be stable I will be able to get reasonably fit again and then how sharp will my mind be.

On one occasion my Mental Health Advocate came to visit me in Shelton. I was outside smoking a cigarette. She told me that the neater you can roll a cigarette the better you are. That is so true. When I am ill my hands shake so much it is almost impossible to roll one. When I am well I can roll them perfectly. I could do that weeks before I was released so does it get you out? No. What really used to bug me in hospital were people asking me to roll their cigarettes for them even when they had not got the shakes. I used to do it and asked them to watch how to do it. They were so bone idle they still asked me. After a time I had had enough. I told them to buy tailor made cigarettes if they couldn't roll them. I am not your flipping lackey. One particular woman was visited by her husband almost every day. I heard him asking her if she needed him to bring cigarettes in for her every time he visited. She always said no and would then scrounge cigarettes from everyone else. She could go and do one as well.

I bumped into my mental health advocate in the street when I was probably at my lowest ebb. She gave me a sandwich to eat when I had absolutely no money and hadn't eaten for days. I will never, ever forget that. It was the best thing anyone could have done for me at that time because I would not have taken money from anyone. Even if they had I would have drunk it. It's a shame she no longer wishes to talk to me but I am not going to lose any sleep over it.

Benefits Agency.

When I worked for the Benefits Agency (the old DHSS) as it was known then, I spent two years here in Newtown and five years in Canterbury, Kent. I worked with so many lovely people here in Newtown. Unfortunately most of them have left and have been replaced by some of the nastiest people you could meet. I bumped into a man I used to work with in Newtown office. His name is Chris and he is one of the nicest, funniest men you could ever meet. He and another lovely man named Ken used to make me laugh so much. I was a very naïve Clerical assistant when I began working there. They would ask me to get them some stripy paint, sky hooks and a left handed screwdriver. Luckily I didn't fall for them. They did however ask me to refill their biros, and I actually thought twice about that one. They were great. When I saw Chris the other day he had some food wrapped in a serviette and begun singing Mae Hen Wlad Fy Nhadau (the Welsh National Anthem) and said they were Welsh cakes. He always tells me if only I had stayed at the Benefits Agency they would have taken care of me and I believe they would have. With the benefit of hindsight I really wish I had. Actually with the benefit of hindsight I wish that I had never, ever heard of Social Services.

In Newtown Benefits Agency we really did not know we were born. On one occasion a man shouted at a member of staff. The police were called and he was escorted from the building. In Canterbury there was a bullet proof glass screen between staff and clients. Some members of staff were issued with death threats. They were told by their clients that they would be waiting outside when they finished work. The Police were then called to escort that member of staff to their cars. That must have felt really horrible. Mind you a lot of staff members' attitudes stunk, (as they do now in Newtown). They were so judgemental and seemed to view the unemployed as the lowest form of life. However I don't think the members of staff deserved that.

William Beveridge brought in the National Insurance Benefits system in order to help the poor and the sick. I happen to think it is, along with the National Health Service, one of the best services this country has. As long as it is used properly. In my experience very few people want to be out of work, and people most certainly do not wish to be ill. I used to ensure that everyone received the benefits they were entitled to. It is a very mixed bag at the DWP these days. Some people I have spoken to have really gone out of their way to help me. Others seem to be intent on clawing the money back. I think that William Beveridge would be disgusted with these people. One man in particular is named Sir??? Robert Devereux. He is the civil servant responsible for increasing the state pension age to 67. He is retiring at the age of 61 with a £1.8 million pension pot. He will receive £85,000 a year and a lump sum of £245,000. He is the secretary for the department for Works and Pensions. His attitude seems to be that I'm ok Jack but the rest of you can work until you drop. My £4,500 in Disability Living Allowance which they refused to pay me has quite probably gone into his pockets too.

Junie Pritchard

When I worked in Canterbury as a Clerical Officer, we were all given a certain amount of cases per day to work on. I used to work so hard on my cases that I would be finished by lunchtime which left me the afternoon to make and receive phone calls. Then my manager used to give me my lazy colleagues cases to work on. What is the point in working hard and of course I didn't look busy, I did it right the first time. When I told my manager that I was going to work as a nanny in the States she told me that if I stayed they would make me an Executive officer. No thank you. I chose the States.

I had a great time there for twelve months but to me there is no place like home. When I returned to this country I resumed my relationship with John. I was living in Kent when I fell pregnant with Joey but John was concerned that as he was a long distance lorry driver he might be away when I went into labour. Therefore I returned to Wales and stayed with my parents a couple of weeks before my due date. My sister Annie was my birthing partner and her poor little hand was squeezed so tightly I'm surprised I didn't break it. I surprised even myself as I only swore once. Annie continually told me to breathe so I said "I am fi;ng breathing". Eventually Joey popped out and I was the happiest woman alive. I had that exact same feeling when Jai was born. As I mentioned John and I split up when Joey was four and I continued to live in Wales and John returned to Kent. He loved Joey dearly and would have done anything for him. I remember on one occasion John and I watched Joey play rugby. I find it quite unbelievable now but Joey had quite a bad temper when he was on the pitch and was sent off after about 10 minutes. John had made the five hour trip to watch him play for ten minutes. John really didn't mind though as he had that much more time to speak with him. Joey just has not got a bad temper at all now, and realises that if you lose your temper whilst fighting in the cage you are almost sure to lose the fight.

CHAPTER 12 SHELTON

It really was not all bad in there. I was first admitted in August of 2006. I was on a high and it was a beautiful summer there. I built up my leave as quickly as I possibly could and went training in the grounds. It was reported to Wasi by the nurses that I ran and ran faster than anyone they had ever seen. However how do you run from what's inside your head. I think it was 6 years ago in the summer that I was admitted again on a high. I seem to suffer from mania in the summer and depression in the winter. I think sometimes I should go and live in a hot climate but I could never bear to be apart from my children.

Shelton is a beautiful building with fabulous grounds and on my good days I felt privileged to be there. I used to imagine what it was like years ago and how people with mental health problems were treated then. I also read a book on what Shelton was like back then and it showed photographs of people in shackles made to work on the land. And ECT was given without anaesthetic and as a matter of course. Oh my life.

Anyhow, the summer of 2012 (I think) I was sectioned again feeling manic. It was beautiful weather, and I decided to sunbathe. There were other "normal" people sunbathing topless so I didn't think it was a big deal. I thought I was far away from the main building not to be seen and took my top off. What a crime. However here comes Craig the gorgeous nurse with a towel to spare my blushes. Luckily I had seen him coming and had put my top back on. He said that some of the nurses on the seriously dangerous persons section had seen me and complained. Had they got x ray vision or what? And what about the other topless girls who weren't deemed as nuts closer by? It was so ridiculous. I didn't hold it against Craig of course as I knew he was just doing his job. In fact Craig could have done anything and I wouldn't have held it against him. Only, joking. Oh no I'm not.

Craig was an absolutely lovely nurse. He was kind, caring, and very good looking. All the patients liked him and we were a little flirtatious with him. Well I was a lot actually but I blame it on my condition. Some of the women used to wolf whistle whenever he walked onto the ward. I would have but I can't do it. But I certainly let him know that I liked him. Honestly I could just gaze at him and feel happy. I even asked him for a bed bath once which I never got. Ha ha, the poor man. Where was the harm?

My family were very good to me but just didn't understand how I was feeling. I think when I first developed this illness they had no clue what it meant and neither did I. At one point they did disown me and I really don't blame them. I was in hospital for two months and only my children kept in touch. I asked the nurses every day if my brothers and sisters had rung, and nothing. At that time I really did feel like one of the forgotten few. These days they understand much more but still have no idea what we go through, and who could unless they have been there themselves.

Anyhow my younger brother Gary and my sister in law Lyndsey took me to see Roy Chubby Brown for my Birthday. I had been allowed leave and off I went. Craig said to me "you don't do so badly do you Junie?" And I didn't. It was exactly what I needed. I laughed the whole evening through. Even though I had been feeling crap earlier on my spirits soared that evening. Thank you so much little bro. However I still had to return to that shithole. My spirits sank like a brick. Don't do too badly? The nurses all get to go home at the end of their shifts. We are stuck in that place indefinitely. I just wanted to go home with my brother. I believe that everyone who has anything to do with these places on a professional basis should spend at least a week locked in there. See how they like it. I also believe that we should have comedians visit the hospital once a month or so.

Years ago Shelton even had its own brewery. Happy days. In my view patients should be allowed limited access to alcohol as

I should imagine, ex prisoners would feel as soon as they are set free they want to go straight to the pub and get hammered because they haven't tasted it for so long.

D.

D was another patient who I think was about my age. She was very poorly and very aggressive. She was also quite a lot bigger than me. She and I did not see eye to eye at all. She used to take cigarettes out of the older women's hands or even from their mouths and smoke them. There was absolutely nothing these poor women could do. I decided to ignore this as although she was extremely rude and intimidating she didn't actually hurt them. God I sound like a bodyguard don't I but I cannot bear seeing people upset. There is absolutely no need. Treat others as you would like to be treated and good manners never cost a penny. One day we were having a patient and staff meeting and D came rushing in from outside. Her face was set in a very angry manner and you could see that her fists were flexed. It was obvious that she was itching for a fight. She walked through the dining room where the meeting was held onto the ward slamming the door behind her. The nurses did nothing to calm her down. When the meeting was over I went back onto the ward. D was becoming agitated, banging objects on the table, wringing her hands and picking at her clothes. She was displaying all the classic signs of aggression. She then walked over to one of the elderly patients, reached into her handbag and took her packet of cigarettes and slapped her. That was it, I had had enough. I shouted at her to give the poor woman her cigarettes back and she came advancing towards me. I stood up in the fighting stance and thought "bring it on". Again because of my kickboxing I was not frightened by anyone, not even a big old beast like D. Two of the male nurses, good old Craig and Simon restrained her. I have to say at the time I was a bit disappointed because I would have loved to lamp her, but at least the nurses were beginning to realise what a nasty piece of work she could be. Craig said to me afterwards "we knew you could have taken her June"

Junie Pritchard

and I knew I could have too but with hindsight I'm glad I didn't as even D is a nice enough person when she is well.

A patient I will call Daisy was completely and utterly spoilt rotten and seemed to think that the world owed her a living. She also gave the impression that she thought of herself as being so much better than anyone else. She told me "oh my mummy and daddy couldn't afford to send me to Oxford so I had to go to Cambridge instead". Oh you poor little sausage. She really didn't want to have anything to do with any of us but she did tell me that she was in the Redwoods because everyone on the outside picked on her. I wonder why. One day she was extremely rude to D. (The girl that I almost had a fight with). D went nuts and threatened to belt her. When the situation had calmed down Daisy had a go at me for not sticking up for her. A) She was the one in the wrong and B) I am not your own personal bodyguard. I don't even like you, you, so why do you expect me to intervene?

CHAPTER 13 The Nurses

The nurses on the whole were amazing. I did not really enjoy nursing people with mental health problems when I was in the army as their behaviour was very unpredictable, and I tried to bear that in mind while I was in there. Most nurses in Shelton would do anything for you. As I said we had nicknames for them all, some were rude, some not. I think the worst we came up with for a not so nice nurse was vinegar tits. I had a run in with most of them at some point, but gradually changed my mind about them as time went on. They were not my jailers as I initially thought but were there to help me. They really did do a marvellous job. It is impossible not to get attached to some of the patients as I did when I worked on the Psychiatric ward in the army. Some of them were so lovable and incredibly funny. And I got attached to some of the nurses in Shelton too.
Bedlam.

Stokesay was slowly turning into Bedlam. All of the rules were being flaunted and we were allowed to get away with it. One evening we would be allowed outside to smoke until midnight, the next we had to be in by ten. We were allowed to watch tv until the early hours of the morning on occasion, the next it was turned off at 8. We just never knew where we stood. One night I wanted to see the moon at midnight as it made me feel close to Jai. We had been allowed out until the early hours several times prior to this. On this particular night the nurses called me in at 11.50. I asked if I could stay out just ten more minutes to see the moon. They said no and two of them began to drag me inside. I was hanging on to one of the posts of the smoking shelter for dear life but they dragged me off it. All that hassle for just ten minutes.

We were not given enough food and fights were breaking out on a regular basis. I remember attending a course when I was a social worker regarding Interpersonal risk factors associated with aggressive behaviour. a) Inexperienced staff b) High rates of temporary staff. Patients like familiarity of staff members c)

Rejecting – hostile attitudes from staff d)   Nurses can provide poor role models re; managing frustration etc. e)   High rates of aversive demands from nurses to patients – not asking patients to perform tasks they are incapable of. f)   Aggression is functional – absence of alternative options, escapes g)   Use of barbs, words known to upset a patient h)   Exploitation of aggression – don't focus on a person's legs if they are prone to kicking i)   Peer group pressure – patients will encourage other patients to be aggressive All of this was happening on Stokesay. Then de de de de duh, a new manager arrived. She was a trouble shooter and boy did she turn Stokesay around. She took back the reins and all of the rules were put back into place and we knew exactly where we stood again. I cannot for the life of me remember her name but she was wonderful. I remember that she was very beautiful and had blonde hair. Hallelujah. Peace reigned again.

I happen to believe that rules are usually there for a good reason and they are normally set in the best interest of everyone. Shelton was in my view an excellent hospital. I realise that more now that I have spent time in four other hospitals. The nurses were a bit wary about us mixing with the men on the next wards. We knew nothing about them or what their diagnosis was. I'm pretty sure that they would be in high security if they were axe-murderers or the like. However they were all lovely and I got on famously with every single one of them. They were far less volatile than the women. I truly believe that MOST of the people I met in there are far nicer than the average "normal" person, and way more fun. But it is not where very few of us wanted to be.

Anyhow I had no money and Dr M was concerned about it. He asked me to put one bank card into the patient's bank and the other one was given to Joey. Although Wasi didn't know it I literally had four pence to my name and this went on for a month. 4p for a month? Holy crap. As I think I mentioned I was a smoker and a nuthouse is not the place you want to be in to quit. How I survived the month I do not know. Well I do know and it was all pretty disgusting. My good, good friend Alfy, the ex jailbird told me about dimps. Dimps are other people's cigarettes that had been discarded. Alf used to smoke them as is but I couldn't face that. I used to break them apart, put new tips in and voila you had a brand new cigarette.

Pats later told me that I should have been entitled to £5 emergency money. I never got it and the nurses watched me carry out this disgusting act. My sister Annie came to visit me and I asked her if she would lend me £5 towards some tobacco. She refused. I was not surprised at all as Annie freely admits that she has problems parting with money. When I can afford it I am going to pay to have her purse surgically removed from her hand.

Obviously I had not enough money to purchase anything. Fortunately there were lots of rose hip bushes in the grounds so I picked lots of them. I then soaked them in boiling water, stirred them up and that made a very nice skin product and shampoo. One of the advantages of living on a farm. The nurses gave me sanitary products, toothpaste and washing powder bless them. Unlike the flipping Police. At the end of that month Joey visited me and brought with him a bag of loose change which he had saved. He apologised that it really wasn't very much. In that bag was a little more than £12. Twelve whole pounds? At that time it felt like a million. Oh how I love him.

When a lady I will call M and I went to the co op on leave, I still only had very little money. I couldn't afford to buy anything but I just wanted to get out of the hospital. When we were there M began to put things into her bag. I thought what the heck are you doing? When I asked her she said "oh come on June we've all borrowed something from Boots". I thought that was hilarious, but I hadn't and didn't intend to start. I really would prefer to be broke.

In stark contrast to my time in Shelton things have now gone from one extreme to the other, and hospitals now have mixed sex wards. How ridiculous is that? One minute you are not allowed to go near a member of the opposite sex, the next you are sharing a ward with them. This has been done to save money. What about saving lives?

I have now been in a total of five different Psychiatric hospitals and Shelton was without a doubt the best. It is now closed as a hospital and is being sold off as luxury flats. There is now a new "Therapeutic Centre" named The Redwoods. I was one of the first patients to walk to The Redwoods from Shelton. Others came over in wheelchairs or by ambulance. On that first admission it was ok in there as I was on an all female ward. What they have done to it now is disgusting. Therapeutic? I think not. I found it absolutely unbearable on my last admission.

Once you are diagnosed with Bipolar you are considered to be a vulnerable adult. But in that appalling place I have never felt so scared and vulnerable in all of my life. Apart from my attacker in the park. And my three overnight stays courtesy of the Police Force. I was in a mixed sex ward. Even my brothers (who are not small guys) said that they felt threatened when they came to visit me there. Apparently a lot of the Redwoods patients simply have nowhere else to go. Personally I would sooner sleep on the streets. When I am mentally ill the last place I want to be is on the same ward as mentally ill (normally highly sexually charged) males. The men would even knock on my door. I was terrified in there. Again put the plebs who are in charge of it in there for a week. See how they come out the other end.

My friend has written a couple of poems for me. The first is based on the incident where that vile nurse tried to stop us watching the Olympics on tv. It goes like this; "Pick your favourite window. Pick your favourite window quick, you're going to go through it, you horrid little prick. I'm up to here, I'm up to there you really make me sick. So pick your favourite window your favourite window, pick." Another text he sent me goes like this; "there are many good reasons for drinking and one has just popped into my head. If you can't have a drink when you are living how on earth can you drink when you're dead? Another little ditty I love is "I'm on the gin and tonic diet. I've already lost two days". Ha I love those poems and I think they are very true. However the drinking ones just cannot apply to me.

My dear friend Bertie and I used to get drunk together and sing this song; "Lord when I die, don't bury me at all, just pickle my bones in alcohol". Bertie is sadly no longer with us. He was in his 70's when I was in my 30's. I used to pop down the road to visit him a lot and I still miss him now. Sometimes I wonder why people have to die. Why can't we stay young forever? I think that's what it's like in heaven. Everyone meeting up. Being young and happy again. Other times I want to die so badly. Old age does not come on its own and neither does Bipolar.

Oh god, I hope this book gets published. I think the last time I made my children proud was when I was working and doing a really good job, and when I won the European Championships kickboxing, but if just one person were to read this book and enjoy it I think they will be proud of me once more.

I really feel for my children. Jai was only ten years old when I first got sectioned and if I had no idea what was going on how on earth was he meant to. I know that initially his father told him I was in hospital with a very bad cold. Understandably I know because how do you tell a child his mum's in the nut house. Poor little man. I don't know what they told him in the end. "Mummy's screws need tightening" or "mummy's living in a funny farm with lots of other strange people".

Jai has this little saying "we are all beautiful in our own way". What a complete and utter crock of shit. You should have seen some of the ugly people I have met. Claire Turner and Fran Foster fall nicely into that category. Jai also says "I like it, I want it, I love it, I got it". Freedom. I love it, I got it. But for how long? Every time I experience a low I think I cannot cope with another. In fact it is worse as you know exactly what is coming. Lord please, take me now. I have begun going to church a lot and someone asked me, how can you believe in God when you have such a critical illness? I do not believe that God has given me Bipolar. It has been brought on by stress and nothing to do with him at all. Just as cancer or any other horrible illness is not God's wish. I find such comfort in going to church and praying at home and I believe that whenever my time is up I will go to heaven and be reunited with the loved ones I have lost. I am not in the slightest afraid of dying and on more occasions than I could possibly remember I have wished for it.

Joey was 19 and present when I was first admitted. He was amazing and it was because of him telling me he just wanted me to get better that I went without putting up too much of a fight. How he coped I just do not know. We were living 7 miles outside town, away from his friends with no one else at the house. Joey's father hung himself when Joey was just 17 and here was his mess of a mother threatening it now. Bless his heart. He seems to have been a grown man since he was 17 but what must have been going through his mind lord only knows. Jaisee is now 25 and I think he has only recently become fully cooked. Sorry Beanie. He has for a while now but if I live to see him into his thirties, he will always be my baby. On one occasion when Jai was only 16 and living with his father due to my illness his father went to Italy for a month. I was sectioned yet again a couple of days later. Poor little Jaisee said "I have lost my mum and my dad within the space of a week." Bless his little heart. It is now April of 2021 and I am going to do everything in my power to stay stable. I try to work out in my gym every day, and make sure that I go for a walk in the fresh air each day too. I take my medication religiously, see Wasi as often as I possibly can and I am now seeing my wonderful Psychologist Ena. Apart from that I cannot think of anything I can do apart from hope and pray extremely hard. I think my sons are a little bit proud of me for quitting drinking, but I do not feel proud of myself for that at all. I would have been proud if I had not shoved so much alcohol down my neck in the first place. I stupidly thought that I might not experience any more episodes if I stopped drinking but have been proved otherwise. I have been sectioned on two occasions since and experienced a low episode not too long ago. That does not mean I am going to start drinking again though. Alcohol and my medication just do not mix and my life would be devastated again, and I just do not want to take that risk ever again. I also believe that if I did drink in town the fun police would be crawling all over me yet again like a rash. Actually I do not feel that anymore. I have recently had cause to help them with their enquiries and I get the impression that they really do now wish me well.

Joey has just told me a joke which I found really funny. It goes like this; A man goes to a bee convention and someone asked him how many bees he had. The man replied I have 500 bees and ten hives. The man asked how many bees he has. I have fifty thousand bees and two hives. The man was appalled and asked fifty thousand bees and only two hives? So he said yeah fuck 'em they're only bees. When I told Jai the joke he did not like it at all. He said mum that's cruel what about those poor bees? Jai it's a joke. He then said but those bees might die mum. Jaisee there are no bees, it's a joke. Oh my life. I can assure everyone that no bees were harmed in the process of telling this joke. I also told him about the man who took his little friend who is only a head to the pub for a drink. He sits the head onto a bar stool and bought him a whisky. The head took a sip and out popped his torso. He took another sip and out pooped his arms. One more sip and his legs popped out. The boy was so excited he ran out onto the street and got run over by a car. The barman said "that boy should have quit while he was a head". Jai did not like that one either. "That poor boy mum". Oh my gaaawd.

CHAPTER 14 BARBADOS

I have always wanted to go to Barbados. Even as a child when my friends were dreaming of Fairy-tale white weddings and babies and things, I was dreaming of Barbados. Thirteen years ago, I paid the grand sum of £6,500 for myself, Joey's 21st and Dave's 60th Birthdays. I ended up getting so high I could have flown the bloody plane and found myself in Costa Del Shelton instead. The insurance company refused to pay up as Dave's daughter who booked the holiday had failed to tell them I had Bipolar. I do not think that she even knew that I had got it. I lost the lot. A pre-existing condition they said. £6,500. And am I bitter? Hell yes. I hate insurance companies. I was kept in for 3 months on that one. Three more months in that awesomely horrific place instead of Barbados. All of my dreams dashed again. Insurance companies are so quick to take your money but trying to get money from them is like trying to get blood out of a stone. The one that really gets me is when they tell you it is an act of God. I wonder if they would call it an act of god if I were to smack one of them in the mouth. Joking. It makes me laugh when people ask me to sponsor them to go and help the children of Africa or other such places. The next person that asks me I will tell them that I would prefer to help the children here, or could they possibly sponsor me to go and help the poor little kiddies in Barbados. I wonder what response I will get. Again I am only joking. I do know that they do incredibly good things to help over there.

Yet again someone has said to me "please don't kill yourself June, think of your children". I didn't deck him as I thought I would but I cried a river when he had left. I think of nothing else. If I spent the rest of my life trying to make up to my children what I have put them through, which is what I intend to do, it just couldn't be enough. I know he meant well but he doesn't have a clue what Bipolar is like and how much it hurts inside.

I must also have quite a strange voice as even at my grand old age some people ring me and immediately ask if they can speak to my mother. I normally reply as sweetly as I can and say that my mother is in heaven so unless you have a really good phone signal it's not looking good.

Drinking

Drinking has always been part of my culture. I was brought up in a pub until the age of 13 and although I was not allowed to drink at that age I loved pub life. The atmosphere was wonderful, always someone to talk to and have fun with. And singing. It used to sound like a male voice choir in there. I loved it. I drank like a fish in the Army at weekends. Alcohol was dirt cheap and that was our way of coping with Army life I think. I then worked in pubs and clubs where drink was prevalent. It's funny though when I went to work in Napa Valley in California where they produced wine I didn't drink at all. I was in charge of two young children after all. I have certainly made up for it since my diagnosis of Bipolar. I used to drink myself into oblivion in order to cope with my emotions. Dr M told me I was self-medicating and that is exactly how it felt. When I drank I never in a million years thought it would become a problem for me. It very slowly crept up on me and I really did not expect it. The amount of mornings I woke up feeling dreadful and said to myself "never again" but I always did. My friend says "I won't drink any more but I won't drink any less". My big brother told me to put the alcohol in the watering can. When I asked why he said "so that the grass comes up half cut". People would say to me if ever I was anxious or upset "have another drink it will make you feel better" and I did way too many times. I do not want my life to be like that ever again. Lurching from one drink to the next. If someone had told me before my diagnosis of Bi polar that I would develop an alcohol problem I would have laughed in their face.

Since my diagnosis I have been called all kinds of names such as retard, not right in the head, tart, slut, you name it I've been called it. I don't think I am any of those things. Certainly not a tart or a slut. I have not had an intimate relationship for nine years. Cheeky gits.

I think giving up drinking is one of the hardest things I have ever had to do. Alcohol is practically everywhere you go. It is on tv, in pubs, clubs and supermarkets. Most supermarkets have the alcohol displayed right by the checkout so that I have to wait in the queue looking at it with lust in my eyes as I wait to pay for my orange juice. It is everywhere, and it is so difficult to watch people relax with a drink and get merry when I am sitting there like a lemon. But I've done it. Joey would cope if I began drinking again, but Jai would be so hurt I just cannot do it to him. I managed not to drink at Joey's wedding. I toasted the bride and groom with orange juice. Joey said he was proud of me and that makes it all worthwhile. Here's a toast to me never drinking again. I am now an alcohol-free zone and intend to stay that way. When I meet my friends now, I either drink coffee or sometimes just good old plain water. Wow I know how to live. I am slowly regaining my confidence and everyone seems to want to be around me right now, so maybe I am not that bad after all.

I went out last night, the first night in an age. I was drinking my usual coffee and everyone else was drinking alcohol. I sat with a chap who I used to have a drink with years ago. He was lovely and told me that it was so nice to see me out. He then told me how hilarious I was when I was drinking alcohol. I was so close to cracking and ordering a drink but I told myself that it might have been funny for everyone else but it was not for me and my children. Luckily I hung on to my resolve never to drink again, but it is so, so hard.

I imagine that being locked up in the nut house must feel very much like being in prison. The longer you are in there the more difficult it is to adjust to coming out. You have to do everything for yourself again, and everything seems faster and busier and your confidence is well and truly knocked. When I am poorly I am anxious about everything, particularly leaving the house. I wonder if people can see or know that I have bipolar and how they are going to react. I say to myself I have coped for three years in the Army and three years in total in Psychiatric hospitals so surely I can cope in my home town. Most of the time, I can cope. Other times I lock myself away and write this book. I really do become quite insular. But I am going to utilise every little bit of advice I have found on Bipolar and do my utmost to stay well. I no longer have any qualms about appearing lazy when I am too ill to get out of bed. I just accept it. No rebukes for me because I really cannot help it. I have accepted the adversity I and my children have been through as really not being my fault. I certainly did not ask for this illness but there is no doubt in my mind I am Bipolar 1 which is the most serious type, but in future I am going to do my darndest to control my emotions.

Fifteen years ago, whilst training for the World Championships, working full time and studying I pushed my mind and my body to the absolute limit and I cracked. Never, ever, again. I now train in my gym whenever I feel like it, normally when I feel anxious and I intend doing no more. I remember a so-called friend (a Social Worker) who came to stay the night at my home and couldn't believe it when I started doing press ups first thing in the morning. But that was my life. I often used to make a forty minute trip to see her. Her daughter and I used to get on very well and her mum would often ring me asking me to go there as her daughter would not talk to anyone else but me. And just who did she think would be talking to my kids when I am talking to yours. I no longer want that woman in my life or any other Social Worker like her. I believe that I have lost the friends I needed losing and have found others along the way. As I mentioned now that I have quit drinking alcohol I drink a lot of water. (Very healthy I think). Jaibo tells me that you can drown if you drink too much water. Maybe I'll use it as my next suicide attempt. Death by water. Not very exciting is it? I want a far more exciting exit from this planet than that. I don't mean to belittle death, but if I don't see the funny side of life I think I will go crazy. AGAIN. Death no longer scares me in the slightest. However I do not want to die from suicide. I want to grow old before I die.

My Scratch Card.

Joey and Hannah were talking about their forthcoming wedding and I was locked up in Shelton still. I was so excited that I bought a very glossy wedding magazine. I couldn't believe my luck as inside it was a million pound scratch card and I had won. I would have won the wedding of their dreams and the rest in cash. I made the mistake of not showing it to anyone other than the woman at the Post office counter. I was home on leave and took it to her. I knew the woman as she is the mother of my niece Donna's husband. She was very helpful at that time and told me to photocopy the scratch card twice and send it by recorded delivery which I did. I went back to Shelton. On my next period of leave I was told that the Post Office was under audit. Nothing had arrived in the post regarding my scratch card. When I went back to Shelton my room had been turned over and all of my paperwork was missing including the photocopies and registered delivery slip. On my next period of leave I asked the lady at the Post Office if she would help trace it. She refused point blank. What? Why? She wouldn't budge. I went into the Post Office on another occasion and a young man told me that it could be traced but it had to be done by her. I then asked my niece to ring her to see if she would have any joy asking the old bag to have a look for it. Yet another refusal. I would put money on the fact that if that had been one of her family's scratch card she would have turned over the whole post office to find it. I don't believe that winning ticket ever left the Post Office. A lot of £8.50 recorded delivery's add up. When I wrote to the head of the Post Office they even had the audacity to say that if I wrote to them again I would not receive a reply. My goodness. How unbelievably rude. What if I had written to my clients as a Social Worker and said that? I would have been hung. How on earth do these large companies live with themselves? I don't know why people have been so mean to me in the past. I think most people believe that when you have a severe mental illness you are void of all feelings and they can treat us however they like. And the sad fact is they can. However it is you who appears to be void of feelings not us.

Jennifer.

One of the nicest people I met there and has since become a very dear friend was called Jennifer. (Not her real name). She was lovely. The nurses commented how we hit it off instantly. We spent hours in each other's company. Jen was warned to stay away from me as I was a bad influence. Thankfully she ignored them. However true to their word I was a very poor role model to have. We used to nip down to the Co-op when no one was looking and bring back alcohol, which we hid in the bushes. Jen was sensible and didn't drink very much but I certainly made up for her. Some rules are just meant to be broken I feel. We had so much fun. We would sit in a shelter with some of the guys and feel completely normal for that short period of time. Bad influence my ass. I would not encourage anyone to do anything they didn't want to do. Often at night time I would join Jen in her room just after checks and sneak back to mine an hour later and so on. We talked and laughed into the early hours of the morning. It reminded me of the Army and University. It was heaven. One night I have to admit I smoked some weed in Jens room and the nurses caught me. Jen hadn't had any. One of the nurses burst into her room and ordered me back to mine and told me to take that smelly stuff with me. We were both tested the next day and I showed up positive. I don't know why they bothered really as I had already fessed up to the fact that I had. I assured them that Jen had not smoked any and luckily they believed me. I don't remember the last time I have laughed so much. I believe that laughter is the best therapy of all. More miserable people should try it sometime. The world would be a much better place. One of the girls heard the nurse inform me that I had tested positive (surprise surprise) and she asked if I was pregnant. I told her no you have to have sex first. I wasn't even punished for that one. I couldn't believe it, but it could have had something to do with the fact that some of the nurses smoked it too. I'm surprised they weren't sniffing cocaine having to deal with us lot but of course they weren't. They were lovely. Jen and I spent most of our waking hours together. She is extremely intelligent and good fun. She went to Private School and says "ya" a lot which I love and she hasn't got a snobby or a bad bone in her body. When we were allowed out we spent a lot of time with a lovely young man named Josh and a slightly older man we nicknamed Jim Bob. We had so much fun together. There was quite a gradient leading up to the Marches restaurant. We used to use the porter's trolley which if we had got caught we would have been in big trouble. Health and safety, etc etc. Anyhow Josh and Jim bob would push the trolley up the hill and Jen and I would shout out moosh moosh and pretend to whip them. Then all four of us would jump on it and roll down the hill. Oh my, gosh, it was fun. I often wonder what happened to the two men. However no one could tell us due to confidentiality. Something the nurses respected. Unlike the Police when they told my employers that I had stolen a non existent kit kat.. Tut tut I am turning over a new leaf. Our lovely law enforcement officers. I mean it honestly.

Benefits Agency.

When I was first ill I was entitled to full pay for the first 6 months and half pay for the next 6 months. I should have had my pension paid to me immediately following that period. This, however, just did not happen. Powys Social Services did everything that they could to avoid giving me a pension at all. For the next two years they refused to pay me anything at all. Joey and I were given the princely sum of £67 a week Income Support. We had to live on that amount of money and my savings which really wasn't much as I had spent most of it doing up our cottage. I also had a mortgage to pay, so I went along to the Benefits Agency where I used to work and spoke with a Disability specialist asking for help. She told me to sell my house. Wow why didn't I think of that? She could piss off and fuck off too. And she was a specialist. Special bloody needs more like. I am not selling my house for anyone. It is what I had worked for all of my life.

Until I got ill I had never taken any time off work in my life, I never went on strike because I felt privileged to work there and sometimes worked two jobs to pay off my mortgage. And I had very rarely had a period where I had not studied in my life. I am very lucky because most Bipolar sufferers do end up losing their homes. Any spare cash that Joey had he used to give me bless him and we just had to muddle through together. He was amazing. After a time I was able to claim Disability living allowance. Phew. However, when you go into hospital, if you are there for more than 28 days they stop your benefits. Oh my god. How are you meant to pay for your home when they do that? And why are we forced to lose our homes because of a heinous illness like Bipolar. Bipolar is a curse. I cannot think of much worse, and we certainly don't request it. When you are disabled and forced to live on benefits they will not pay one iota towards your mortgage, however your rent is paid for you. Why? I cannot see any reasoning to that whatsoever. I was so lucky I didn't lose my home and probably forced to live in a one bedroom flat on a crappy housing estate. And nobody gave a damn apart from Wasi and my children.

On one occasion I had to visit the Benefits Agency to get my benefits re-instated. I explained to this excuse of a human being that I had been discharged from Shelton two days ago and she gave me a telephone number to ring. I told her that I had no credit on my mobile so I asked if I could use one of the four telephones on the wall which were meant for claimants use. She told me to use a pay phone in the town. Her whole attitude stank. I felt too ill and worn down by it all to argue with her so I left. People like her should really be ashamed of themselves, and I really don't know how they sleep at night. If I had treated people the way she treated me when I worked at the DHSS I would have expected to be sacked. Someone told me that all the money that is not given to the people who are entitled to it gets paid to management as a nice big fat bonus? How can that be? Those people should be shot, and I would have loved to be the person in charge of the gun. Again, think of Robert Devereux.

Back to Shelton.

Paul and I hit it off immediately. He had long black curly hair that he wore in a ponytail and John Lennon style dark glasses. He was so cool. He was normally dressed in black and he was a whole load of fun. Every moment we were allowed out we spent together. He was amazing and what was even more amazing was the fact that we came from the same town. I had never seen him there and he is definitely the kind of guy I would have remembered. He was so funny. He used to say to me "hi Juney, how are your tits pits and naughty bits? We also had the same taste in music and would sit in the garden chatting and listening to music for hours. He was the perfect gentleman. Paul was discharged before me and he rang me from his home on the night of his discharge and asked me "what is the meaning of life Juney?" I'm f'ed if I know. I was stuck in the nut house and had absolutely no idea. I was so concerned about him I asked him to ring his Social Worker and I relayed my concerns to the nurses. The next day he was dead. He had overdosed in the night. I was probably the last person he had spoken to and I loved him like a brother. That day I ran out of the hospital and got absolutely legless. I didn't give a damn what the nurses said or did. Breathalysed yet again. Failed yet again. Does this face look bothered?

My Social worker was also Paul's and when I told her what had happened all she said was "we know about Paul June, these people are not your friends". Not my friends? I live with "these people". And most of them are the nicest people I have ever met. Her name was Pauline Rigby and I wanted to smash her teeth so far down her throat she would have had to put a toothbrush up her arse to clean them. My god, have I had some very good lessons in how not to be a Social Worker. All my leave was at risk of being cancelled again, but luckily Dr M at ward round was really understanding about Paul and my leave remained in place. Ha. Up yours Pauline. She is right up there with Laurraine Hamer as the worst Social Workers in the country. Thank god someone in there had an ounce of compassion. I love Dr M. He understood me better than any other person in there. Pauline also assured me that she would complete my Disability living allowance forms as I just could not concentrate enough to complete them myself. I then found that the lazy bleep had not bothered and I lost £4,500 in benefits. I tried my best to appeal but they just would not budge. How the hell do they think I can be disabled for years, get better and then be disabled again. God they make me so angry. To date I have lost £1100 due to this illness and nobody apart from Wasi and I gave a flying F. Plus of course my million pound scratch card.

CHAPTER 15 Annie G.

My best friend Annie sent me this brilliant text, it really cheered me up and goes like this; "I have just heard on the news that someone checked into the psycho ward wearing a thong and nipple tassels, riding a goat. I'll come and get you this time Juney but this shit has to stop". She then apologised and was concerned that I might be offended. Annie I loved it. It so helps when people make light of my illness. Annie has since passed away and she was the best friend I have ever had. She was also one of the best Social Workers I have ever met and I so wanted to be like her. I now think of her as my Guardian Angel and she tells me off if I am naughty and laughs at me when I am good. I told her to please do not walk behind me as I may not lead. Do not walk ahead of me as I may not follow. Please just walk beside me and be my friend. And that is exactly what she did. I really wish she was still here. The measure of love is when you love without measure, and that is what I felt for Annie.

Another joke goes like this: A man and a woman who had never met before but who were both married to other people, found themselves assigned to the same sleeping cabin on a trans –continental train. Though initially embarrassed and uneasy over sharing a room, they were both very tired and fell asleep quickly, he in the upper berth and she in the lower. At 1am the man leaned down and gently woke the woman saying "look I'm sorry to bother you, but would you be willing to reach me another blanket? I'm awfully cold." "I have a better idea she replied, just for tonight, let's pretend we are married". "Wow" he exclaimed thinking that his luck was in, "that's a great idea". "Good" she replied "get your own fucking blanket". Sorry Vicar.

A 31 year old woman has been sexually assaulted with a hoover nozzle and left for dead. Police say "although she is in intensive care she is picking up nicely".

Would you like to buy a 42 inch LCD television for £50? The volume button isn't working, but for that price you can't turn it down.

A man runs into a pet shop, puts a bomb on the counter and says everyone has one minute to get out. A tortoise at the back shouts "you bastard".

Marilyn Monroe is one of my idols. I have a photograph of her on my bedroom wall. She once said "I'm selfish, impatient and a little insecure. I make mistakes, I am out of control and at times hard to handle. But if you can't handle me at my worst, then you sure as hell don't deserve me at my best". That is exactly how I feel now. She was a Gemini too, just like me. It is the sign of the twins. Maybe there is a link there, one twin having the highs and the other having the lows. We are also meant to have a mixture of 12 different personalities. Almost one for every day of the week. And she ended her life at the age of 36. I recently found a mug in my cupboard all about Gemini's. It says Gemini the twins. Gemini is the sign of communication and dexterity. As the typical Gemini is charming and quick witted they make lively and interesting companions. They are often creative and can be involved in the arts and literature and they tend to be involved in several projects at the same t ime. And this is the biggy for me it says that suitable careers are journalist, AUTHOR, linguist and courier. Author. Oh pleeeease let it be me.

When I was down and out, no-one, apart from my children and Alfy wanted to know me. But just remember, on the way to the bottom you make a lot of stops. You sure as heck know who your true friends are and who are your fair-weather friends. Now that I am stable it seems that everyone wants to be my friend. Do you really think that my memory is that short? If you didn't like me then I don't want to know you now. My friends are now mainly the people I go to church with (sincere apologies for my colourful language). My friends there do not judge me, they are always nice to me and seem to accept me just the way I am even though I told them from the get go I am different to other people. I do not want to go for "just one drink" with anyone. Does that sound harsh? It is not meant to be. I would absolutely love to but I know that I just can't do it. I sometimes see some of my ex colleagues from Social Services and most of them try to speak with me. These days I do my best to ignore them. I really do not wish to know you. Apart from my old manager named Terry and the lovely admin staff. They are far more caring than the Social Workers themselves. As for the others please just leave me alone.

I have written something in June of 2010. It says "Smile though your heart is breaking". Why? Why do I have to smile when I hurt like this? But I still do. Oh my god it hurts so much. I would rather give birth to ten kids in succession than go through this mental torture. And I would have, if the children were adopted. (Only joking. But then again maybe not). I do not know what apathy is and what's more I don't care.

Time for a joke I think. An elderly lady decides her body has got out of shape, so she joins a fitness club to do some exercise. She signs on to do an aerobics class for senior citizens. On her first day she bends, twists, gyrates, jumps up and down, and perspires for an hour. But by the time she manages to get her leotard on, the class had finished.

Gosh, I never used to swear. Honestly. I remember swearing once when Joey was about 15 and he said "Mum that is the first time I have ever heard you swear". Now I think I have developed turrets or something. I can no longer converse or express myself without it. I am ashamed of that too. Shame, guilt, sorrow and despair. They are all at the forefront of my mind when I am low. I also had to be extremely Politically Correct as a Social Worker. Boring, boring, boring. We had all our black boards replaced with white boards. If we wanted a black coffee, we had to ask for a coffee without milk. These days, I say exactly what I want, when I want, just in case you hadn't noticed that yet. And if I want to call Jai's little black rabbit "nigger boy" then I damn well will. And before you jump down my throat, I am not racist, sexist, feminist or any other kind of ist. I just happen to find it funny.

Stokesay.

Sometimes women would be brought into the ward on stretchers and they didn't look as if they would make it through the night. A few of us would sit outside their room and pray for them. The transformation in the morning after just one good night's sleep was incredible. They were both physically and mentally exhausted. My friend used to call older people coffin dodgers. She felt that everyone over the age of 60 should be put in a pit and the ones that were able to climb out could be free. The ones that were still down there would be left there. She was only joking (I think).

Most of the women in Stokesay were so poorly they had neglected their appearance. Me too, when I was low, but on this occasion I was on a high. I went home on leave and hit my favourite clothes shop in the world named Severn Island. My friend Julia runs it and I'm convinced that she buys everything with me in mind (only joking of course) but I love everything in there. She helped me select lots of lovely outfits. As I said I was on a high and we joke now that I almost bought the whole shop. I have given up alcohol and smoking. I could give up shopping but I am not a quitter. When I returned to the funny farm with all my goodies we had a fashion show. Some of the women had done each other's nails, hair and makeup and for that evening at least we felt like real women again. A few of us even had a dance on the ward. I love dancing. On one occasion the Police came to my home because someone had told them that I was dancing in my living room. Unbelievable. Why on earth was anyone looking in to my living room anyway. Whenever anyone looks down their nose at me now for being in a Psychiatric hospital I think to myself, yes I have Bipolar, I am being treated for my illness. You are obviously not. You have three choices in life: give up, give in or give it your all.

Sleep is important to everyone. My mum used to tell me that

sleep is the greatest healer and I believe her. It is particularly important to Bi polar sufferers. If we do not get enough sleep we will get high or low, and mainly in my experience low. Dr Mohamad told me that the older I get the more likely I am to get the lows. Oh be joyful. He can be such a happy little bunny sometimes, but I am grateful he always tells me the truth. There is absolutely no point in dressing up this illness and I believe that being forewarned is forearmed. I know that Dr Mohamad is my psychiatrist not my friend but that is how I view him. I feel that I can tell him my innermost secrets and I know that he will not tell a soul. I trust him completely. I tell him things that I would never tell anyone else. I am sure that he has felt absolutely exasperated with me on occasion but he does not let it show. Bless him. Oooh I get by with a little help from my friends. AND in the fifteen years I have known him I have NEVER made a complaint about him because he has never given me a reason to.

I would give my right arm to be rid of Bipolar and one poor girl in hospital did just that. She was so poorly love her and wanted to end it all. She jumped in front of a train and lost her arm. (I would like to mention that around about the time of my illness a friend of mine had an accident at work and lost his arm. Understandably he was awarded £150,000 compensation. I lost my mind at work which I truly believe is way more painful. I was awarded nothing, a big fat zero from the wonderful caring profession).

That poor, poor girl. She was so sweet but absolutely sick of feeling desolate. Bless her heart. There were so many mangled bodies there through suicide attempts that had gone wrong. Self-harming was rife also. I mentioned the young girl in the four bedder with me who had arms twice the size that they should have been from continually slicing them and re slicing them with razor blades. Oh my god she was so nice. She was young and pretty and she played football with me. I love football and we started to play football amongst ourselves in good old Costa Del Shelton. I am ashamed to say that I picked up the football from outside a Primary School which had been kicked over the fence. Instead of throwing it back over like any model citizen should do I took it back to hospital with me. For some ladies it was the only time they went outside at all. We were crap, but we had great fun. We were also going to go busking. Some of the women were really talented musicians and we thought that we could have some fun and make a little money at the same time. I am not a talented musician by any stretch of the imagination so I was going to be the one holding out the hat looking gormless. We were going to call ourselves "the Shelton Shufflers". Thank god we were not allowed as the fuzz would have probably locked us up for vagrancy. I was told that if you did not have enough money for a cup of tea you could be arrested for being just that, a vagrant. And I had 4 pence for the month. I was doomed. If one of them didn't lock me up the others would. I want to go home.

Yesterday a severe stutterer was sent to prison for drink, driving. He was given six months, but the police don't think he will finish his sentence.

It was difficult to accept that I have Bipolar. In one respect I always knew I was different. I think I was an ADHD kid. In the army I studied Psychiatry. Not because I wanted to practise it, but because I wanted to know what was wrong with me. I did not experience the extremes highs and lows that I do now, but there was something there. However I never once thought that I was a manic depressive and truly believe that if Claire Turner, Amanda Lewis and Clive Bartley had not put me under such extreme pressure, and the intolerable way they treated me following my breakdown I would never have developed this truly disgusting illness. As Ena, my Psychologist says, I managed perfectly well with life until the age of 44 and began working for that woman. Most Bi Polar sufferers develop it in their 20's.

When I was studying for my Diploma I had a choice of which team to do my placement in. When I considered doing my placement with Claire Turner people told me that she was a bitch and that she was weird. Stupidly I thought she can't be that bad, but how wrong I was.

Later on I also studied Psychology, Counselling skills, Life Coaching and Social Work, but was still none the wiser. I think that my only problem in the past was maybe hyperactivity and a thirst to learn. It took the stress of working for Powys Social Services to give me Bipolar. I also sat the European computer driving license. You wouldn't think so now though. On a couple of occasions I have needed my sons help to find work on my laptop that I thought I had lost. Jai says to me "this is what to do if it happens again Mum". Then he goes da da da da da on my laptop keys so quickly I tell him that I don't remember the first key you pressed let alone the last. I was not brought up with computers ok? You have a great advantage over me you little ingrate. This book is proving to be a nightmare to complete and I really will take my laptop for a long walk off a short cliff when it is complete.

Wasi really did save my life the night he sectioned me as I was so out of control and wanted to really harm myself to help take away the emotional pain and agony I was feeling. He has also saved my life on several occasions since. And if you are bored stiff with this book it is his fault because he suggested I write it. I really believe though that he doesn't realise what a horrible little specimen I can be. Oops. Hey ho. Away we go.

Since being diagnosed I have found all the information I can on Bipolar and there is absolutely no doubt in my mind that I have it. And I absolutely hate it. I don't know why I have got it, or what I have done to deserve it but it is here and I just have to learn to live with it. At this present time I am considered to be stable. Even now though, it is so hard to live with. I continually ask myself if I am behaving normally. As sometimes I really don't know. I keep thinking about the lovely nurses who said to me "always be yourself June". But these days I hardly know who I am any more. I know that I am not a bad person as I would not harm a fly but I am well aware that Bipolar could always rear its ugly head again. I am also well aware that my sense of humour has become very dark so if I threaten to knock someone's lights out or anything similar I promise you I really would not. I am always fearful that people may be offended by my humour and find myself having to explain that I am only joking just in case. If I laugh a lot I am afraid that people will think that I am manic and have me sectioned. If I cry I am so afraid of going on another low and the thought of feeling suicidal terrifies me. It is hard to form new relationships as I really don't know when is a good time to drop a bombshell like that. Hi my name is June and I am Bipolar. I have spent a total of 3 years out of the last thirteen in Shelton and other similar places. But were those 3 years wasted? No of course not. I am a firm believer that no experience is wasted. I was talking to my son Joey today. He said that I just gave too much of myself to Social Services. And I did. I used to do absolutely anything they asked of me. I certainly was a willing horse. They say that hard work never hurt anyone. But it did. In fact I almost died. If only I had not worked for Claire Turner.

Joey isn't really aware of the persecution that followed from the Police and Social Services as the poor boy had enough to worry about, and that certainly had an extremely adverse effect on my Mental Health. But I am not going to let you get me down. Chief Executives are like nappies and need to be changed for exactly the same reason. They are all full of shit. I would like to point out that this is not directed at the current Chief Exec as I know nothing about her other than the fact that she bothered to write back to a little retard, so, so far so good. But, then again, maybe not. I also met the most amazing people in Shelton and lived in another world that I hardly knew existed.

Women would come and go out of Stokesay. Some I liked some I didn't. The same goes for the staff but not on such a regular basis. If you really got on well with them it was hard to see them go. The opposite was also true. Some women were really horrible, so were a couple of the nurses and I was glad to see the back of them too.

Edna is a 45 year old woman. One day she has a heart attack and is taken to hospital. While on the operating table she has a near death experience. Seeing God she asks, "Is this it? Is my time up?" God replies, "No, Edna, my child. You have come here too soon. In fact you have another 43 years, two months and eight days to live." Upon recovery, she thinks to herself, I may as well make the most of it whilst I'm here. Edna decides to stay in hospital and have a face lift, liposuction, breast implants and a tummy tuck. She even has someone come in to change her hair colour and brighten her teeth! Afterwards, she gets out of hospital but, while crossing the street on her way home, she is run over by an ambulance and killed. She arrives up in Heaven in front of God and is completely furious. "What's going on?" she asks God. I thought you said I had another 43 years? Why didn't you pull me from out of the path of the ambulance?" "Oh, sorry Edna," replies God, "I didn't recognise you!"

When people threaten suicide and they really mean it, it is so awful. The thought that, that poor person feels so badly about themselves that they want to end their own life is abhorrent. I have heard other people make an idle threat to kill themselves just to get what they want. I think that I have become quite hardened inside. When people threaten suicide and I know damn well they don't mean it, I'm like go ahead do it then I really don't care. Suicide is absolutely not a joke. I have even been out with men who have said if you leave me now I will kill myself and I know they haven't meant it. Does this face look bothered? Go ahead honey I'm leaving anyway. And have they done it? No of course not. How dare they use that threat to keep me with them? Most men who have threatened to do that have gone on to get married very quickly indeed. Still want to end your life darling? I will go and find you a rope for your massively big head. I think that most men are looking for mothers not lovers anyway.

Anyhow I remember being well enough to go to the Greek Island of Crete. I went with Jai, Joey and Hannah for two weeks. Even though I was well enough to fly, the way I felt did not change when I was there. The kids had gone off to a water park for the day and I remember lying on a sun bed, one of my favourite places to be on holiday and was hurting so badly that I was lying on my tummy hoping that no one would notice me sobbing my heart out. I believed at that time that if I were a dog in a fraction of the pain I felt I would be put down. And that was me in a relatively stable period. Even though I was so happy to be with the three people I love most in the world I still felt that way. Bipolar is so horrible, I wish so badly that I could be rid of it.

An elderly couple arrived at the airport just in time to catch the plane. "Do you know what?" says the elderly lady, "I really wish I'd brought the piano with us". "What are you talking about?" says her husband, "Why on earth would you want to bring the piano?" "Because", says the elderly lady, "I've left our tickets on top of it".

CHAPTER 16 SOCIAL WORK

As a Social Worker you definitely get to see the ugly side of life. I saw and did things that prior to this work I thought unimaginable. Things like that stay with you, and you are not allowed to discuss it with anyone. It also rubs off into your private life. I remember allowing the boys to go to the gent's toilet on their own when they were little and waiting vigilantly outside the door in case there were paedophiles in there. It also rubs off into your home life, you just cannot help it. Especially, when, some clients found their way to my home. The little buggers are so crafty. They even got hold of my private mobile phone number without my knowledge.

My sons are now friends with a lot of my ex clients and I am too. It's great. And I know I am blowing my own trumpet but they tell Joey that I was the best Social Worker they had ever had, and that makes me feel ten feet tall. Some of the young people I worked with even call me mum. Once again the old trumpet is blowing but the experiences with the absolutely useless Social Workers that have been allocated to me who's practise has been nothing short of life threatening I realise how good I was. And what really gets me going is the fact that they seem to forget that I was a Social Worker and know exactly what they should be doing. As I said their practise could have ended my life and left my sons without their mother. I so feel like shouting at them "I have Bi Polar disorder, I am NOT stupid". But I won't. I will play the game and act like a dumbass until they do something that might harm me again and always remember that I cannot trust them. Not one inch.

CHAPTER 17 EVEREST

Everest doors and windows and Everest kitchens are awful companies. It took them 18 months to complete my kitchen when they found out I have Bipolar. Talk about discrimination. Two idiots who behaved as though they were halfway through their NVQ's (Not Very Qualified) turned up at my home and took the old kitchen out. They then asked me where the new kitchen was. How the heck do I know? You are from Everest. They had previously asked me to pack away everything in my kitchen prior to them coming. There were boxes everywhere in my kitchen and dining room and it looked as though a bomb had hit it. One of the idiots rang Everest and they were told that the kitchen had not even been made yet and that would take at least two weeks. What??? I could not believe it. The stress of this sent my right back into Shelton. I even cried down the phone to a man named John Lawler who was in charge of the work whilst I was in Shelton and I told him where I was. I begged him to get the work completed before I got home. He assured me that he would. But did he? Did he heck? He was at my house one day measuring up or whatever he did to look busy one day when I was home on leave and he had the gaul to say to me "I bet your son is glad to have you home". Poor Joey was living in this bomb site. And the man didn't give a flying f that I was still in Shelton. They even took my gorgeous colourful handmade Italian tiles off the walls without my permission. They stole from me and nearly burnt my house down.

A few months before Everest had fitted my patio doors and had done something to my electrics which their own electrician tested and recognised a fault. He informed me that there could have been a house fire. My children could have been burnt alive while they slept in their beds all thanks to them whilst I was in hospital. Fit the best? Fit Everest. I really do not think so. The final letter that they sent me stated that they would finish my kitchen as a good will gesture. Good will gesture? To finish a job, that I had paid a huge amount of money, to complete eighteen months later? Yet again not even an apology. I am watching the Soaps and Ken Barlow is having a go at Pat Phelan regarding a kitchen which is going to take two weeks to complete as opposed to one as had been originally agreed. One week? Two weeks? Try 18 goddamn months with Everest, and we could have been burnt alive, and quite possibly my neighbours too.

I have to say that Barclays Bank were amazing. Their sales rep was called Alan Cross and I told him almost immediately that I had Bipolar because he needed proof of my income which included my Disability Living Allowance. Somehow he managed to get me to sign a Home Improvement loan with a very high interest rate. Oh my god. I was frantic when I found out and I rang Barclays to ask for a lower interest rate. They were amazing and helped me so much. I couldn't believe the way Everest had treated me and a huge Bank like Barclays showed me more compassion and I hadn't even met them. I will make amends if my financial situation changes and it will be my pleasure. Thank you Barclays Bank.

I have to tell most companies that I am involved with that I have Bipolar because of my income. I live on a small works pension and disability benefits. They often ask for proof of my income. I have no idea whether they think that because I am Bipolar they can treat me however they want or because I am a single woman. But most people do try to take advantage of me.

I used to be a staunch Liberal Democrat supporter and worked as an activist for Lembit Opik. He is lovely. He said the same as Joey "there is nothing wrong with you June, you just give too much of yourself". Unfortunately he did not get re-elected.

I have just been reading some literature on Bipolar or Manic Depression and this is something I really will cling on to for dear life. He states that; the mood swings from high to low sometimes become less severe with age. Oh Pleeeease. Age is a high price to pay for maturity but if it enables me to stay well I really do not care. It is a case of mind over matter. If you don't mind it doesn't matter. Being young is a fault that diminishes daily anyway. We do not stop playing because we have grown old. We grow old because we stop playing. Stephen also states that more has been discovered about Bipolar disorder in the past ten years than was discovered in the past 50. Who knows in the next ten years there may be a cure and I sincerely hope that I am alive to see it,

When I was seeing Dave I met a man nicknamed Harry the bag. He told me that he had been in prison. Harry came to sit with us and he came out with the best compliment I had ever heard. He said "sorry to intervene" and looking directly at me he said "you look radiant, salubrious, impeccable, divine and voluptuous". Isn't that cool? It was much better than Dave telling me I looked tidy. I have found a small piece of paper that I kept from Shelton and my friend Sally Mac wrote when her husband became religious. It says "It's bad enough with bloody football never mind Jesus". I love them both.

When you are in hospital you obviously have huge problems of your own, but it is so difficult to get well when you are surrounded by other depressed people. There is no alternative at the moment. If you are ill enough to be sectioned you are sent to hospital. At the moment I am wishing, hoping and praying that I never go back into one of those places again. But I am the Queen of wishful thinking.

CHAPTER 18 BRO HAFREN

Easter is coming soon and I am as mad as a hatter, and mad as a March hare. What's a girl to do? A lovely lady called Ali who works in administration at my local Mental Health Centre once told me that even when I am as crazy as a box of frogs she still thinks I am normal. She is so much nicer and kinder than all of the professionals who work there put together.

I have just been watching Mo sing in the final of the Voice. He sang "you've got to hold on". And I believe that we have to do just that when we feel suicidal, hold on for dear life. Life will get better even when you do feel that there is no other way out, we will want to live again, as I do now, however each time I spiral into another low the harder it seems to cling on to that fact.

Jeremy, Clive, Claire and Amanda, mean nothing to me now. I wrote this a long time ago and have come to realise they are not even worth wasting my time thinking about. Actually I no longer hate them as I realise the only person I was hurting with that emotion was me. A big part of me even forgives them because I now realise that even though they treated me in such an abhorrent way they could not have foreseen that I would develop Bi Polar. No one could have. Least of all, me. I probably won't forget completely what they did, but when I do think of it I will use it as a reminder not to treat others in that disgusting manner myself.

Nicknames I have been given many nicknames over the years but one of my favourites was given to me by my little friend in Shelton called Marriane. She named me Juniper Berry. I absolutely love it, but the ones that tops them all for me are Pats' nicknames for me are Slutty and Smutty. Jai was quite upset when he heard her call me that but he is used to it now. My friend Jen calls me ICK. I told her I was a coffeeholic, alcoholic, shopaholic, and a chocaholic, and not necessarily in that order. I am also a kleptomaniac, but I am taking something for it.

When I lived at my parent's pub because my initials are J.P. one of the customers used to call me Justice of the Peace. I would love to be just that. If a little old lady was brought in front of me for stealing food to feed her grandchildren I would let her off and make the Police pay for the food. And so on.

My son Joey's nickname has always been Joe Bear which is very apt as he fights in that cage just like a Bear. Jai's nickname is Beanie but I have recently begun to call him Jaibo and you can call me whatever you like.

Sleeping.

Sleeping is one of my favourite things. It feels like the only time my head will switch off. I love snuggling up in my bed with Alfy the teddy bear without nurses shining a torch on me every hour.

Another piece of useless information is that I was told the more Occupational Therapy you take part in the sooner you can get out of there. Right? Wrong. I attended almost every session they had going when I was well enough and still I was stuck in there. I was also told that once you find your way around Shelton it was time to leave. Right? Wrong again. I used to visit people on the other wards, I did nature treks all around the grounds. I had a shoe box full of conkers, feathers and pretty leaves. What for I don't know, it just felt like a nice thing to do. But nothing seemed to get me out of there

Friends.

Even though my stuck-up Social Worker told me that "these people are not my friends," I have made many lifelong friends in Shelton. I have been in several Psychiatric hospitals in both England and Wales and as I have said Shelton was the best. We had the loveliest nurses and nicest patients on Stokesay and Whittington ward. Compared to other places I was blessed. Most of the nurses also if they were not so professional, I would have chosen to be my friends. I never ever want to go back into one of those places, but if I had not been in there what would I have written my book about? I have always loved writing and my teachers always said that I could become an author if I wanted to, so I really hope they were right and that you enjoy this book.

I think if you suffer from any illness, especially if it is potentially life threatening you re-evaluate life, especially when you have a mid life crisis and go through the change at the same time. I think it makes you appreciate things and in particular people all the more. I ask myself "what have I done with my life?" and "what do I want to do in the future, if I have one?" If I am going through the change I hope I will change into something good. I really can't see past this book at the moment and don't know how I will spend my time when it is complete. It certainly won't be writing another one. Actually I am now writing another. I so love writing. If I hear something that I find funny, or maybe a beautiful line in a song I have to write it down. Even if someone has made me angry I write it down and then no longer feel the need to have a go at them. I find it so therapeutic. However if anyone thinks that writing a book is easy then they are a better person than I am. It has taken me years. So many times I have felt like throwing my laptop into the river. However I am glad now that I didn't. Apparently Spike Milligan wrote eighty books in his lifetime. Eighty? If I live to the age of two hundred I could not pull that off. Amazing.

Family and Friends.

Mental Health by no means only effects the person who is suffering. It affects everyone close to you too. How my children have coped I really do not know. Both of them worrying about where I was, and what was being done to me. I'm so sorry. Again I blame you Claire. I remember how horrified I was when my mother told me she had undergone 12 sessions of ECT, because she believed there were monkeys on her back. My poor mum strapped down and electricity poured into her brain. Oh my god, I felt terrible for her and I didn't find out until years after. My boys knew when I was having it done. No one knows how, or even if it works. Apart from the attack on me in the Park and the four day in the Redwoods it was the most terrifying experience in my life, so how did my children feel? Bless their hearts. Having said that Wasi explained the whole process to me and I felt so suicidal and nothing else was working to drag me out of it.

I trust Wasi completely and would do anything he suggested to get well and he has proved to be right time and time again. I would not have gone through that treatment for any other Psychiatrist but I believe that Wasi is the best. I would also love to give Fran Foster and Lauraine Hamer a little bit of ECT. I think I might miss their heads and put it into somewhere far more intrusive on their bodies.

Once more I would like people to ask themselves why I have never ever complained about Wasi or any of the hundreds of other professionals I have worked with ONLY the two aforementioned women.

I felt that Fran Foster was a pretty useless Psychiatrist but I had nothing against her. I just found our consultations pointless and as I said more beneficial to her than me. I realised right from the start, that Lauraine, and she was my Social Worker for many years that she was pretty incompetent but I loved her and had absolutely nothing against her either. However the worry and concern they caused my sons alone is enough to make me despise them.

I intend to make everything up to my children as much as I possibly can though. I know I am an ok mom when I am stable, but when I am in the middle of an episode, either end of the scale they struggle to cope with me. BUT they have always been there for me, no matter what. I am also very nice to them as they will be choosing my nursing home or God forbid which funny farm I end up in.

I have become completely disillusioned with a GP named Doctor Porter at my local surgery. I was feeling extremely suicidal and I desperately wanted to see Wasi. I was told that I needed a referral from my GP. I made an emergency appointment with Porter and he assured me that he would refer me. Eleven days later I had heard nothing. I rang the surgery and he had not bothered to make the referral. I wonder if I had not rung the surgery would he have made the referral at all. I feel sure that if I asked him "am I going to live? His response would be "yes, but I wouldn't recommend it", in a hopeful tone. When I was a social worker if one of my clients had told me they were feeling suicidal I would have acted on it that very minute. Not 11 days later so that the person may no longer be with us. He so obviously does not care.

I spoke with good old Doc Porter recently. I said the word bloody (bloody is in the Bible, Bloody is in the, book, if you don't bloody believe me take a look) and got the whole no abuse will be tolerated crap. Oh my goodness. That was the only time I swore but on three or four occasions he threatened to put the phone down. He then suggested I leave the practise and go somewhere else. What? Why the hell should I go just because he has an inability to count? Why don't you leave the practise? I felt like shouting at him "look I am not ringing for a cosy little chat. I don't even like you. Please could you just give me my life saving medication and then I will piss off and fuck off". But obviously I didn't say that in case he died of a burst blood vessel. I have been with that surgery on and off all of my life, and remember the excellent doctors we have had in the past, such as Dr Mc Vey, Dr Wilson and Dr Harries. And now we have him. Oh be joyful.

When I was in hospital I opened the door to a six foot beetle who smacked me around the head and told me to f off. Apparently there was a nasty bug going around. I hope Doc Porter catches it. Joke. Oh my life. Be careful what you wish for. I have just heard that a young vulnerable adult has head butted Doc Porter. Obviously I do not condone physical violence in any shape or form but I will make an exception in his case. Tee bloody hee. No I would not wish that on anyone, but I cannot say that I was surprised.

I am going to tell a joke now which he probably won't understand but maybe someone could explain it to him; A 7 year old and a 4 year old are upstairs in their bedroom. "You know what" says the 7 year old. "I think it's time we started swearing. When we go downstairs for breakfast I'll start swearing first then you". "Ok says the 4 year old". Mum comes from the kitchen and asks the 7 year old what he wants for breakfast. "Shit mum I'll have co co pops". Whack. He flew out of his chair crying his eyes out. Mum looks at the 4 year old sternly. "And what do you want for breakfast?" "I don't know" he blubbers, "but it won't be fucking co co pops". Both these children have now been asked to leave Newtown Medical Practise.

My hairdresser Diane at Hair Affair. (Next to the Elephant and Castle) is amazing. When I go there not only does she do exactly what I want with my hair, it is also like going to a therapy session. She is hilarious and very caring. I have been going to her forever. All the girls in there are lovely but I think Di is the star. They joke about "isn't it wine o'clock yet?" and absolutely everything. She also seems to sense when I am not feeling 100% and will give me a hug. On my last visit I asked what she was doing that evening. She replied "I'm going on a slutty sleepover". Ha ha, isn't that great? (She has recently met a really lovely man and I couldn't be happier for her). I may go in there feeling a little low but I always leave feeling great. Thank you Di.

Smiling For some reason I smile a lot. I think it is probably laziness as it takes less muscle's to smile than it does to frown apparently. My father used to hate it, my superiors in the army did and so did my kickboxing coach. The amount of times I was told by all of them that they wanted to wipe that smile off my face was in the hundred's. To heck with them. Why don't you try and make me? It also used to get me out of a lot of trouble. I was smoking in the toilets at School and a lovely teacher named Dr. Leighton caught me. I smiled at him thinking I'm in for the high jump now, and he just said "get out of here smiler and don't do it again". Phew. At College I was in trouble again for going on a trip to London to the Stock Exchange as part of my Business studies course. I thought to myself that while I'm down here I might as well visit my friends in Kent for a couple of days. I informed my tutor and as it was the weekend I could go. He asked if I had informed my parents and with my fingers crossed behind my back I told him that I had. One of my class mates grassed me up and told my tutor that my parents weren't on the phone. (I rang my mum at work on the Saturday). When I returned to College I was hauled in front of the Principal. He said to me "June you are above average intelligence and you are wasting it". I apologised and smiled at him. He then said "you can't get through life with only that smile of yours you know". He then said "however, on this occasion you can. Now get out of my office and I don't want to see you back here again. Gosh I thought I was really looking at expulsion this time but made a mental note to be better behaved in future. I did and I passed the course with flying colours. I said to him "if it is any consolation sir I had a rotten time" "Did you June?" "No". Why can't I just quit when I am behind.

This is how little my ex-husband knew me as one Christmas he bought me a very swish leather brief case with brass locks. Did he really think that I would visit families, who were invariably poor dressed in designer clothes and carrying an extremely expensive looking leather briefcase? Just how did he think those families would feel. Here is a Social Worker who has everything and their children have nothing. Talk about the haves and have not's. I used to wear casual clothes and carried my paper work in a bag. What he failed to realise is that I have plenty of talent and vision. I just don't give a damn.

Spending cash.

One of the things you do when you are on a Bipolar high is spend, spend and spend some more. Once I bought Jaisee a dirt bike when he was 13 and had never expressed an interest in dirt biking at all. We kept it for a while and then sold it. On his 14th Birthday I bought him an f'ing rabbit. Not the best present for a 14 year old boy. Flopsy has sadly passed away, but Jai has got his own back on me and bought another little rabbit we have named Murphy. And guess who takes care of him? Moi. Unfortunately Murphy has sadly passed away. Wasi is so lovely and easy to wind up I told him that I had given Murphy a very dignified burial (he was dead), and that I had put him in a shoe box and dumped him in the bin. I didn't of course but Wasi's face was a picture and he said "that is not a dignified burial June". I just found him so funny I did not correct it and left it at that. I actually boiled him. No, honestly I did not do that either, I buried him. However apart from the dirt bike I don't regret buying anything. I have a large cupboard in my bedroom full of gifts that I had intended giving people but haven't yet. Occasionally I take a peek in there and it is like going shopping without actually leaving the house. I have two bin bags full of cuddly toys bought with my grandchildren in mind. Currently I am managing my own finances but occasionally have to hand over my bank card to my little sister if I feel a manic spend coming on. But as I tell her "it is the little voices in my head that tell me to go shopping". God if that were true and I did hear voices I'm sure I would be banged up again. And I hate to bang on about not drinking but I have been talking about money so here goes. You save an absolute fortune when you don't drink. And the calories too. Alcohol is absolutely full of them. Now I can eat whatever I want without feeling guilty. People say that I have lost that dehydrated look of a drinker and I look and feel much healthier. I drank so much that I could barely afford to eat, and I got to the stage where the alcohol I was taking home with me was cheaper and cheaper. There is a saying; drink poor liquor and you'll never be sicker. And it is true.

I don't blame anyone for drinking. I used to love the taste and the way it made me feel. But eventually it turned on me. I was a slave to it. I couldn't trust it anymore. Once my best friend it became my enemy.

Alcoholism is an illness. I changed because I might have the sickness of alcoholism. My tolerance weakened. Alcoholism does

Junie Pritchard

not come in bottles. It comes in people. I drank for happiness and became unhappy. I drank for joy and it made me miserable. I drank for sophistication and became crude and obnoxious. I drank for friendship and made enemies. I drank to soften sorrow and wallowed in self-pity. I drank for strength and I became weak. I drank to feel heavenly and came to know hell. I drank to erase problems and saw them multiply. I drank for my precious freedom and became a slave. I drank to cope with life and invited death. I felt as though I could not function without it. And all the positives are taken away from you when you address your drink problem.

Giving up drinking is one of the hardest things I have ever done, but now eight years on it is one of the best things I have ever done. Alcohol is everywhere, and when you are in a pub or restaurant it was so difficult to contribute to the conversation. You feel as though you are the designated driver every time you go out. I no longer feel that. If people don't wish to talk to me, that's up to them. At least these days I know what I am talking about. I am back in control of my life.

Jaisee was my biggest saviour there. He absolutely hated me drinking so whenever I fancy a drink, I think of him. Another thing that swung it for me was when I was in one of my local pubs and a beautiful woman was getting quite seriously drunk at the bar. Her teenage son came in and asked her to go home with him. She refused and eventually told him to f off. The poor lad looked crushed. She appeared to be a perfectly nice woman but just needed that one or two more drinks. I do not wish to be that woman. I also do not wish to be the grandmother who has to visit her grandchildren in a contact centre because I chose drink over them.

When I was drinking heavily no one wanted to know me. I don't really blame them, but to my mind I was still the same person. Everyone, that is apart from my children, and my friend Alfy who also had a drink problem. He is fantastic. He has however been to prison on a few occasions for fighting and being drunk and disorderly. When you listen to a person's life story, you can often understand why a person turns to drink. It is normally to forget. Alfy is off the booze now too and I couldn't be prouder. Alfy has worked hard most of his life, but he lost his job, his wife and home in one foul swoop. Who wouldn't turn to drink? He is now forced to live on benefits. He practically lives on fresh air, but he still bought me my teddy bear who I have named Alfy after him. He even visited me in Shelton love him. A lot of the patients quite fancied him, but poor Alfy does not have the confidence to see it. We used to have such fun together. One drunken evening I was showing off my head kicks. I missed and landed on my butt. He still brings that up today. See? There but for the grace of god go I? I have also caused him a whole lot of trouble.

When I was a teenager, I was a massive Bay City Roller fan. I had all the clothes, the t shirt, tartan trousers and stripy socks. The lot. My, did I look a pillak. Anyhow the Rollers were playing one night in my area and I desperately wanted to go. I asked Alf if he would take me and he agreed as long as it was ok with my parents. I said sure. My dad told me I couldn't go as I was only 14. We had a few words and I went to my bedroom. I climbed out of the window, shimmied down the garage roof and presented myself to Alf. The concert was amazing UNTIL I got home. Six of the best for you, young lady. No problem. It was well worth it.

Alfy really did make my evening recently though as I was under the impression that my dad hated me. Apparently, my father had said to him "please stay away from my favourite daughter", meaning me. Wow. My dad did like me after all. Poor Alf didn't have a lot of choice though. On one occasion he told me that he was going to a local venue that had live music. He drove a really cool Ford Capri which I jumped into the back of and hid. Halfway there I shot up out of the back seat almost giving the poor man a heart attack. He always used to take excellent care of me though. No wonder my poor dad threw me out. I can't believe this but Alf has made me feel so good. He asked me for a photograph of myself to keep him alive when he feels suicidal. He said I regularly save his life. Oh my goodness. I can't tell you how good that makes me feel. I have lots of male friends but it takes a lot to convince them that you just want to be friends. But we usually get there in the end. Lots of men have tried it on with me but Alfy is one of the only male friends I have that has never done that. He is quite the gentleman. My lovely jailbird Alf. I love him to pieces.

ECT.

Joey has shown me an Only Fools and Horses sketch. He was worried in case it might upset me but I found it hilarious. It goes something like this. Boycey, Trigger and Del Boy are sitting in the pub. Boycey tells them that a woman they knew named Mavis goes in to a psychiatric hospital for ECT every 3 or 4 months and is plugged into the National Grid. Lights have been known to dim as far away as Basingstoke. Trigger says that apparently she's perfectly normal when she comes out. Boycey then says yes until she gets her electricity bill. Thankfully I didn't have to pay mine. I prefer it when people make a joke out of my illness. I do not want sympathy or pity from others because I believe we all have our cross to bear and do not forget the true euphoria I have felt.

The Pub.

Occasionally when I was allowed out into the grounds I used to jump over the wall which separated Shelton's grounds and the pub. My friend Ken took me to Shelton the other day (which felt very surreal) to take my photograph outside it for the cover of this book. They have now put a huge wooden fence there. Spoilsports.

I was feeling really quite poorly the other evening and I rang Shrop doc, my local out of hour's medical service. I spoke to an absolutely lovely GP named Dr Pryce. He made me feel tons better just by talking to him. He said that I sounded sensible though. I really hope that I am not sensible and boring. I could just imagine waking up to his voice every morning asking if I'm ok. I don't think I would feel suicidal ever again. I have been tempted to ring him again and ask if he was unattached and would he like to go out to dinner. However, it would probably be considered completely unethical, over familiar and inappropriate behaviour. Let's lock her up again and this time, throw away the key.

My friend Helen tells me that if ever you have the chance to be naughty, grab it with both legs. But I can't. My kids would say I was demented and ring the Emergency Services. Local nut job harasses G.P.

I am known in my town (amongst other things) as the Social worker who went nuts. Well Jeremy, Clive, Claire and Amanda, I will show you just how nutty I can be. I no longer live under the oppressive regime of Social Services or Shelton. I am not a mental defective. I am me.

In hospital a lady used to call me a white witch. I had no idea what she meant by this but apparently the white ones are the good ones. Phew. I was also told I was a medium. I told her I was a size small. I am certainly not a medium, or an average in any shape or form. The male patients in hospital said that I was an Angel with broken wings. Bless them. When I go to sleep at night now, I dream of nice things. I no longer imagine that there are monkeys on my back or that the devil is in my room. When I am happy, I think that I am happier than most people. When I hurt, I hurt that much more. But that is the nature of the untamed beast known as Bipolar.

But right now I am stable, I have my freedom and I intend to make the most of it. When you have been caged for so long, the feeling of freedom is amazing. What do you call a pea when it lands on the table? An escapee. That is me. A little pea who has escaped from the nut house.

At one point I told Sergeant Bullock that if I was in a wheelchair he would not be patronising me the way he was, and if I had a bandage around my broken head maybe he would be nicer to me, but I really don't think he would. I believe he gets a kick out of inflicting pain onto people. I honestly think that there is something wrong with the man and that he should seek professional help. I think that it is such a shame that there are men like him on the force as it tars others with the same brush. I can't wait to discover how the Police and Social Services respond to this book. See how you like a little bit of victimisation yourselves. Here I go again mean mean mean when most of them are just doing their jobs.

Lainey.

Lainey and I had been friends for years. We met at Social Services but she had the good sense to get out long before I became ill. She came to visit me in hospital and I was allowed to go into town with her. Oh my goodness. What a sense of normality. Typical Junie though I just had to flaunt the rules and I had a little drinky,poos. We ordered one small glass of wine each and the barman liked us and gave us another large glass each. I obviously had the choice whether to drink it or not and of course, true to form, I did. When I got back to cell block H I was breathalysed. The flipping thing showed that I had drunk 25 units. What? I wouldn't be standing if I'd had that amount but they cancelled my leave. It was almost worth it though as the sense of normality I felt that afternoon was immense and I strove to get out of there as soon as possible. When I next saw Wasi at Ward Round I told him the truth regarding the wine. I was only gone 2 hours. How on earth do they think I managed to drink 25 units in that amount of time? Wasi to the rescue yet again. He reinstated my leave. Phew.

CHAPTER 19 Shelton

The thing about Psychiatric Hospitals is that you are removed from the Community. You are considered to be a danger to yourself or others. I harmed myself a little bit but never others. I just thought it's my body... I can do whatever I want with it. But apparently you can't. I got on well with almost everyone (apart from the one I call The Olympic Nurse). It is a strange existence and one that I previously knew very little about. You are considered to be a nut job and you are living alongside other nut jobs. Sometimes things went wrong. Drastically wrong.

A lovely young girl was visited by her boyfriend and his friend. They appeared to be lovely young men. We were sitting together in the smoking shelter and everything seemed fine. I went inside to go to the bathroom and when I got back outside the poor girl appeared to be fitting. The two lads did a runner. I called for the nurses and pandemonium broke out. The doctors were called, and alarms were going off everywhere. Nurses came running from the male ward and the whole place was in panic mode. It turned out that the young men had given her some illegal substances. Oh my god, I thought that she was going to die. I don't for one minute think that the boys had tried to hurt her, but whatever she was given mixed with her psychiatric meds was almost a lethal cocktail. The doctors and nurses were amazing and were there in seconds. Thank god they managed to bring her round but the poor little thing was extremely ill for a long time.

I also met my little friend Jess on Stokesay Ward. Jess was possibly late teens to early 20's when we met and I fell in love with her straight away. Jess is a little ray of sunshine. She even knew my son from the School bus run. Jess is smiley, bubbly and pretty. We spent hours chatting and drawing and colouring. Jess is an amazing artist. Unfortunately she was sent to a secure unit for her own safety. I missed her so much. Yay. She is free again. She has been stable for a long time now and I am so immensely proud of her. I also met a beautiful woman named

Ginny on one of my admissions. Ginny is an extremely well educated and eloquent woman. She looks beautiful and she is. I have recently begun seeing her again and it is wonderful. It is strange. All of my best friends are nutty. Definitely the best people to spend time with. I believe that if you have a crazy friend you have everything.

I remember being taken as a child to see my grandfather on my father's side in a Psychiatric hospital. (See? I've got no chance). Mental illness runs on both sides of my family and none of them were particularly athletic. I found the whole experience quite disturbing and I certainly didn't want that for my little Jai Beanie.

It was not long before I found myself in The Priory in Bristol. I had already quit drinking when I went there but I attended a 12-step addiction programme just to get me off the ward. I'm sure it has helped a lot of people but I found the whole thing a huge bore. A 12-step programme going on for weeks and weeks. Why don't they just tell us to take 12 steps away from the bar? Job done. Another thing about The Priory that was depressing were some of the ex addicts they invited to talk to us. They would bang on about having to still attend AA meetings every week and eleven or so years later they still want a drink. How flipping depressing. How is that meant to help us feel better? I certainly don't want one. Well occasionally I do I suppose. It is not a craving, I just fancy one and I have never been to an AA meeting in my life. You don't have to feel like a bag of crap for that long. I know that I can never say never to alcohol, but right now I really do not envisage me ever having one again. I think of poor George Best the footballer, who had a new liver due to alcoholism, and all it took was one of his fans to buy him a drink and he was back to square one again. He later passed away due to his condition. Alcoholism is an illness and people should not be condemned for being so. They require help, understanding and support and hopefully they will work through it. Alcoholism is an awful way to die too. Firstly, your liver packs up followed by the rest of your organs. What a horrible way to go. In Bristol there were shops there that sold legal highs. They got away with it apparently by changing the ingredients slightly in the drugs whenever the Police raided them and began selling them all over again. A couple of young people used these drugs an awful lot. I did feel sorry for them as for a time they seemed very happy, but the comedown was awful. They would become aggressive and extremely abusive. One young girl even called the nurses "nonces". Gosh I hate that word. Those poor nurses. They used to keep us awake all night shouting and screaming. What I found bizarre was that the young girl was thrown off the addiction course. Surely that little one needed the course more than anyone else. Does that seem ridiculous to you? Or is it just me? Artificial intelligence is no match for natural stupidity.

The man in the room next to me used to smear excrement all over his walls. The stench was almost unbearable. I used to work with children who used to do that and we called it "a dirty protest", but I had never known of a grown man doing it. He would be sent elsewhere and it took the poor cleaners days to clean his room. He would then come back and do the whole thing over again. What on earth do you do with a person like that? I think that I would have shoved a wire brush up his arse. Sideway's. I was not surprised at all that he was single.

When I got home I worried about Jai in particular. It was difficult for him to see me go from an active person to a practical invalid in such a short space of time. I was so thin. My arms and tummy were wrinkled. I looked and felt like a 90 year old.

Anyhow, I found myself back at home. I was able to spend a lot of time with both of my sons and this helped immensely. I was trying so hard to get better but I ended up getting much worse, and was sent to another hospital in Brecon. Oh my god was I ill. All I could think about was ending my life practically every minute of every day. I spent all my time planning how to do it. (Unfortunately there is always a way no matter what safeguards they put in place and people do die in those places). But I didn't have the guts. Whoever thinks that suicide is a coward's way out has absolutely no idea what they are talking about. The pain that I felt in my head and my heart was indescribable. It was not a headache as you might think a few paracetamol would take care of. The pain was in my mind.

I would hear about other people dying, some even my age and younger, and I always thought why wasn't it me instead of them? My sister in law named Rosey rang me every single morning I was in Brecon and she and my brother Leslie took me out as often as they could which was lovely. Thankfully I didn't kill myself and right now I am stable and do not want to go anywhere. AND I made it to Joey and Hannah's wedding. Yay. I didn't drink and possibly run the risk of ruining their day. I toasted the happy couple with orange juice. Yay all over again.

I have just texted my friend Ken moaning that I had spent all day typing up my book and had only managed 14 pages. I told him that if this book doesn't get published, I was going to smash up my laptop. He replied; "I think 14 pages is amazing – for a girl!! Don't even think about smashing up your laptop, we can leave it unattended at New Street Station and watch the Army blow the fucker up to kingdom come (after you sell a million copies and do all the chat shows in both the UK and Kazakhstan)". Gosh he is a star. I think that he should be writing a book not me.

An elderly lady was asked "would you like sex or a good book?" "Oh come now" she says "you know I can't read".

Shelton.

Most of the Patients on Stokesay and Whittington (the men's ward) were the most generous, giving people I have ever met. I only had to pass one of the guys on the way to the Marches restaurant and they would offer me tobacco. (Shame I was in the Redwoods when I only had 4 pence and was smoking dimps). Luckily I was always in a position to share my tobacco with them too. Everyone was so kind but I still desperately wanted to get home. The only person who could make that decision was Wasi, and the day eventually came (after 4 months) when he said yes. The man from Delmonte said yes!! Yay, bloody, yay. No more smashing of plates or mirrors to harm themselves with. No more crying or wailing in the night. I was free. Thank you, Wasi.

Wasi has always told me that I could oppose his decisions and go to tribunal to try to get them overturned if I wished to do so. I know some women that did that. However I have always known that whenever Wasi has sectioned me it has been absolutely necessary and I trust him completely. He is the exact opposite of Phillipa Walker who kept me there much longer than necessary. I mistakenly trusted her. She would tell me that I was allowed home. I would arrive home and within a few minutes they would either ring me or send the police to my home to tell me to go back to the hospital. I didn't even have the time to unpack. It was an hour's journey each way. She really is horrid. I now wonder if my favourite nurse Craig knew what was going on. I like to think not. My ex-husband had to make that journey nine times in one week. All of that had such an adverse effect on my Mental Health. I didn't know whether I was coming or going. I cannot stand the woman. She was always wearing black, which is meant to be slimming. I would have hated to have seen her dressed in white. Ha I am such a child. I think that she had a brain cell once, but it died of loneliness. I also believe that she once had two brain cells but she was pregnant at the time.

Trying to get out of there was horrendous. You have to sit in a room with 4 or 5 people and they treat you as if you are in front of a parole board trying to get out of prison. There are nurses present. Your Social Worker when she can be bothered to show up and a Psychiatrist. Good old Phillipa Walker asked me had I behaved myself? Ooh yes ma'am. And have you done everything that has been asked of you? Ooh yes ma'am. And do you think that you fit are to be let out into the Community? Oh yes ma'am, absolutely ma'am. Why don't you go and fuck yourself ma'am? I don't really know how the conversation got onto this subject, but I was telling her that when I get home I was going to buy Joey steak for his tea. She then asked me why I don't buy minced beef instead? Whaaaat? What on earth has that got to do with anything? Joey is a cage fighter not a ballet dancer and who gives a flying f anyway? She then asked me why I bought so many clothes? I replied, "because I am a woman" and thought to myself if you want to go around looking like a bag of shit every day go ahead, but I don't. It is the little voices in my head that tell me to go shopping. They are also saying go on Junie knock her nasty head off. Joking of course. If I'd said that to her, I'd probably be looking at another six months.

Just who do they think they are, playing god with people's lives? I live alone and have no partner to ask "ooh could I buy a dress this weekend please darling? Or hang it in the back of the wardrobe only to make an appearance when you think he can stand the shock. It is my money and if I want a new dress, I will darn well buy it. This is my life and I want to be at home with my kids not kept in here to keep the peace.

When I was under Phillipa Walkers so called care, I was very much what Pat's and I called a swing door patient. Allowed out and then swing back in through those bloody doors again at the drop of a hat. I honestly was not at home long enough to do anything wrong. I didn't even have time to make a phone call before the Police arrived at my door. And if you don't believe me then just check the records.

I have an excellent joke for her: an elderly couple (named Mr and Mrs Walker) are getting ready for bed. Phillipa is standing in front of a full length mirror. She says "oh my goodness, my hair is so grey and I have so many wrinkles, my stomach is fat and so are my arms and legs. Please tell me something positive about me to make me feel better". Her husband replies "well there's nothing wrong with your eyesight".

It used to annoy me when Psychiatrist's, and almost every other member of staff used to bang on about my drinking, but funnily enough I would go to the shop when I had leave and both psychiatrists and nurses would be there with a trolley half full of the stuff. What hypocrites. Sometimes they would call out an out of hours GP and they would reek of alcohol.

Because my Social worker bothered at last to show up at my ward round I was allowed home. Walker actually said to me "don't hug me or I will say you are on a high and keep you in". Hug her? I wanted to deck her. Ha I am going to be in so much trouble if this book gets published but I really do not care. You told me I was trouble and are no good so here I am. When I am good I am good but when I am bad I am better. You also have to sometimes be bad to know what good is. People should do the jobs they are paid to do and if you are no goddamn good at it get another. I hear she has left now, probably with a whacking great pension because she played god with people's lives. I hope that retirement doesn't suit her at all and she a) gets even fatter or b) withers away to nothing. God I am such a child, and again I am only joking. I am told that everyone has a good side but I believe that hers was her back.

Wasi would never have kept me in that long. His aim was always to keep me in the community and at home with my children. Dr Walker's aim was to keep me there as long as possible, but my nursing days are over and I am not prepared to nurse anyone in there for free. Get lost. Anyhow here I am at home after 4 months and it felt so strange. You go from having a ward full of people to talk to, to home where it is quiet and peaceful. Initially I couldn't stand any noise. I couldn't be in a room with the tv on or even any music playing, which is so out of character for me and very difficult for my family to deal with, so to begin with I spent most of my time in bed. I slept a great deal when I first got home and the rest of the time I lay there thinking and thanking god for letting me come home. And please, please god keep me alive.

When I was kickboxing, I was extremely disciplined. I rarely drank to excess. I have to admit I turned up for training once on a Saturday with a hangover and my goodness did that stop me doing it again. Training was hard enough without having to stop a couple of times running around the track to be sick. I vowed never to do it again and I didn't.

Joey, Jai and I are as close as ever, Joey seemed to understand what was happening with me, but poor Jai had no idea. We had no idea what Bipolar was. I had never even heard of it before I got it so I made it my business to find out. I read every single bit of information I could find on this condition and found that my diagnosis was spot on. I am Type 1 Bipolar. Aren't I the lucky little git!! I then found myself spiralling into a low again and it was not long before I was re-admitted.

I was severely depressed. Depression to a Bi polar person is the worst feeling ever. I have experienced short spells of depression in my life before but NOTHING compares to this. It is indescribable. Death is honestly preferable to feeling this way. It is horrendous. Anyhow here I am again. Locked away from civilised society. Thankfully this time I avoided the High Dependency Unit and went straight into the Mother and Baby Unit wishing that God would take me. I just could not get out of bed and face anyone. On this occasion the nurses were even more amazing than usual and brought my medication and food and drink in to me. I could not eat a thing. All I wanted to do was shrivle up and die. I looked at Joey and Jai's photographs all of the time and believe that they (as always) got me through it. And eventually I did begin to get through it. I began to venture out of my room at meal times and got to know the person in the room next to me. I was next door to Pats. Pats, believes she lives with Freddy Mercury and Paul Newman. She believes that when she coughs, or feels low it is Newman's fault and Freddy is her husband who loves her and takes care of her. I used to hear Freddie's music being played almost 24/7 which I was ok with as I love Queen. It also used to cut out the noise of the woman crying and sobbing in the room on the other side of me.

Pats had two little dolls in her room, tucked up in towels in her wash basket. They were hers and Freddie's twins. One was called Joanie after her second name and the other is Freddie, for obvious reasons. She nursed them constantly and even made the noises a baby would make, which could be very grating. I went into her room one day and told her to shut the twins up or I would put gin in their bottles to make them sleep. She went ape and threw me out of her room. That is the only altercation Pats and I had and even that I found funny. She and I had lots of visitors to our rooms but I couldn't believe it as one day a woman came into my room and asked if she could pee in my waste paper bin? What??? "I don't bloody think so. "Bog off". Pats, I and two other ladies were quite often in her room. The three of them would smoke in there and blow the smoke into a carrier bag to avoid being detected. That did not look healthy at all to me (not that anything about smoking is) so I used to smoke outside. After my first admission the smoking room was closed and a shelter was provided outside. It didn't bother me too much as I am a bit of a fresh air freak. It wasn't too pleasant in the rain and snow but it always seemed preferable to a carrier bag.

Life to me is about having fun. Find a job that you love and you will never have to work again. I loved working for Social Services and I did have fun. I loved the Army and the Benefits Agency and I had fun there too. There is a saying in Welsh; "Paid a Poini". It means don't worry. And I didn't used to. I knew that I had done a good day's work therefore I did not worry. Don't worry, be happy. My manager at the Benefits Agency in Canterbury told me once that she couldn't tell the difference between a client's phone call and a personal one. Treat everyone with respect I feel. I even had a couple of males ringing me back to ask me out. Unlike most of the Benefits Agency staff I have had to deal with since becoming ill. "It is not your money you nasty people".

Even though Shelton was a shit hole as Patsy describes it and obviously holds extremely ill patients, I still managed to have fun.

Most of the staff had a sense of humour too, thank god. Some had a face like a slapped arse and were definitely in the wrong job. A couple would have been better off in the Gestapo and tried to rule us with a rod of iron. F off. I had read several sections of the Mental Health Act which I felt applied to me and I knew my rights. The staff there seemed to work the opposite way round to the police. I believe the higher rank you hold in the Police the more nasty you are. In Shelton however the higher position you held, nine times out of ten (excluding that old bag Walker of course) the nicer they were.

One day I was on a high and decided to have some fun so I blew up a condom, tied it and sent it into an office where a male Psychiatrist and nurses were working. You know when you get that sinking feeling when you've done something and thought, shit, I think I've gone too far this time. That's the feeling I got. (Or maybe it is just me). None of them in there could have seen who had done it as I only stuck my hand through the door, but I heard JUNE. I walked into the office and he just laughed and asked if I would like it back. I told him I have no use for it in here therefore he could keep it. Thank god he had not had his sense of humour removed on the way in as some of the nurses had and we had a laugh about it. Some of the nurses though definitely mistreated us. One poor lady had problems with her bladder and had no idea when she was going to pee. She spoke to me about it and she was understandably embarrassed. I told her not to worry as the nurses would understand. They were nurses after all weren't they? On one occasion she came out of her room and was making her way to the toilet. She had an accident in the corridor. A nurse went mad and started shouting and shooing her back into her room as if she were a cow. (I was brought up on a farm so I know). I laid into the nurse shouting that she couldn't help it. She was making her way back to the nurse's station. I told her the poor woman needed a bath. It's a pretty bloody poor show when the patients have to tell the nurses how to do their own jobs. A short time later we were told that the poor lady had cancer of the bladder and was moved to another hospital. And that nurse had treated her in that appalling way. I really don't know how some of them sleep at night.

Another poor lady used to wet the bed. Obviously she reeked to high heaven. She would regularly ask me to hug her and I thought oh please not again, but I did. She would refuse to take a shower or a bath. One day she asked one of the nurses if she would help her to have a bath. I thought to myself, yes!!! The nurse refused to do it and told her to come back tomorrow. What? This was her golden opportunity to get the poor girl cleaned up and the nurse refused. We had to live with that poor woman and quite possibly she would refuse to bathe tomorrow. Some of the nurses really were bone idle. The poor woman smelt so badly they should just have put her in a wheelchair and shoved her through a car wash.

Following the closure of our smoking room (which I find completely understandable) they closed our beloved Marches restaurant, to save money obviously, so we all had to eat on the ward. What a joke. There weren't even enough tables and chairs for all of the patients. If you were not served first you may not get served at all. There was just not enough food for us all. My little friend Alison Cowell was on one occasion given a plate of peas as that was all they had left. Little Ali was so thin you would have seen every pea going down if you looked closely enough. How could we not have enough food? We were in hospital for goodness sake hoping to get better. We weren't going to do that unless we were fed. We all complained like mad and were eventually given sufficient. The food was ok, nothing to write home about, but adequate. However Pats was not a happy bunny. She used to write notes to the chef with suggestions of new recipes. She used to call him Oberon, king of the fairies as he was gay. His name was David. David loved it and began to vary the menu. I think David felt very unappreciated as a chef. He was given such a low budget to feed us on it was almost impossible to do so, and we did tend to complain a lot. Then we

Junie Pritchard

began to compliment him, (whenever we saw him) or write him little notes of thanks and he seemed much happier in his work. Good old Oberon. Fair play we did have a patients' forum and I made damn sure I was on it. That's where we got our food budget increased and it's where we got lots of things changed. At least they listened to us in Shelton unlike Bronllys.

CHAPTER 20 Theft

Theft is rife in these places. The doors to our rooms had no locks therefore as soon as you leave the building other patients know that they could go into your room and steal whatever they want. It's kind of like pasting on Face book the fact that you are going away on holiday and your house will be empty. They have a disclaimer on the wall which says that anything that gets lost or stolen is not their responsibility. Whose f'ing responsibility is it then if we can't lock our doors? I had a beautiful Welsh gold T bar necklace stolen which my parents had given me for my 21st Birthday. I was gutted. I informed the nurses and as I already guessed, was told there was nothing they could do. How about searching people's rooms for it? It was so unusual they would have spotted it a mile off. On one occasion the teddy bear which my jailbird friend Alfy bought me went missing. Alfy the teddy bear has been with me to every one of those places and keeps me company at night. I cannot sleep without him. I had had enough. I told the nurses that if they didn't find him I would. Alfy (the real one not the bear) used to tell me that in situations like this I should hold my head up high and my hands under my butt. Not this time Alf. The nurses did retrieve my teddy for me but refused to tell me who had taken him for fear of reprisals. And there would have been verbally. How dare they? I didn't help myself to their possessions so why should they get away with taking mine? One little girl named Alison's room was like an Aladdin's cave full of other people's property, yet the nurses refused to do anything about it. On the flip side of that I found a beautiful amber ring. I handed it into the nursing staff and asked if no one had reported it missing could I keep it? The next thing I knew it had found its way onto that very nurse's finger. Nice.

I believe that no matter what safeguards and however vigilant nurses are, if you want to kill yourself badly enough you will find a way. No one can be with you 24/7, even though the nurses, psychiatrists, everyone there, worked so hard to prevent it. Looking back, although I believe Bipolar is the most heinous illness I have ever known, apart from Schizophrenia, and there is no cure, I do not wholly regret my time in there. Sometimes the 3 years of being locked away seems like a waste of my life, but I would not have been able to write this book and give people some kind of insight into what it is like in these places and what Bipolar is really like. I also so want people to realise that patients in there are ill, but very often do get better. As I mentioned earlier, I believe that no matter what safeguards and risk assessments are carried out, if you want to kill yourself that badly you will do it wherever you are.

These are the Personal Risk Factors that members of staff have to judge us on in hospital: 1/ Poses and treat mental health needs 2/ Change of routine 3/ Matching staff and client 4/ Lack of information i.e. inadequate care plans 5/ Alcohol and drugs The Environmental needs of a client: 1/ Heat 2/ Overcrowding 3/ Lack of Community Support 4/ Noise 5/ Lack of staff 6/ Lack of communication. We were meant to have an hour's discussion with our designated nurse every day. However this very rarely happened as they did not have the time. 7/ Clients inappropriately dressed i.e. too hot, too cold, or too revealing Very few of these risk factors were met in Shelton Hospital. The worst was the threat of being attacked by another patient, and I could take care of myself, so I have no idea how scared some of the more frail patients felt. And the noise. Women screaming, wailing, and crying, 24/7. Aaaagh. It drove me nuts. On the whole I felt that Shelton was an excellent hospital and the staff they were very competent. My attitude was well we're here now so for god sake shut up and get on with it. There was also overcrowding. When there was nowhere else for women to go they were brought into Stokesay and sometimes put to bed in the corridors, and when we were overcrowded some of us had nothing to eat.

Here is a list of risk factors a patient may present: a) What specific challenges does the patient pose? Me? Lots. If you don't do your job right I will sure as eggs are eggs, let you know. b) What personal, environmental and interpersonal risk factors are known to be associated with this person's behaviour? Mine must be bad because they keep locking me up. c) How can the factors be removed or modified so as to reduce the possibility of aggression? Stop locking me up. Primary risk factors associated with aggressive behaviour 2. Interpersonal risk factors associated with Aggressive behaviour. 1) Inexperienced staff – there were many. 2) High rate of temporary staff. Patients like familiarity of staff. Too true. 3) Rejecting, hostile attitudes from staff. There were some. 4) Carers can provide poor role models re; managing frustration etc. I don't blame them for feeling frustrated. Nursing in a Psychiatric hospital is a thankless task. 5) Inconsistent approaches – can lead to bedlam as it did on Stokesay Ward until the wonderful new manager arrived. 6) There is a high rate of aversive demands from carers to patients – not asking patients to perform tasks that they not capable of doing. 7) Aggression is functional – absence of alternative options i.e. escapes. There is a lot of aggression in Psychiatric hospitals. A bunch of severely ill people, all expected to get along. It just didn't happen and if you did manage to escape on occasion you were brought back by the Police. 8) Use of "barbs" words known to upset a patient. Only one nurse did that to me and she almost ended up going through the window of her choice. 9) Expectation of aggression. Don't focus on a person's legs if you think they are going to kick you. 10) Peer group pressure – patients will encourage other patients to be violent or aggressive. Theories of Aggression. Instinct theory – Aggression is innate, biologically determined and functional. Aggression provides a powerful mechanism via which heightened arousal generated by aversive events can be reduced. Fight or flight. I will stand up and fight anyone if I feel it is necessary, but my usual response is that of flight. Fly away to freedom just like a bird. The general Personal risk factors associated with aggressive behaviour are as follows: 1/ Aged between 15 and 30. I am way past it. 2/ Male. I personally think this is sexist but maybe it is true. However, the nurses told me that they would much prefer to break up two males fighting than two women. Men tend to throw a couple of punches and it is all over. I witnessed women scratching, gouging, biting and pulling hair as well as punching and kicking. It really wasn't a pretty sight. 3/ Previous history of aggression – I have none 4/ Recent stressful life events – I had many 5/ Dual diagnosis – notably schizophrenia. Thank the Lord I have Bi Polar and nothing else. 6/ Disinhibition caused by drugs/drink. I was disinhibited even without those things. I even chatted up the manager of the hospital, poor man. I also asked Craig if he could give me a bed bath for goodness sake. He knew I was joking of course. But that is the nature of Bipolar. 7/ Severity of intellectual disability. My Psychiatric report states that I am severely mentally impaired. I make perfect sense to me. I am just not sure I am on a level playing field with the rest of the world. I am going to show the world that I am normal. I do not have low intelligence because I have Bipolar. My brain may on times be a little bit scrambled and I am possibly wired up differently to other people, but they are not any less superior. Occasionally I just come undone. Why won't people just meet me in the middle? I am losing my mind just a little. 8/ Unmet physical, social and emotional needs. I feel that these were met in hospital as some of the nicer nurses would even give me a hug if I had been crying. 9/ Co-existence of self-destructive behaviours. Absobloodylootely. This was rife on Stokesay. Men and women would bang their heads on the wall, and bite, pinch, and cut themselves. Anything, to create an adrenaline rush for themselves to hopefully alleviate the excruciating mental torture they were experiencing.

Paul Smith's model – based on 100's of assaultive/aggressive incidents. His model indicates that aggression is not inevitable – you can direct people away from aggressive behaviour. The nurses were very good at this. Particularly, Craig and Simon. Intervention is able to change the behaviour except at point of crisis. This is sometimes unavoidable. There are very few nurses compared to patients and they cannot watch us all of the time. As I mentioned earlier when fights do break out it is horrible. Women are far more dirty fighters than men for some reason. Adrenaline increases strength and physical muscle tension. Body temperature rises and vision focuses on the trigger. You do not see the wider picture. A person may become verbally aggressive, agitated, banging objects, wringing hands. DIVERT PEOPLE NOW, when you see the above signs. With no intervention wholly hell can break loose and it so often did.

The thing with Bipolar is that it never gives you a chance to build up a resistance to it. As soon as you feel almost well it strikes again, and at my age now it is more likely to be a low. Oh my god, please help me. I absolutely abhor Bipolar. I so want to be normal. No highs, or lows, just normal as I was before I worked for Claire Turner. Please somebody put me back together again.

So the best thing is, to get as much sleep as possible. Sleep is the greatest healer. The next thing (and who am I to talk) is try to drink as little alcohol as possible. Alcohol has such an adverse effect on your medication it really is not worth it. Thirdly take your meds. If you want to come off them do it with the support of your Psychiatrist. Most of them really do know what they are talking about. Next, never be ashamed of having Bipolar or any other form of mental illness. It is not something we have chosen or can help. I am ashamed of some of my behaviour when I am unwell, but of the illness itself? No I am not. We have a critical illness just like diabetes. No one runs them down. It is something we just have to learn to manage. Unfortunately these days mental illness is rife. One in three people suffer from it. 1 in 3!!!! Is it nature or nurture? Obviously lots of mental illnesses are not as serious as Bipolar, but for that person it is still hell I'm sure. You really feel that you are never going to come out of a low and the sad thing is some people don't.

These days I am horribly well much to the disgust of Social Services. Ha!! I am seeing Dr Mohamad again and I now see a lovely Psychologist who wants to be named as Ena Sharples for the purposes of this book. I have only met with her on three occasions and already feel better about myself. Maybe there is hope for me yet. This is a poem that someone gave me: "Down by the river where the green grass grows, where Junie washes her clothes. She sings, she sings, she sings so sweet, she calls for her playmate across the street. Playmate, playmate will you come for tea, come next Sunday at half past three. Cream cakes, tea cakes, everything you see. Oh won't we have a jolly time at half past three". I think that it is lovely.

Someone else told me that when you stick your two fingers up you are thinking to yourself f off. The two finger sign originated from the Archers. They used their index and middle finger to hold an arrow with. If an Archer was captured the enemy would cut those fingers off. Archers would stick up their two fingers to show the enemy they could still fire an arrow. I may not have all my faculties but I do have my two fingers. Not quite as sweet as the poem but interesting to me none the less.

Social Services, the police and the CPS Unbelievably at one point actually sent me to Probation. We even had a laugh about it as I used to work closely with them in my role as a Social Worker. When I walked in there the lady asked me who I was there to discuss. She couldn't believe it when I said this time it is me. Probation? I ask you. I blame Claire Turner, Jeremy Patterson, Clive Bartley Amanda Lewis and the police for me even developing this illness. Oh and Jane Jones the manager in Welshpool. They repeatedly hounded me hoping that I would kill myself rather than allow me to leak all that I knew about them.

I have read my Psychiatric report written by Dr Wasi Mohamad, MB BS MRCPsych, DipCBT who I have the privilege of being my Consultant. This report was written on 23 March 2007, and states; "Clearly the areas around June's occupational work need addressing and if she can be provided with support in the future, she has a much better chance of maintaining her improvement and preventing any major relapses". PREVENTING ANY MAJOR RELAPSES? Provided with support? My fat ass. They used and abused me even more. Jane Jones, that nasty manager in Welshpool was absolutely horrible to me. I did not sweat blood and tears to qualify as a Social Worker to spend my day making coffee and make my clients feel that I was the have and they were the have not's.

Sometimes I really wonder why people go into Social Work, and like the Police the higher up the ladder they go the more horrible they are. They show no compassion towards their clients, so why do the job? Any connection between their reality and mine is purely coincidental and if I have said anything in this book to offend it is purely intentional.

Am feeling a bit guilty right now, as my friend who was in Shelton with me, told me about a nurse who self-harmed. Oh my god. If I drove any nurse to do that to themselves, I am truly sorry. I wasn't always nice to them I'm afraid as initially in my manic state I saw them as the enemy. People who were my jailors who would not let me go home. When I eventually regained my faculties I realised what wonderful caring people they really are. Apart from the Olympic nurse, of course. Beeeich.

Some people in my home town, even those who I considered to be my friends have told others that I am not right in the head. How dare they? If I am not right in the head, then I must be wrong. I've heard that said about a lot of people in the past, I just never ever thought it would be said about me. The label I really despise is spastic. What on earth is a spastic? I don't even know what it means but the word is bandied about all over the place. I have just looked up its meaning. "Spastic; suffering from cerebral palsy with spasm of the muscles. Weak feeble, incompetent". How dare people label others as a spastic? I will show them how weak and feeble I am as my muscle spasms cause me to smack them in the mouth. Once more I am joking. I really have never and will never harm anyone. And I truly believe that not one single person who has spent time in my company has EVER felt threatened by me. Please judge me for me not a label society has placed on me.

I am going to show the whole world that I am normal. I am not of low intelligence. I am ME. I am Bipolar. I am neither wrong in the head nor a spastic. I experience extreme highs and desperate lows but for the most part I am normal. I am listening to music, typing up this book and am about to make my own coffee. Yay. I am free. I am slowly regaining my confidence and everyone seems to want to spend time with me so I don't think that I am really all that bad. And if you don't like me please just stay away from me.

Lucky.

Some people say that I am lucky as I am currently not working, and they think that I am living off a big fat Social Work Pension. Am I heck? My pension is piddly. Lucky???? Not to be well enough to work. What is so lucky about that? I recently spoke with a nice Police man. Yes I did say nice in the same sentence as the Police. Anywhoo we had quite a civilised chat and he mentioned that he likes the idea of retirement. I told him that I would love to work again. He then said "the grass is always greener on the other side". Three years spent being locked up? Experiencing suicidal thoughts what feels like one hundred million times. Four very serious attempts? Just how green did he think my valley was then?

If Social Services had treated me better, I honestly believe I would not have developed Bipolar and feel sure that I would be in management by now on a whopping great salary and a very good pension. Right now I live on a tiny little pension and benefits. Every second or third week in the month I worry as to how I am going to manage until pay day. It is horrible. Do you know that most people's sleepless nights are due to having no money? We live in a civilised country. This should not be allowed to happen. Oh please some of you rich people give some to the poor.

Instead I do jack, and my income is far, far less than it should have been. How is that lucky? The next person who tells me I am lucky I am going to deck them. Only, joking. When I tell people I am retired on ill health grounds some even say "god I wish I'd got your doctor". No, you bloody well do not mate. Believe me you do' nt. If only they knew. They really have no idea how I feel, and I can't blame them. If you've never felt something yourself how can you possibly know what it's like for someone who has. You can sympathise and even empathise with me, but unless you have Bi polar you have no idea, and every time I feel well enough to go back to work I fall ill again. Yes that's me. Lucky, lucky lucky.

On the flip side of that some people who know I have been locked away for three years of my life ask how I can keep smiling and stay positive. The thing is if I keep looking over my shoulder, I will not see what is in front of me. Others look at me with pity in their eyes. I really do not want that either. Please just treat me as you would anyone else.

Oh my goodness. I have just been told that the Children and Families team in Newtown are now at Special Measures, which means that children are being neglected. Adult services are also under investigation. Why are the people of Powys putting up with this? Nobody seems to care. I wrote a very nice letter to my local newspaper which I call the County Crimes. It is really the County Times and they didn't even print my letter. We are not sheep, why are we putting up with this? I thought that things would improve now that Jessa and Amanda had left but they haven't. Jeremy Patterson was TOLD to leave Powys with a £170,000 payout for failing to protect children. Unbloodybelievable.

We were told in Shelton that if we were annoyed or upset with someone to write a letter to them and then put them in the bin. I think that that is a great idea, but I tend to send mine. It is so much more fun. The Chief Executives of Powys are obviously not capable of doing their jobs so give the job to someone who can. I tried ringing Jeremy Patterson once but was told that I had to go through his Personal Assistant. They refuse to speak to us minions. I can just imagine the conversation. PA says, "Excuse me sir I have a phone call for you. Shall I endeavour to tell her to fuck off?" Probably for the best as I feel sure I would develop a serious case of turrets if ever I got to speak to him. I often wonder what I would do if I met him. I think that I would give him a side kick (and my sidekicks are very good) and tell him it was involuntary movement due to my medication to treat this disgusting illness you caused me to have. (No I wouldn't, but I can always dream). I only have one nerve and he is bloody well on it.

I hope this is a phase or part of the menopause but I really get a kick out of pissing people in Authority off right now. Particularly when people don't bother to do their jobs at all, are incompetent or just huge liars who have no ethics at all. God I could write a book. Oops, I forgot, I am. As I am sure the same applies to people with physical illnesses. That also has an effect on their mental health. When you become mentally ill you can have weeks and sometimes months when you cannot face getting out of bed and that has an effect on your physical health and every time it happens, you literally have to crawl your way back to fitness. If you have to spend all of your time at home until someone can take you out in a wheelchair. Of course you will feel down. All of these issues have to be addressed. Disability of any kind is abhorrent and the best thing that the government can do is to give them the money that they need to pay for their care NOT set up Mickey Mouse agencies to give us the misapprehension that you actually give a dam about us. "Oh sorry I can't help you. You have to be lying on a slab at the mortuary to be given any help or support otherwise have a nice day. And if there is anything else I can help you with take your mobile into the coffin with you and I will put you on hold allowing you to listen to Vivaldi for half an hour and then cut you off. Goodbye. Have a nice afterlife".

Bipolar is almost like a drug. When you have felt that buzz you feel the need for the buzzes to be bigger. It is like chasing the dragon. That is one of the reasons I drank as most of my highs have occurred when I was drinking. Sometimes it is tempting to feel that euphoria again. That is the manic side of my illness. I no longer want that. I now wish to be in complete control of my faculties which drinking made me lose. I was brought up in a pub and my parents owned a farm also. I have also worked in pubs and night clubs and drank a lot in the Army. However, I know that I can never, say never, but I no longer want to be that person. I don't blame anyone else for drinking as it is an enjoyable, social pastime but I just have to accept that I cannot do it.

Drinking a) has an adverse effect on my medication and b) my medication does not have the chance to work properly when I drink. I drank alcohol in pop bottles in hospital in front of the nurses. I felt what the eyes don't see, the heart doesn't grieve over. Drinking in there was a little bit of relaxation and an awful lot of up yours. I pushed every single boundary in that place as I have done all of my life really.

I believe that there have to be rules and laws as I would not want to live in a lawless society, however some rules are just meant to be broken and occasionally Mark Twain is right when he says that the law is an ass.

I considered myself a multi-tasker. I went to parties, I smiled, I talked, enjoyed great food and I had little drinkiepoos. I also used to enjoy cooking with red wine and sometimes I would even add food. I have recently heard on the news that there is supposedly a link between alcohol and cancer therefore they are hiking up the prices. I do not believe that for a second as half the population of Newtown would have it if that were the case. It is a way of the government making yet more money out of us. My sister Joycey also made a very good point when she said "if they are pushing up the prices of what THEY feel is bad for us, why do they not lower the prices of things that are good for us". A punnet of strawberries cost about £2 yet a bag of sugary sweets costs a pound. Where on earth is the sense in that? Just me again? Hey Ho.

Since my diagnosis the mental health professionals and sometimes my family (not my children) seem to want to mould me into something I am not. I feel that the professionals (not Wasi) would prefer me to be on a low as opposed to a high as on a low I don't cause them any hassle. All they think about is what makes life easier for them. Everyone questions how much money I spend. I know that they have my best interests at heart but I feel like shouting "f right off, it is my money and I will spend it as I wish". I think that going to Cuba has put me off ever going abroad again, I do not run a car so what on earth do they think I am going to spend my money on. I feel that everyone around me wants me to be normal (no one more than me), but what they seem to forget is I am not. Actually my sisters are brilliant now and when I tell them that I have ordered a new dress they tell me that I deserve a treat bless them. I also love buying shoes. Anyone would think that I was a centipede the amount I own, but I am not. I just have a right and a left foot just like you normal people.

I believe (hope) that I will be well aware in future if I feel a manic spend coming on and will hand over my bank card to my little sister Joycey.

One weekend I was allowed leave. Section 17 of the mental health act. The most important section of all apart from discharge. I went to watch Joey fight. Joey is an awesome cage fighter and he let me tag along. It was amazing. Joey was fighting first and I was shouting my medium to large mouth off, which just happens to sound like a foghorn. He won of course and I felt as if I was on cloud nine. Peeps told me that they heard me several rows back. I don't know whether that is a good or a bad thing. I think it is good as when I was making my way back to Joey's wife Hannah people said to me "well done mum". Joey has recently won the highest Amateur Championship belt there is. As they say "a quitter never wins and a winner never quits". My son is certainly no quitter. The guy that Joey fought that night was no slouch either. Joey did not have it easy but he won. Whoopee. All of that preparation, the hard work, the fitness, that is needed to fight in a cage. The stamina required, the awful diet, and the mental preparation had paid off. Joey Rice, that's my boy. I could not have been prouder. And I know for certain that his father would have been proud of him too. Oh wow what an amazing night. I spent the evening with Hannah watching my gorgeous, gentle son Joe Rice, fight in a cage with nowhere to go. At least when I fought my opponents were able to run off the mats which was very lucky for them.

I was so happy. It was 1.20 in the morning and there were no lights out. No one fighting each other apart from in the cage. As I have mentioned when I fought it was on mats. I have been to Joey's gym and did some very light sparring in the cage. I found it terrifying and would never step foot in there ever again let alone fight someone in there.

On another occasion I was allowed home to watch Joey play guitar with his band at a local village hall. Joey went to The Guitar Institute in London and is an awesome guitarist too. I caught a bus back to Newtown but there were none going to the village where Joey was playing. I thumbed a lift the rest of the way. Poor Wasi would have turned in his grave if I'd told him so I didn't. When I arrived there the band had already started playing. Everyone was sitting down in rows very quietly. I thought this is more like a tea party than a rock concert. I was very manic and asked my brother and sister to get up to dance. More people followed suit and danced with us. At one point I jumped on the stage, pointing at Joey. It felt great. For me anyway. My brother took me back to Shelton and when I had calmed down, I thought oh my goodness, what a pain in the ass I must have seemed and what did people think of me. However, Joey, bless him, told me he was not embarrassed at all and his band members told him that it was really boring until I showed up. I honestly don't know how my kids cope with me sometimes. I will try to do better in future.

I am extremely lucky as I now live with my little Jaisee in a beautiful stone cottage that everyone thinks is quirky. I eat my meals when I am hungry, I am free to make a cup of coffee when I want one and can even stay in bed all day if I want and more importantly, I see my sons almost every day. I am so proud of both my sons and my beautiful, inside and out, intelligent daughter in law Hannah. She always makes me smile. She also buys the best, most thoughtful gifts. Joey is so laid back he is practically horizontal, yet he works so hard. Jai is a lad and a half. He is so funny and clever. Both boys are handsome. Joey in that well hard but with compassion look and Jai is a wonderful good looking little romantic with attitude.

I have recently had a birthday and Jaisee bought me some gorgeous dining room chairs and Joey and Hannah gave me a coffee maker for my bedroom. YES!!! I never have to leave my bedroom unless I wish to sit on my beautiful chairs. I wonder what the nasty management at Bronllys hospital would have to say about that. A certified nutter armed and dangerous in charge of a coffee maker. Hannah has never known me without this illness and she and Joey have visited me in every hospital I have been in. I have difficulty dealing with my emotions and felt suicidal every time they left. Every time Joey would say "I wish I could take you home with me mum" I felt as though my heart was breaking in two.

Sometimes I wonder if I will ever get married again. I am not sure the man has been born who could cope with me. According to my lovely Psychologist the happiest people are married men. The next happiest are single women, next are single men and the least happy are married women. Mmmm I think it's a case of staying single for me. I have really gone off the idea of having one of those man things in my life. I do not wish to pick up dirty boxers that he has discarded on the floor six or so inches away from the wash basket or having to put the toilet seat down and does not have the ability to change a toilet roll. I do not wish to cook or clean up after someone who is bigger than me. I do think however that I could put up with one for a week, as although I have a hammer, a saw and a hedge cutter which I use on a regular basis, I would ask this male to do the jobs I cannot do and once the jobs are complete show him where the door is and ask him to walk through it.

I want to be happy in my own right and not rely on a man to try and make me happy.

When I was in Shelton and was allowed off the ground's I saw a van drive past with the slogan "husband for hire. The answer is "yes" now what's the question?" That is what I need for a week or a fortnight. Perhaps I should marry a Gynaecologist as apparently they have a good old knees up at Christmas.

I am a very sociable person and according to Craig my nurse, because of that fact it is harder to cope with Bipolar. I was never happier in there than when all of us women were sitting in the Common room or in the smoking shelter having a chat. I just love people, but not enough to counsel them anymore. I liked everyone until they did something to lose my trust. I do not like dishonesty. You have to have a very good memory to be dishonest and very few people do. That is why I am telling the truth, the whole truth and nothing but the truth, (which is damning enough) in this book. I know that I cannot be sued for libel or slander due to that fact. I also do not like people who force themselves on others and invade their personal space. And moaner's. I just cannot cope with them. Especially those people who moan about the weather. Some people will moan when they are too hot, too cold or even when it's raining. Whatever, the weather is doing. I feel like saying "we live in Wales for goodness sake, it rains. If you don't like it why don't you move? I really would be happier without you. Or as my nurse Kelly would say "could you just tell somebody who actually gives a shit!!!"

Junie Pritchard

When I nursed in the Army, we did not have male nurses. There were male guards (if that is the correct term) on the doors of the Psychiatric wards but all of the nurses were female. It is a far nicer balance of having male and female nurses now. We had lots of fun in there as I decided I just had to make the best of a bad job. Craig in particular had the worst time from me. When you are on a high you have a tendency to become over familiar with members of the opposite sex and I used to flirt relentlessly with the poor man. I blame it on Bipolar but I think it is also just the kind of person I am, and felt one day that maybe my flirting had gone too far. I apologised to Craig and bless his heart he said that it was people like me that made the job fun. Phew!!

Thank goodness I had my faculties in order enough not to flirt with the pastor, but we did nickname him Jesus.

These days I do not have the confidence to flirt with anybody as I am far too worried as to what they think of me. And I do not have the confidence that alcohol brings you. I believe Craig was born to nurse. He and many others were amazing. Others were definitely in the wrong job, but my attitude was, you signed up for the job so get the hell on with it

We used to have a little shop in Shelton where we could but newspapers and chocolate etc. I spoke to a lovely young man who was running it. I thought that he would have made an amazing nurse and asked him if he would consider it? He replied "I would if all the patients were like you June". Oh bless his heart. He thoroughly made my day.

Why does red wine taste so good if it is so bad for me? One of the Psychiatrists said to me "I bet you're hilarious when you are drunk". I have always drunk but rarely to excess. I loved it. My favourite times have involved alcohol. But I was drinking heavily at the onset of my illness. When I first developed this illness I had no idea what was happening to me. I did not know what I was feeling as I had never felt this way before. It was very frightening. My mind was scrambled and my emotions were so strange. I felt so depressed that I wanted to die or self harm, then as high as a kite the next. I did not know how to cope with those thoughts.

When you are on a high your thoughts race, which is really very frightening. You feel as though your head is spinning. It is so horrible. Your speech becomes rapid and people cannot understand what you are saying, which makes you feel like a complete idiot. You become very irritable and if anyone came close to me when I was unawares I used to jump a mile as they frightened the heck out of me. I dreaded the postman arriving in case there were returned direct debits. Going to the cash machine and realised I had maxed out my overdraught yet again. Drinking helped me cope with those thoughts at the time. Not so later on. Alcohol turned from being a friend that I relied on to being my worst enemy, although initially I didn't realise it. All of the staff in the hospital wanted me to stop drinking but thinking I was clever, I still was. I would go to the shop and buy shots and hide them in the lining of my coat, which I hard torn especially for the job at hand. We also used to deliver alcohol through friends' windows. It could always be done. How I expected to get better I do not know, but hindsight is a wonderful thing.

When you are high and feel euphoric you cannot see the wood for the trees.. "There is nothing wrong with me mate. It is you who seems to have the problem". BUT when you come down from that high, the desperate low that follows you know damn well that you are ill but have no idea what to do to fix it.

Prior to developing Bipolar I had never been in trouble with the Police and I had a very healthy respect for them. I didn't even have any points on my driving license. Now all of a sudden I had got myself arrested on four separate occasions. Life just seemed so unfair. I was terrified they were going to send me to prison. How would I explain that to my boys? Your mother is a drunken jail bird. Each time I didn't even know what I had been arrested for.

Junie Pritchard

Six years ago I attempted suicide by taking a month's worth of medication. I was in a coma for four days, had my stomach pumped, and spent the next 8 months wishing I were dead. Every single, long, long day. I could not speak for weeks due to the tubes they put down my throat in order to pump my stomach. (At least there were some up sides for the boys). I felt dreadful, looked dreadful and really was no use nore ornament to anybody. Following having my stomach pumped I spent the worst four days of my life in the Redwoods. Now they can stick the Redwoods where the sun don't shine. I refuse to spend another night in there on a mixed ward. I will either escape or they can carry me out in a body bag.

I spent the next 8 months in and out of Psychiatric facilities and did not feel well at least until the following year. And the police who broke into my home to get me out of there were well aware of that fact and yet again they were all over me.

A really horrible WPC called Julie rang me and asked me to attend the Station with an appropriate adult. It transpired that someone had supposedly found a huge bag of what looked like cannabis on my property and they assumed it belonged to me. I had never seen so much of the stuff and it certainly wasn't mine. Yet again I was fingerprinted and was asked to sign what felt like fifty million documents. This happened three times and the last time I was there Julie told me that it was not cannabis at all but a leaf that looked very much like it. Then what the hell are you trying to do me for then you short, fat little poisoned dwarf? How on earth could she be allowed to treat people like that?

I still was not over my last suicide attempt and the Police asked my Social Worker if I would drop the complaint about the pepper spraying that I had made against them. I believed that I would get nowhere anyway as they are a closed shop, so I dropped it. The poisoned dwarf then magically disappeared. She did not even have the courtesy to let me know that the case had been dropped. I think that some of the police are devoid of any emotion when they put that uniform on and they see it as them and us. They seem to believe that they are the good guys and that everyone else is a nasty little criminal. And if you cross one of them you cross them all and they go out of their way to dish up some dirt on you. I'm sure that that ignorant woman will go far in the force.

Come on Julie try and arrest me now. It is so so easy for you to arrest me when I am extremely ill isn't it? And she was well aware of that fact. You would not have such an easy time of it now I am well I can assure you. A flipping bag of leave's. And yet again (and I am sure she will be wringing her hands with glee if she reads this) all of that had an adverse effect on my mental health.

I know that I am lucky for a million reasons. I am physically healthy so what's the big deal? I could be having to manage in a wheelchair or have to cope with a learning disability. Why can't I just appreciate my life for what it is? Ungrateful so and so. As you can gather from this book I have to be aware of turrets like symptoms leaking into my speech. I never used to swear. Now it has become second nature to me and I feel that I can no longer converse or express myself without it. I am ashamed of that too.

CHAPTER 21 Bristol

In that desperate eight months that followed my overdose I was sent to the Priory in Bristol. I live in Powys. How is anyone meant to visit me there, but my lovely nurse Graham arranged it for me because I would rather go absolutely anywhere other than the Redwoods on a mixed sex ward. It held both private and NHS patients. The Priory appeared to be mainly for addictions. I spoke to some of the people there and they told me that to go in there privately cost £750 a night. What??? I wouldn't pay a brass farthing to stay there. It was just a funny farm like all the rest but it served better food. A few of the patients told me that their employers were paying for them to stay there. What??? My employers wished that I was dead, and still do. I think I was in Bristol for about 6 weeks. It was miles away from my home in Wales and Joey could only visit me occasionally. Fair play to my sister Annie and her husband they came to visit me and it was lovely. Jaibo and I used to text and telephone often and together they got me through it. Jai has never visited me in hospital and I am so glad of that fact. I would not have liked him to see me in any of those places, he was much too young.

There were so many young people in there of both sexes who suffered from anorexia and bulimia. Some were so frail and weak they could not get out of a wheelchair. The poor little things. I do not fully understand why young people strive to keep themselves so tiny. Perhaps it is pressure from the media or their peers. It was all so sad.

I believe that the help and support from my children and my family got me through that hellish 8 months in the end. I was in hospital in Bristol when Joey and Hannah came to visit and they announced their engagement and named the day as the following May. Oh my goodness I was overjoyed. Until they left. Yet again I cried what felt like a river. I just wanted to go home with them. Why can I not be with my family? I felt determined to stay alive. The wedding was all that I could think about. If I was not there Joey would have neither of his parents present. I just could not let that happen. I just had to get better no matter what it took. I began exercising in my room. I attended every course they offered me just to get off the ward. I was going to bed at 8.30 every night depending on which nurse was on duty and would give me my meds. What goddamn difference does it make to them if I wanted to go to bed early? I did not particularly gel with any of the patients there, or the nurses so why would I want to stay up?

All that I wanted to do was sleep so that I switch my suicidal thoughts off. However some of the nurses had a real "I think I'm god" complex. The Psychiatrists prescribe your meds for you, but some of them used to refuse to give me the medication the Psychiatrists did prescribe for me. You are nurses not Psychiatrists, what is wrong with you? I also wonder what they did with the medication they refused to give out. It was horrible in Bristol. I did everything I could to get well again. I did everything my Psychiatrist told me to do and I began eating and drinking as much as I possibly could, but I continued to lose weight. These days I am half bulimic. I eat and eat and eat but I forget to make myself sick. Oh god please let me stay alive long enough to see Joey marry the girl of his dreams. My children are my world and I would die for them. I can only imagine what I have put them through over the last fifteen years and I apologise from the bottom of my heart. I cannot change the past but in future I will do everything in my power to be the mother I want to be and hopefully one day, make you proud.

I have been reasonably stable for almost five years now apart from the Cuba incident where I so low and it lasted for months. I have not had an alcoholic drink for eight years and hope that if I continue to abstain from alcohol, I will not experience another high. I really hope and pray that if I avoid stress in my life I will remain stable for the rest of my days but deep down I know that this won't be possible unless a cure is found. According to Stephen Fry 70% of what we believed to be true seven years ago has been proven to be not true at all. I am hoping that no cure for Bipolar will soon be proven to be untrue.

Now I go to bed and think of nice things' like Joey, Jai and Hannah and I pray for them every night and morning. I think of things I have to look forward to, Jai's 25st Birthday, a holiday perhaps, grandchildren, and just hope that this will all be enough to keep me alive. It should be more than enough but Bipolar can just hit you 'bang' out of the blue. But, but but I am alive now and my handsome cage, fighting super hero, Joey, my beautiful super intelligent daughter in law Hannah Banana, and Jaisee, my delicious, sensitive young romantic all love me.

Freedom. Right now I am lying in bed, my favourite place to be, writing this book. I can drink as much coffee as I want, when I want, without having to beg a miserable nurse if I can make one. The only noises I can hear are birds, the occasional traffic going by and the ticking of my clock. No shouting, screaming or wailing. AND my gorgeous little Jaisee is back living with me and Joey and Hannah visit often. My idea of heaven. I cannot believe my luck. Oh please god make it last.

Living the Dream.

People say to me that I am living the dream and to all intents and purposes I suppose I am. I am retired. Therefore have all the time in the world to do what I want to do. I could save up and go anywhere in the world I wanted to (however I have heard that some states in America won't even let bipolar sufferers in). I could save up and buy a flash car, but I don't want one. I used to drive a really cool purple classic mini cooper. I loved driving it as all the children used to wave to me as I drove past them. However, whenever I was admitted into hospital it would be left standing and deteriorating. I have now sold it and walk everywhere. I no longer sit behind the wheel of my car and say to myself "Go Junie and don't spare the horses". These days I travel on Shanks's Pony.

This is how mean I am. I lie in bed listening to the radio reporting on traffic hold ups all over the country and smile to myself and think how lucky I am not to have to do that. I know where I would rather be. None of this matters to me because of Bipolar. I would spend every last penny I had to be free of it. THEN I would be living the dream.

A person's health is everything. If you have your health you can achieve anything you want to. I am always fully aware that I have this condition, and do not feel relaxed enough at present to really be myself, but the person I am right now Joey's and Jai's friends seem to like and I am so proud.

Sometimes what I would really like now is to meet somebody for me. Just me and nobody else. I know that this contradicts what I have written in the past but I kind of would like to now. I guess it is a tall order for a Bi polar person. There is a book called "The secret world of a manic depressive". And this illness was always kept a secret. Quite frankly my dears I don't give a damn who knows any more, otherwise I wouldn't be writing this book, but I do find it embarrassing.

Not by the illness itself just the things that it has led me to have to do i.e. being sectioned. Oh hello what have you done in your life that's interesting? Well, I have spent a total of three years in a lunatic asylum and I was not on the payroll there either. Is that interesting enough for you? Maybe I am experiencing a midlife crisis. Who am I? What have I done with my life apart from being locked up for a total of 3 years in Psychiatric hospitals all over the country? Apparently, I am also going through the change. I just hope I change into something good. I think I am getting over my crisis as I now realise what I have got. I have two wonderful sons who love me dearly. Mother's day is coming up soon and they had better show how much they love me otherwise they will be shot. I am only joking of course. The little darlings. The measure of love is to love without measure.

It is strange when you have a mental illness. Initially people are scared of you. People I have known all of my life used to cross to the other side of the street to avoid me. One man who I had been in Primary School with even asked my sister in law if it was ok to talk to me???? I have Bi Polar I am not mute!!!! I think that most people think you are an axe murderer or something, so if I joke about knocking someone's head off they really think I mean it. But of course I don't.

Sometimes I feel desolate, desperate, suicidal and on occasion believe that the boys would be better off without me, so why not do it? Then I look at my sons' photographs strategically placed in front of my medication and hope and pray that that will be enough to keep me alive. So far it has worked. I cannot remember the last time I had a high. Not that I want one as even though you feel true euphoria, I don't want that either. I just want to be normal as I was before this truly awful illness hit me.

Some Bipolar sufferers I know deliberately don't take their medication so that they can experience that high again. No thank you. Definitely stability for me pleeeeease.

Right now I think that people who I meet believe that there is nothing wrong with me. WRONG. Some people have even said to me that I have been putting it on and that there is nothing wrong with me. What absolute idiots. Do they really think that I would have been locked away against my will for three years away from my children and undergone 12 sessions of ECT if I was putting it on? Why the heck would I put it on? Living on a pittance as opposed to a good Social Work salary? Yeah sure I have put it all on. I tell you what, why don't you try it just for a day and see if there are any benefits to having Bipolar at all, because believe me there are none.

It is lovely being stable. The highs I experience with Bipolar are incredible. But and this is a big but you become extremely vulnerable and risk being sectioned. Once when I was on a high someone asked me if I was on speed. I thought to myself I really don't need it darling. Stuff that. Some people have even offered me cocaine saying that it would make me feel better. I do not wish to go on a high, or a drug induced "journey". Just give me normality any day please. This is where I want to be forever and a day, but I am well aware of the fact that it can rear its ugly head again at any time. Still, my marbles are all present and correct these days so I intend to make the most of it. Motivation determines what you do ability and attitude decide how well you do it.

Sometimes I do not have the motivation to get out of bed. And each time I feel well enough to even contemplate going back to work I fall ill again. Yes life's an f'ing dream. That was then and this is now. Happiness is now where sadness was. I have a lovely life now. I have been ashamed of my behaviour, whatever I did to get me locked in the police cells, what I did to get a life ban from that pub but as Wasi reminds me I was ill. Guilt is a wasted emotion and I no longer feel it. I am not a bad person. I see that in the way my sons have turned out. I do absolutely nothing now that I am retired other than what I want to do. I take care of my home and my garden. I live independently, manage my own finances and actually feel quite normal for the first time in an age, and I am just a metaphor for anyone who has been there before. I'm busy doing nothing all of the whole day through. Do you really wish it was you?

I socialise whenever I want to, but don't drink alcohol and I am enjoying writing this book. Even if other people hate it, it has been a very therapeutic process for me. If you really do not like it you can throw it away. It is completely biodegradable and will not create any more holes in the ozone layer. I sincerely hope you enjoy reading it, but if you don't you can always use it as toilet paper or to light the fire with.

There was once a man who had an obsession for tractors. His walls were covered in posters of tractors, his mantelpiece covered in tractor plates. Tractors tractors, tractors all over the house. His wife, naturally, because she was sane, hated it. So she gave him an ultimatum – the tractors or her. After much thought he decided to get rid of the tractors and promptly took all of the memorabilia to the dump. He returned home to find his house on fire and that the smoke was preventing his wife and kids from finding the door. So the man took a massive deep breath. He sucked in with all his might. The smoke sucked out of the house and his family escaped. Later on, a fire fighter asked him how he did it. "That's easy" he replied. "I am an ex tractor fan".

The female janitor at a man's building asked if I would chill and smoke some weed with her. The man replied "no I can't deal with "high" maintenance women".

The band Electric Light Orchestra are telling me to hold onto my dreams, and my dream is to become a successful author so here goes. None of the names in this book have been changed to protect the guilty, only the innocent. I think I am living life as normally as I possibly can now. I say think because I am always extremely aware of my condition and the thoughts of "am I behaving normally" are almost constant. I am living with my youngest son Jai who does me the world of good and would do anything for me, even though he finds it difficult to spend time with me sometimes. I can be very lively on occasion which I think he finds irritating, but don't make me walk when I want to fly. I occasionally have to cook for him. I really don't think I am cut out for cooking in fact I only have a kitchen because it came with the house.

When you are retired on ill health grounds and locked away for three years of your life you feel useless, worthless and all the rest of it. I should imagine redundancy is pretty hard to take too, however there is usually the possibility of moving on to another job. I don't think I will ever be fit to work for anyone again. I just cannot handle stress any more. Who would want to employ me with my sick record anyway? BUT and this is the biggy, I now see it as a positive. I am FREE. No one can tell me what to do anymore. My freedom means everything to me. I am very much enjoying being a DNB. (A do nothing bitch). I never want to be locked up again, never in a month of Sundays, and in the past the highs are always followed by a devastating low which I do not know how I would cope with again. I most definitely wish to stay stable even though it does feel a little boring sometimes. When you have experienced the highs of Bipolar it is difficult to know where your baseline is and you feel a little flat. However, the highs are just not worth the risk.

Bipolar rarely gives you the chance to build up a resistance to it. As soon as you feel almost well it strikes again, and at my age the episodes are more likely to be lows. Please stop the world, I want to get off. I sometimes feel that now I have a heart of stone. I discussed this with my psychologist Ena. She is the most unlikely Ena I have ever met. She is incredibly intelligent and interesting. She makes me laugh also which is definitely a plus in my eyes. I also tell myself that what doesn't break you makes you stronger. I feel as if I have been completely broken to end up in a Psychiatric hospital and enduring ECT but now with the help of Dr Wasi Mohamad and Ena Sharples I am being put back together again. Who knows, with their help I might just be considered to be normal again one day. I sincerely hope so.

I went to see Ena this week and was five minutes early. I mistakenly asked a woman in the waiting room how she was. Oh my god. She went on to tell me what a bad back she had, that she had to have her feet sorted due to diabetes, her legs were aching, and she had a bad cold. Her husband was outside waiting to be helped in because he had had a hip replacement. All of that in the space of five minutes. I was losing the will to live. Of course I felt sorry for her but all of that fades in comparison to Bi Polar. Almost everyone tells me about their coughs and aches and pains and all the time I am thinking I'm sorry but I cannot cope with hearing about your illnesses as well as my own. You've got a cough? Stop smoking. You have aches and pains? You're getting old it comes with the territory. In future could you all just tell me I am fine thanks, because every day I have to get through this shit show of a life living with Bi polar.

Junie Pritchard

Every morning I pray for "One day at a time sweet Jesus, is all I am asking from you. Please give me the strength to do all the things that you ask me to do. Yesterday's gone sweet Jesus and tomorrow may never be mine. Lord for my sake, teach me to take one day at a time".

Life is definitely what you make it. I laughed with Ena about the people who moan to me and she told me in future to ask people if they are alright instead of how are you? I will certainly do that as I really don't want to hear about other people's illnesses. I know that sounds harsh but I just cannot cope with it. I love going to see Ena. As I said she is incredibly intelligent and we discuss almost every topic under the sun. I'm bored, I'm bored, no wonder you are the chairman of the bored

But I was never bored chatting with Ena. If I were to tell people how I really feel I might end up in hospital again. "Oh today darling I feel so wretched I want to die". No one wants to hear that, particularly not my children.

I will try not to look back anymore, and once this book is complete, I will only look ahead to a hopefully brighter future. My Psychologist really is amazing and will hopefully get to the bottom of why I am Bipolar. I know there is no cure, but I really would like some answers. Ena thinks that it is quite possible that I now have a chemical imbalance in my brain and the chemicals I take every day in the form of medication replaces the ones I am missing. It also seems strange to her and I wholeheartedly agree that I led a perfectly normal life until Claire Turner, Amanda Lewis, Clive Bartley and Jeremy Patterson were in charge of me and treated me like crap following my breakdown which they caused me to have in the first place.

Sometimes when I tell people I don't drink they will say "go on one drink won't hurt, you're not an alcoholic" I think "am I not?" I have never been diagnosed as being so and have thankfully never done any damage to my liver. My mind then plays tricks with me and says have a drink. What if I am remaining abstinent for no good reason? But I tell myself that for me, one drink is too many and two are not enough. And I am fully aware of the effect it has on me mixed with my cocktail of medication and I refuse to do that to myself. Then I think of my children and I don't want to take the risk. Initially it was extremely difficult not to drink as alcohol seems to be everywhere, but now I can honestly say I don't want one. I no longer crave it and my life is so much improved without it. Give me a cup of coffee any day. And I have managed to stay out of hospital for almost five years now. Yay, go me. Oh sorry I do have a sip of communal wine at church once a week and even then Jaisee asked me "what percentage is it mum?"

As I have mentioned I am fondly known as "Trouble" at my Church. I say my Church not because I own it but more from a sense of belonging. I like to think that I behave impeccably whilst I am there. I only take a sip of Communal wine even though I would love to glug the whole Chalice. I cannot wait for the day that I am the person giving out the wine as they get to down whatever is left. I would say to everyone as soon as it hit their lips "that's it that's all you're getting" then I would drink the whole thing to myself. You guys can have the bread but this baby belongs to me". I am only joking of course but I really have thought about it.

Thankfully I have not been in any trouble for a number of years now and I hope that I never will again. I read somewhere that staying out of trouble is boring. I think you can only really say that if you have never been in it. On previous occasions when the Police have tried to pin something on me and I knew that I was innocent I have waivered my right to see a Solicitor because of that fact. I will NEVER do that again. The thought of being done for Criminal damage when I accidentally tore a piece of paper belonging to a little biddy widdy Policeman. Being accused of having a bag of leaves on my property which I had never set eyes on before. For goodness sake. I will always have a Solicitor present even if I have a wild wee in the bushes in the park and they try to do me for indecent exposure, my Solicitor will always be present.

Two tourists are travelling through Llanfairpwllgwyngyllgogerychwyrndrobwlllantysiliogogogoch and argued about the pronunciation. They stopped for lunch and asked could you please pronounce where we are very slowly. The blond girl leans over the counter and says "Burrrger King".

CHAPTER 22. MY LIFE NOW

My life is ok right now. I have two amazing sons and daughter in law who I love more than life itself. I own my home and I have a little money to spare. For short periods of time I can live in harmony and I try and run from Bi Polar, but it is always there in the back of my mind/s. If I am crazy, why do I not feel it? I know it is not normal to have suicidal thoughts to the degree that I do and occasionally I became extremely manic. I have not been manic for a long, long time now and according to Wasi the older I get the more likely it is I am only going to experience lows. Cheers Was. What a little bundle of joy he can be sometimes. However, I am glad that he doesn't try and dress up my illness and tells me the truth. Forewarned is forearmed they say.

On occasion I will discuss this illness with people. I hope that I never moan about it and try to gloss over it. So many of them tell me "oh I think that I have got that as I sometimes get depressed". I try my best to stay calm and of course I feel sorry for anyone in that situation but inwardly I feel like shouting "have you ever been in a Psychiatritic hospital? Have you ever attempted to take your own life? Been given twelve sessions of ECT? Have you ever been so manic you are literally climbing the walls? No? Then the chances are you have not got it". Your average depression is NOTHING compared to a low of Bi polar.

I am constantly aware that I have this horrendous illness and continually ask myself "am I behaving normally?" Because if I am behaving normally why am I classed as mentally impaired? And why have I been locked away from the "community" for three whole years? My friends and family tell me I am behaving normally at the moment but still the questioning is always there. Right now I don't think anyone would guess I have a mental illness. Everyone says I look so well, which is great and another good reason to cut down or cut out drinking, you do look much better but it still feels as if it is raining in my heart.

There is a certain look to someone with an alcohol problem. I can now spot a heavy drinker a mile off, bless them and I definitely had that look. You can never say never to drinking alcohol but I just hope and pray that I don't. I want to be an alcohol free zone for the rest of my life.

I thought that I had completed this book however there has been another twist to my story.

I had been relatively stable for the last two years and it was lovely. I decided that as I had not been on holiday for the last six years due to illness and lack of cash I would go to Cuba. It meant me selling my moped and blowing all of my cash but I thought it would do me the world of good. Originally there were meant to be four of us going. Two males and two females. However two of the people dropped out which left me and a guy named Kenny. We were going for two weeks in November of 2017. Wasi had very sensibly I feel, left Powys and set up his own private clinic. I am so proud of you Wasi. Anyhow at that time I was seeing a psychiatrist named Fran Foster. She practically gave me her life history. Every time I saw her. I think our sessions were more therapeutic for her than it was for me. When I mentioned that I was writing a book she told me that she was too. When I mentioned my sons she told me that she has a darling little son who is in boarding school and has never given her a day's trouble in his life. He bloody wouldn't give her any trouble if he was never at home would he? This is about me not you. I don't even particularly like you and so many people I have spoken with since feel exactly the same way.

Prior to my holiday I felt so well and felt no benefit for seeing her, I asked Fran Foster, my, I do not know what to call her other than a Psychopath in the making to discharge me. I asked her if I were to become ill again could I see her immediately as opposed to going on a waiting list. She assured me that this would be the case. I would never have asked for discharge if I did not have access to a psychiatrist immediately with my history of mental illness.

On the Friday prior to us leaving I had a pre-arranged appoint-

The Forgotten Few

ment with my Care Co-ordinator Laurraine Hamer. I had been prescribed three Valium per day but the GP's had not included this on my prescription. To have obtained the extra Valium I needed I would have had to make an emergency appointment with my GP. The surgery will not issue prescriptions over the telephone. Laurraine offered to obtain my Medication either from my GP or Fran Foster and bring it to my home. I knew that Fran was in the building as I saw her in her office.

With hindsight I should have asked Fran to issue it there and then but she was with a client and I trusted Laurraine. I went home and waited for her. I know from my own experience as a Social Worker you can often work well into the evening. If you bothered to do your job properly that is. I heard nothing from Laurraine. I just assumed that she was running late and I'd left it too late to contact the GP's. I intended to do so the following morning. I could not get through to the GP's on a busy Saturday morning and Kenny was anxious not to hit the heavy traffic. Kenny is a 78-year-old man and the last thing I wanted to do was make him anxious. So we left for Gatwick. I was not overly concerned as I had enough Valium with me for one a day and a prescription for one a day more. I had been prescribed three a day for some time. The second day I was there when Kenny was having his old man nap I approached the travel representative and explained my predicament. She was lovely and she took me to three different pharmacies but none of them stocked Valium and had not even heard of Bipolar. We returned to the hotel where she rang other pharmacies, but nothing. Oh my god. What on earth was I going to do now? I didn't even realise I needed a plan until it went wrong. I racked and racked my brains as to what I was going to do. I thought of flying home but Kenny did not want me to do so and I thought that the relaxation of a holiday may be enough to stop me feeling so anxious. So I stayed. The holiday was the worst of my life. I was more anxious than I had ever been before. I tried to eke out my Valium as much as I could but I felt suicidal and was suffering severe withdrawal symptoms. I was experiencing tremors in my hands and could not even get a cup of coffee to my mouth without spilling it. People were looking at me and I was terrified at the thought of being sectioned in a Communist country. I was so scared. Oh please, please god get me home. I told Kenny again that I wanted to fly home but he assured me he would take care of me. Kenny had spent his life savings on that holiday and I did not want to ruin it for him. I can honestly say I have never prayed so much in my life, not even in Shelton. I begged god to get me home and he did.

Not ONCE in the whole time I was in Cuba did I think that Lauraine had tried to hurt me. I knew what a useless Social Worker she is but that thought never once entered my head.

Two days before we were due to leave Cuba, I text my sister and explained to her that I felt so incredibly ill and asked her to make an appointment for me with Fran Foster. The admin staff who are lovely told her yes of course, that would be no problem, and they would get back to my sister. Joycey rang again and was then told that Fran would not see me and that Laurraine had said that she was due to see me on the Thursday anyway. What??? (I arrived home on the Saturday). I was feeling so desperate and suicidal and the two people who were responsible for my care refused to see me. Wasi has even been to see me in the middle of the night on his night off in the past.

When I eventually arrived home I was suicidal, jet lagged, and the time change for taking my medication had all taken its toll and I could not get out of bed for days. I could not believe that they were doing this to me. I rang the Police and reported them for what I truly believe to be attempted murder. The police stated that it was not a case for them, that I needed to go through Social Services. What? If you truly believed that someone had attempted to end your life who would you call? Social Services or dial 999. I cannot believe that these two women are still working for Powys.

We are now in April of 2021. The holiday was last November 2017. Quick aren't they? I wonder if the Harold Shipman case took so long. Somehow one of my GP's, a Margaret Jones (again no doctor) had found out about my complaint and rang me. She stated that these two women did not try to harm you June. (How the f does she know?) She very abruptly asked me if I was suicidal now. I told her no and that was it. She put the phone down. I then wrote to her saying that I thought that I would be judged in a court of law, not at my GP's surgery. Margaret Jones has known me for what feels like forever and would not have known Fran Foster or Laurraine Hamer very long at all as they are not originally from Powys. I have also not made a single complaint in my life before developing this illness so why on earth does anyone think I would start now? What could I possibly hope to gain from it anyway? Thank you Margaret bach.

I was an avid Sun news paper reader as they exposed the Baby P incident, so I rang them asking them to print my story and they did not want to know stating that they felt it could all be a symptom of my illness. I have Bi polar disorder, I am not delusional or psychotic. My mental health is significantly worse since the whole experience as I believe (and I say believe as I cannot prove it as yet) that those two women wished me dead. What was meant to be a relaxing experience turned out to be the holiday from hell, all due to Social Services, and the Local Health Board. I no longer believe that I will get anywhere with my complaints as who is going to believe someone with Bipolar over these two organisations.

The feeling of no one believing you is really really, unpleasant but I know the truth and I swear on all that is holy I am telling it.

I am extremely aware of the fact that since developing this illness people think that they can do whatever they want to me and get away with it and the sad truth is they can. However I know in my heart of hearts what they attempted to do to me. I really loved to travel but after visiting Cuba and the possibility of being sectioned over there I don't think I want to go abroad again. I have also been told since, that the withdrawals from not having the Valium could have caused me to have a fit. If I did experience a fit would it be followed by more? I lost a stone in weight over there which I could ill afford to lose. My children said that I looked like a skeleton when I got home. Who on earth loses a stone on a two week all inclusive holiday? Laurraine Hamer has even met both my sons. She is the mother of three sons. How on earth does she think her children would feel if she had committed suicide in Cuba or worse still got sectioned in a communist country? I know that I sound bitter and twisted when I talk about these women and that is because I am. I think anyone who found themselves in my position would be too.

What I also find interesting is that this is a revised version of my book. As I said I went to Cuba in 2017. This book was first published in August of 2019 on Amazon for the whole world to see. They were fully aware of the allegations I had made in my book but absolutely nothing has happened. If I were a professional, (in fact I still am as my Social Work qualification has not been stripped from me because of my Bi Polar) I would move heaven and earth to disprove those allegations but they have done nothing. And would you like to know why? Because they are guilty and if a proper investigation were to be carried out interviewing the Admin staff at Brohafren and my sister Joycey that fact would be proven.

Also WPC Rottie Rotweiler you told me that there would be repercussions for me if I published my book mentioning Sgt. Davies. Where are they? Two years later and nothing so why don't you just go and chew on a bone bitch. That is the correct term for a female dog right? I would hate for you to think that I was being as rude to her as she was to me.

When I obviously refused to work with Laurraine ever again another bleached blonde and high heeled creature, named Rebecca

Jones came to visit me. She told me that she was well aware of what happened in Cuba with regard to Fran Foster and Lauraine Hamer. She said "I am here to help you June". We discussed my retirement and she went on to tell me that she had retired but has returned to work two days a week because she liked to help people. Well bully for you darling. Whatever you want to do to make you feel as if somebody needs you. I certainly don't. I think that the money she earns through doing good for other people (not) really should go towards some Botox because she was in desperate need of some. She left my house assuring me that she would bring my medication to me the following day. But did she? No of course not. I have not set eyes on her since. Unless she has had the desperately needed Botox and I didn't recognise her.

Wow the results are in and the verdict is? Nothing at all will happen to those two women. They said that they were sorry about my ruined holiday. Ruined holiday? A ruined holiday is when your kids want to come along with you (only joking darlings I would go to the moon and back with you as that is how much I love you) or the pubs have run out of alcohol. THAT is a ruined holiday. Not wondering every single day what is the best way to kill myself and experience severe withdrawal symptoms from the valium they had deliberately not given me.

I am now seeing Dr Wasi Mohamad again on a private basis. I would prefer to spend my last penny to see that man as opposed to Fran Foster. I really feel like using all kinds of expletives here, but that woman is not worth the bother. And my vicar might read my book.

The stigma attached to being in a Psychiatric hospital is still rife. I am not sure how I would have reacted to someone with such a severe mental illness if I had no experience of it myself. I sincerely hope I would have treated them with respect. I think so. In fact I know so.

I remember going out one evening and a girl was joking about her friend and said "don't worry about her she's on leave from

Shelton". I thought shit so am I. For real. I went to See Dr Wasi Mohamad today. On the way there I had been a little bit tearful. I went straight in to see him. As usual I felt tons better just being there. I answered all of his questions but other than that I was happy just to gaze at him. We discussed my local Mental Health team moving to new premises. He said that Fran Foster was feeling stressed. YES!!!! As I said though he only sees the good in people and said "bless her". I thought to myself "bless her my fat ass" I think she will be a little more than stressed when this book is published. Tee hee hee. He really made my day. However when I went to the rest room I was horrified to see that my eye makeup had spread itself all over my cheeks. (Probably from the tears that I had shed). I looked like I was auditioning to become a band member of Wizard, not going to persuade my Psychiatrist that I was fit to be let loose amongst the general public. Somehow though I managed to convince him that I was. Aaaah. Bless him, not that witch Fran Foster.

My sons and I often talk about grandchildren. Jai is really keen to fall in love, get married and have children. Joey and Hannah both want to establish their careers first. The thought of having grandchildren keeps me teetotal too. That is all fine and dandy and I just hope I stay alive long enough to see it all. I will get well again. I have everyone rooting for me however our life expectancy isn't very high a) due to the amount of heavy duty medication we have to take and b) the very real threat of suicide. I'm sorry if this all sounds a bit morbid and I have tried to make light of it but there is a very dark side to this illness also, and the pain and anguish is indescribable. I cannot begin to tell you what the depressive stage of this illness is like as there are no words to describe it. You are in such emotional pain and turmoil that it makes you bang your head against the wall. I have done that myself and witnessed other women do it and it is such a disturbing sight, it scares me. And self harming. Oh my goodness the sights I saw.

I have stayed out of the funny farm for almost five years now. A minor miracle. Yay, bloody yay. I want a drink to celebrate but I know that I can't. I will make my umpteenth coffee instead. One huge step for Junie, one small step for my loved ones.

The weird thing about being teetotal is that everything is the same. You don't get that high of being drunk, and neither do you get the hangover the following day. But there is nothing I can do to celebrate or commiserate. I really believe that I will be on a mini high if this book is a success and I now accept that justice will never be served and these days I believe I experience a mini orgasm when I have finished the ironing I do not have a man in my life and have given up smoking. I will ask Wasi if the next time he thinks I need sectioning could he please put me in a nunnery.

In the last fifteen years following my diagnosis I have become quite hard. I honestly feel like I don't give a damn about anyone other than my family and friends. But of course I do. When you have been crapped upon by so many people from such a great height as I have, particularly the ones who are paid to help you, i.e. Social Services and the Police you do become hardened inside. They are the very people who have wished me dead. BUT revenge is a dish best served cold. Actually I no longer want revenge. I no longer hate anyone. I no longer view anyone as my enemy but as Sir Winston Churchill say's "you have enemies? Good. That means you have stood up for something, sometime in your life". What is Sir Winston Churchill most famous for? He was the last white man to be called Winston.

I felt so anxious after Cuba. I felt nauseous all of the time and had to force myself to eat. It also made me shake as if I had Parkinson's most of the time. All of those symptoms had gone before that wretched holiday. For a long long, time I felt as if I was almost back to square one, and those two women, Fran Foster and Laurraine Hamer knew exactly what would happen to me without the Valium. They are both still in the caring profession and as I said have both been promoted. Frightening isn't it?

Why don't you both take a year out to find yourselves? You may even find yourselves in a funny farm or a prison cell. Thanks to Fran and Lauraine yet again I went to bed every night wondering if I will see my children again or will I end it all. The poor things must feel the same bless them.

When I have had suicidal thoughts in the mornings for some time I go into Jai's bedroom as I do every night to kiss him goodnight. I know how very much he loves me and I feel ashamed and disgusted with myself for even considering ending my life and leaving him. Each night I pray and pray to God to please keep me alive. And every night I cry myself to sleep. I don't think that anyone has wished me dead before other than the very people who have a duty of care for me. It is quite a strange feeling and one I have never felt before.

When one does feel suicidal there is an absolute compulsion to do it. And yes of course I think of my children. I think of nothing else but. I love them more than life itself. I would gladly give them any organ in my body. Even my heart but of course they already have that. Having Bipolar is like a permanent death threat hanging over your head. You never know when serious thoughts of suicide are going to enter your head. It is difficult to plan ahead because you don't know how your mental health is going to be at that time. Bi polar is similar to an addiction you just have to take each day as it comes. I have a little coin which I read daily. It goes like this; "God grant me the serenity to accept the things I cannot change, courage to change the things I can, and wisdom to know the difference".

When I first became a Social Worker I wanted to change the world. As I said Juney land is a happy place and I wanted to make everyone else happy too. However I did it until my head broke and I now realise I cannot change the world only my own little corner of it. I really do not think I am cut out for domesticity as I hate cleaning and don't particularly like cooking. If the boys on occasion tell me the house is a little untidy I tell them "look, it is me or the house, we can't both look fabulous".

I am a little upset at the moment as my little fairy from the bottom of my garden is pregnant. How did she manage that you might well ask? The poor little thing sat on a toad's tool.

I have always loved boxing and watched a documentary with Frank Bruno the amazing boxer who also has Bi polar. He stated that going to the gym helps him focus, so I have converted my shed into a gym and it really does help. I imagine that I am knocking anyone's head off who has hacked me off that day. I also have a fab new machine at my gym. It does everything! Kit Kat's, Maltesers, crisps......I sometimes give the machine a good kicking and steal a Kit Kat. Are you police officers going to come and arrest me? Come on make my day.

Of course I do not want that. I never want to be arrested again. EVER.

It also helps when I am feeling anxious. I come out of there feeling a whole lot better. I am also spending a lot of time writing this book and that in itself is so therapeutic. It has been a very difficult process but a worthwhile one and as I keep asking "please judge me for who I am and not the label society has put on me". I truly believe that without this book, having the opportunity to tell the truth about the way people have treated me I would have remained in a very dark place. I would have been the person they consider to be nuts and they would have got away with it all. I now accept that they always will get away with it all and if my life is worth just a promotion to Fran and Lauraine so be it. But I know, they know and God knows what they have done. Is that fair? No it is not but I have always fought fairly in the past. I have also been shown how to fight dirty but would never ever do that.

My friends used to say that I should have been born with a Government Health Warning on my back, so maybe I was a little crazy back then but just didn't know it. One of my friends who I used to play football with actually had a card printed saying;

Junie Pritchard

"June Pritchard, party animal for hire". But boy what fun I have had.

CHAPTER 23 WASI

I have seen Wasi today. Yay. I had not seen him for two years. We reminisced about some of the stunts I had pulled. One in particular was when I flew to Nice. This was in the early stages of my Bipolar and I didn't realise that Wasi had complete responsibility for me and when I did not attend appointments he becomes very concerned. Anyhow I didn't realise any of this and jetted off to France. My Social worker rang to find out why I had skipped my appointment. I explained that I was at Gatwick airport and was going to France with a very old friend who was a doctor. She seemed reasonably happy with this explanation but on my return I told them that he was a doctor of Physics not medicine. Poor Wasi. I really don't know how he copes with me. I asked what they would have chosen, the South of France or a dingy little office in Newtown? Wasi told me that I should write a book and at last I could tell him I have.

Oh my goodness the saga goes on. I went to see Wasi and as always came away feeling better than when I went in. I got home and began to put my medication into Dossett boxes, which is a minefield when you are taking so many tablets a day, and most of them look the same. I realised I hadn't got enough for that night. I spent 2 hours ringing the GP's, Home Crisis team and Shropdoc which is extremely stressful in itself as I am well aware that without my medication I could commit suicide or worse still get locked up again. Shropdoc assured me that I would be ok for one night but get them in the morning. These are repeat prescriptions; Dr Mohamad had made no changes to my meds therefore they should have been waiting at Boots for me. Surprise, surprise they were not there. This happens every single month. I believe that Doc Porter can't even count because he always gets them wrong. When I see Wasi he writes to my GP's with a copy to me and another to my Care Coordinator. Following my complaint about them, I have received a letter from Dr Porter stating that the letters they receive from Wazi are not always clear. Can't you f'ing read now either? Wasi speaks perfect English. I can understand them easily and have much less medical training than he has.

On another occasion they had not prescribed my Valium. I rang the surgery and spoke to that pratt Porter. He told me that he would prescribe them for me and that I could come and pick them up right away. I don't suppose that he knows that I no longer have a car, but obviously knows my address. Even if I had driven it would have taken at least twenty minutes to get there. Walking would have taken me half an hour. I felt so ill that I could not face the walk. I rang the home treatment team. One of the nurses who was based ten minutes away agreed to pick them up, but not before telling me that I am responsible for handling my own medication. You bloody try looking after it when you are taking sixteen tablets a day and they all come in dribs and drabs. Anyway, she left straight away but when she got to the surgery it was closed. Doc Porter would obviously have known that. Oh how I dislike that man, not enough to head butt him, I left that to somebody else. And they wonder why I get anxious. My Care Co-ordinater (whose job it is to get my meds sorted by the way) has often commented that she doesn't know how I stay so patient with him.. The trick is never expect anything and you won't be disappointed. I fully expect my meds to be wrong each month so I just have to deal with it. The same thing happened again this month. Yay.

I have not had the need to see a GP in ages as physically I am absolutely fine. I don't even know who the GP's are any more but I have to see a nurse on a regular basis to have my blood levels checked and an ECG in case there is a problem with the levels of medication I am on. Since good old Doc Porter has retired (it could be a coincidence) but the atmosphere in the surgery is so much better. Even though they are working under extreme pressure due to Covid everyone is extremely proficient and pleasant, and my medication has been spot on for months now. Maybe Porter was horrible to members of staff as well as patients, who knows.

People have been a little concerned about my mental health recently due to lockdown and I am well aware that others have really struggled with it bless them. But to my mind being on lockdown is a million times better than being locked up.

There has recently been an assault in my local park. The same park I was attacked in. On this occasion the park was cordoned off by the police. At least this time they were attempting to do something about it so why couldn't they do the same for me? Still at least there is hope for women in future.

A woman goes into the Police Station and tells the Duty Officer that she had been graped. The Officer asks "don't you mean raped?" She replied "no there was a bunch of them". At least in my case there was not even a pear of them.
The Sun newspaper would not print my story so I am doing it myself. My father was right. He told me that if you want a good job jobbed, do it yourself so I am.

Occasionally I will bump into someone I know in the street and they ask me what am I doing now? I am too embarrassed to tell them I am disabled so I tell them about my book. They then normally go on to say "oh so you're not working then?" I think "blimey are you my father reincarnated?" Not working? I have shed blood sweat and tears over this book (well not the blood bit, no more self harming for me) but I have spent years writing it and if you happen to think it is ok, then it has all been worthwhile.
I felt a bit fed up today so to cheer myself up I watched my wedding video backwards. I love the end where I take the ring off, go back down the aisle, jump in the car and fuck off

I am getting a bit fed up of these racist jokes. As I said I am not racist or any other kind of ist I promise you. I treated black people the same as anyone else even when I was young. When I was a kid my best friend was black and we played together all the time. Until my dad sold him. Chin chin and lashings of gin. I

Junie Pritchard

feel a bit bad about telling that joke but you have got to be bad to know what good is.

I have just received a text message saying "every time I see you I smile. When you walk, I laugh. When you speak I get excited. For some reason retarded people amuse the F out of me". Gee thanks. Today has not been a good day either. I have been looking through my bank statements and Sky TV has periodically taken the grand total of £595.12 from my account. I ordered Sky last year and engineers came to my home on three separate occasions. While the engineers were present Sky was working fine but as soon as they left my property it stopped working. I really wanted to be able to view Sky so I rang them again. They assured me that they would send an engineer to my home on a particular day between 1 and 5pm. No one arrived so I rang and cancelled the service which I had never received. I rang Sky today and they denied that I had rung to cancel, therefore were unaware that I had no service. A) I did ring them. And B) if their engineer didn't bother to show up to enable me to have a service in the first place and I had returned my Sky boxes how on earth did they think I was going to be receiving a service? I asked them if they would be prepared to pay almost £600 for a service they hadn't received would they be happy. They replied "no". So why on earth do they expect me to? To top it all off they then told me that they were going to approach a debt collecting agency as I owed them another £200. What? I really was losing the will to live at this point but I didn't swear at them once.

When I was studying law, which I admit was a long time ago and the law may have changed for the worse, I was told that to create a binding contract I had to be receiving a service which I would then pay for. I have never received a service from them so what exactly am I paying for? At the end of the conversation, the idiot on the other end of the phone asked "is there anything else I can help you with today?" What does she mean anything else? She hadn't helped me with anything other than ruining my entire day.

My Mental Health Advocate rang Sky on my behalf trying to appeal to their better nature but they really don't have one. Prior to ordering Sky I had a box which enabled me to watch free view tv. I got rid of that box when Sky's engineer fitted theirs. Thanks to them I am now unable to watch any tv at all. Goddamn It might make me resort to having sex. Apparently most babies are conceived during a power cut with no tv to watch. And they wonder why I am annoyed with them. I will give you 50 million guesses. I rang them AGAIN as I was terrified of the bailiffs showing up at my door. I spoke to a lady there. I overheard her discussing me with her colleagues and told them that my Mental Health Advocate had rung and she called me mental. I would love to show her just how mental I can be.
They even had the nerve to send me a text asking how I rated their service on a scale of 1 to 5. I replied "what do you fucking think?" Again I am only joking. I didn't I just felt like it.

I wonder if you have to pass an idiocy and rudeness test before they get their jobs with Sky as she would have passed with flying colours. I heard on the news today that Sky has been bought out. They described Sky as one of Britain's favourite companies. Who says? Certainly, not me. Tomorrow I will contact the Ombudsman. First Everest and now Sky. What the heck is wrong with these people and just what kind of stress do they think that they cause a "mental" person.

It seems to me the bigger the company they are the more ruthless they become. That's probably how they made themselves big in the first place. Anyhow, I am not going to spend the evening worrying about these useless, money grabbing companies as life really is too short. The Sky is the limit
I see Wasi on Wednesday and I'm sure he will put everything into perspective for me. As he always has done.
Lots of poor people with Mental Health problems lose everything including their home and sometimes even their children. Is it hardly surprising when huge companies treat us this way?

However I am one of the lucky ones. I love living in my little cottage with my children, family and friends calling and meeting up for lunch. Obviously not a liquid lunch but a very enjoyable lunch none the less. If I hadn't got Bipolar my life would be practically perfect. I tell myself how lucky I am with everyone and everything I have.

The one that really gets me is when people tell me that their wife has left them and they were depressed for weeks and they say "I know how you feel now". Have you got Bi polar? No. Have you felt suicidal every day for months on end? No. Then you have no idea how I feel. Oh you poor little sausage. Have you ever asked yourself why she left you anyway, you miserable self centred bore? The pain and anguish you feel with this disorder is nothing in comparison. I am not trying to belittle depression but there really is no other feeling like Bi polar.

People like Robbie Williams, Stephen Fry, Catherine Zeta Jones, Frank Bruno who all have this disgusting illness and appear to be living normal lives and Sir Winston Churchill who also suffered from Bi Polar and called his depressive stages "his black dog". They are my inspiration. I mentioned that Hitler had it also. Not a very good claim to fame and no inspiration to me at all.

I seem to have one of those stupid faces that people just want to moan to. Please please dont moan to me. Go and see a Counsellor if you need to but please don't moan to me. See how hard I have become? Maybe it is because I feel so bad myself I just cannot cope with other people's problems anymore. I did it for ten years at Social Services and my head cracked. I obviously do not wish anyone any harm, but I am sorry I just cannot cope.

I was talking to a man I'd never met before and after a short time he asked if I would meet him for coffee sometime. It was a beautiful sunny day and he went on to say "we're going to pay for this." I asked what he meant "we are going to pay for it." He replied "it will probably rain for the next month". Oh my goodness another flipping moaner. No way did I want coffee with him so I said my goodbyes. Why do people do it?

I have recently met a man who I quite like. He may not be my Mr Right but he is my Mr Right Now. Uh oh my possible Mr Right has turned out to be Mr Wrong. He appeared to be more interested in my body more than my mind but unfortunately they both come as a package. But does this face look bothered? Absolutely not! I am free again.

There's a new Belgian lager on the market exclusively for women. It's called Fellas Artwats. Don't they realise that girls just want to have fun?

These sayings just about sum up men and women for me.
Here are the male version: Why beer is better than a woman: You always know how much beer costs. You don't have to wine and dine beer. Your beer will always wait patiently for you in your car while you play football. When your beer goes flat you just toss it away. Hangovers go away. A beer doesn't get jealous if you grab another one. Beer labels come off without a fight. When you go into a bar you always know you can pick up a beer. Beer never has a headache. A beer won't be upset if you come home and have another beer on your breath. You can have more than one beer a night and not feel guilty. You can share a beer with your friends. You always know you're the first one to have a beer. If you change beer you don't have to pay maintenance. A beer doesn't demand equality. You can have a beer in public. A beer doesn't care what time you come home and a beer is never late. And women: Women just know: Q. How many honest, intelligent, caring men in the world does it take to do the dishes? A. Both of them. Q. How does a man show that he is planning for the future? A. He buys two cases of beer. Q. How many men does it take to change a roll of toilet paper? A. We don't know; it has never happened. Q. Why is it difficult to find men who are sensitive, caring and good looking? A. They already have

boyfriends. Q. What do you call a woman who knows where her husband is every night? A. A widow. Ouch. Q. Why are married women heavier than single women? A. Single women come home, see what's in the fridge and goes to bed. Married women come home, see what's in bed and go to the fridge. Man asks god: "God why did you make woman so beautiful?" God says "so you would love her." But god, the man says "why did you make her so dumb?" God says: "So she would love you."

We are having a beautiful summer this year in Wales. However there are a couple of flies in my home and I cannot bear to kill them. I just tend to ignore them. Jaibo absolutely hates them. The little weasel has just told me that we have more flies in our house than I have brain cells. I have let him live as he may have a valid point. And am I bothered? No not one iota.
When I go into town or anywhere where there are lots of people I still become very anxious. I tell myself that I have spent three years in the Army, three years in Psychiatric hospitals all over the country so I'm sure I can cope with this. It doesn't really work but I tell myself anyway.

I am home now writing this book having been discharged into the Community. I am even allowed out without a nurse these days. Whooo lucky me. Whether you are high, low, or stable when you are Bi polar you feel as if you are constantly walking a tightrope, just dreading falling off and getting ill again. It is so horrid. I absolutely abhor Bi polar. I hope in time it gets easier and I only think of it occasionally rather than constantly.

A recent report in my local newspaper said that 76% of 14 year olds living in our poorer housing estates regularly binge drink. Who on earth is looking after their children? Joke.

Pringles condoms; once you pop you just can't stop. Burger king condoms: home of the whopper. Andrex condoms; soft strong and very long. Polo condoms; the one with the hole. Oops.

A smile is a sign of joy. A hug is a sign of love. A laugh is a sign of happiness. And a crazy friend like me…..that's just a sign of f'ing good taste.

Stallholder on the market shouts "blow up dolls £40". Guy says to him "I bought one here yesterday and it went down on me"… Man shouts "blow up dolls now £80".

I have just been arrested. I was in my car dying for a pee, so I did it in a coke can. Police stopped me and asked what was in the can? I am now being done for possession of canopiss. Hard luck WPC Julie. I don't even drive.

Jen and I are going to life drawing classes next week at my local art gallery. I have stipulated though that if we draw each other she has to make my tits look much bigger. She said she would be delighted. Ginny is joining us next month. Yay. Way to go us nutters.

I have been to the cinema to watch Mama Mia 2. I sat there without tremors or shakes and it so made me laugh. One particular line I liked was when two women clocked this absolutely gorgeous older man, and one of them said; "Oh please let his wife be dead". Ha ha I love it.

The only person I would like to apologise to in this book is Dr Wasi Mohamad as even though he suggested that I write a book I feel sure that he had no idea how disparaging towards services I would be, or how hardened I have become. So sorry Wasi. I take full responsibility for my actions.

My favourite hymn is Amazing Grace. I feel that the first verse so applies to me. "Amazing Grace, how sweet the sound, that saved a wretch like me. I once was lost but now I'm found, was blind but now I see."
I feel that my head speaks a language that no one understands,

but now my soul is restored to where once was a hole and I am who I was born to be, even though tomorrow may never come for me for all I know.

Bi polar. Me? I prefer the term "emotionally action packed". We are experiencing a huge undertaking in Newtown at present. We are having a bypass built around the town. My friend has just told me that the leader of the Eco Warriors has died. I thought he was serious until he stated that he died because he refused to have a bypass.

He also told me that a little test tube baby is pulling through and has printed on the back of his t shirt "my dad's a wanker". I know quite a few of them. Perhaps I should go into the t shirt printing business.

My friend Glyn has just visited me and we have been discussing World Affairs. He said that the world has gone mad. I replied "no I think it's just me". He then said "well if you are mad there should be more of you about". Aahh bless.
A young boy went into School and apologises to his teacher for being off School the previous day. He explained that his grand-dad had got burnt. The teacher asked "was it serious?" The boy replied "I think so miss, they don't fuck about at the Crematorium".

I saw Graham Jennings the CSO in town the other day and he gave me his best make your heart melt smile (Sorry Mrs Graham but you know the one I mean). He really is a nice guy as the first time I met him was at a School fete which I took my mum to. My poor mother was bent over and had severe tremors in her hands due to the Parkinson's. He treated her like the absolute lady that she was which was lovely but Graham darling you were a little too nice as all I heard on the way home was "who was that lovely young man Junie?" His name is Graham mum. Who was that

lovely young man? His name is still Graham mum. A twenty five minute trip home, over and over again. What is that young man's name Junie? His name is Bill mum. Aaah Bill. Next time Graham please ignore the old biddies. You can cause huge problems for their families. I am joking of course. He has an air about him that makes you feel safe. I really don't think that he would let anyone hurt me however ill I become. Bless him.
Graham is also a black belt in Karate. He used to teach it in the next room to my kickboxing classes. I used to occasionally take a sneaky peak. He was amazing and I definitely would not want to fall out with him. Not that I ever could I don't think as he is just so nice.

On the 20/12/18 I rang the Police and asked if they could verify that Sgt Davies was the officer involved in my attempted rape case. The young lady explained that she could not give me his/her name. However she was pleasant enough. I rang again in order to cover myself and said that my book will be published early next year???? so unless you tell me otherwise it is staying as Sgt Davies. She said that I would have to write and ask his permission beforehand. What?? He/she didn't write to me asking if they could do jack shit in an attempted rape case. She then said in a very aggressive manner something along the lines of "if you publish a book you will have to take the consequences" Yeah really? Do you think Enid Blyton had to take any of this shit?

My taxes go to you to take care of me not to threaten me. She sounded like a cross between a thug and a Rottweiler.

A young woman from Newtown Police Station rang me today regarding the request I made for an audio transcript I requested of the conversations with Robocop. She informed me that the first call (with the pleasant lady) had been answered by someone in Newtown and that call had been recorded. She proceeded to inform me that the second and third call had gone to Robocop in Brecon who do not record their calls. I asked for Robocop's name and they said they did not know it. I told her that I found that very coincidental, but she continued to lie. It would have been so easy to send an email asking who was on duty that day in Brecon. This basic bit of policing has obviously proved too difficult for her. What f'ing hope have we got of them actually solving any crimes? It doesn't bode well for the future does it.

I wonder why the station in Newtown does record calls, but Brecon doesn't. Surely the people of Brecon deserve the same level of service (or complete lack of service in my case) that the people of Newtown do? She told me untruths from the beginning to the end of the conversation. In my view she should be made to go on the Jeremy Kyle show and made to take a lie detector test which she would fail for certain. Also if she doesn't improve her lying techniques she really won't go very far in the Police force.

When you call the Police you are told that you are through to Dyfed Powys Police. ALL calls are recorded for training purposes. It does not say all calls apart from Brecon are being recorded. This does not make sense to me at all and if it doesn't make sense it is not true. She absolutely lied her tits off.

When I think of good policing I have to mention Aileen. I bumped into K, the young lady who had developed a drink problem. She was very drunk and becoming verbally aggressive, not to me but towards passers-by. Aileen arrived and low and behold she did not put K in a head lock or handcuff her. In fact she did not attempt to restrain K at all. She calmed her down purely by talking to her. When Aileen left Kim did also. And do you know what Aileen did? She came back to see if I was alright. Now that is how Policing should be done. Ten out of ten to the girl.

Policing reminds me of a Jethro joke I've heard. The police pulled him over whilst driving. The Police officer asked him how much he had had to drink. Jethro replied "I've had 8 pints of lager, 3 whiskies and 4 brandies". The officer then asked him to blow into a breathalyser. Jethro asked him "don't you bastards believe anything?"

Methinks that they are the ones who tell lies. I have been told that the recordings exist and that I have to contact Data Protection, but I really cannot be bothered

How do you know when a blonde is having a bad day? When her tampon is behind her ear and she can't find her pencil.
I'm a blue tit and I've had a bit. I'm a dove and I've had some lurrrv. Then there's a duck…..who say's "I'm a drake and there's been a mistake".
I spend an awful lot of time in my sister Joycey's shop now. We have such fun together. She is bombarded with phone calls from different energy companies bless her. I just love answering the phone to them. They ask if they can speak to the owner. I sometimes tell them that she is having an illicit affair and has eloped. Other times I tell them she is dead. And you know what? They still try to make a sale and ask if there is anyone else they can speak to? NO!!!
As I said Joey runs a gym named Empire Gym. I have trained there in the past but I now have my own gym. OH MY GOD. Ladies, if you want to see some amazingly fit men go to Empire gym. Don't worry if you don't train hard, just oggle. (Please don't tell Joey I said that). Work as hard as you can. The women are fit too of course but they are not what I concentrate on. I have been told that the fittest people are cheerleaders, but after seeing

Junie Pritchard

both, my money is on the Mixed Martial Artists.

Here is a photograph of my gorgeous, handsome son at Empire Gym.

This is my beautiful romantic son Jai. Do you think for even one second that these boys should have to live without their mother? Laurraine Hamer and Fran Foster so obviously did.

I am going on a bicycle ride with my friend Dickie tomorrow. I have not ridden a bike for years. If I get a little bored I am going to remove the saddle and really have some fun.

I have recently been Baptised at All Saints Church. Wow. What an amazing experience. I feel so happy. I now believe that even if I get sectioned into one of those truly horrendous places again that God will be sitting beside me holding my hand. This is a photograph of my very dear friends who sponsored me. Joey and I are in the middle.

Junie Pritchard

Oh my life. I have just had coffee with my ex-client who is still my friend. He has told me about the amount of sexual abuse he suffered at the hands of female Social Workers when he was a minor here in Powys. He has told me their names and has witnesses to some of the abuse. I one hundred per cent believe him but it is not my story to tell. I have advised him to contact the Police but he does not want to. HOWEVER if any service treats either me or my loved ones (and he is included in that) in an untoward manner I WILL whistle blow and I will metaphorically blow Social Services in Powys apart.

I have now given the young man's name to Social Services in the hope that he gets the help he so desperately needs and these despicable Social Workers are banged to rights

On a very serious note, if you are anywhere near Shrewsbury in Shropshire and feel unhappy or worse I thoroughly recommend paying Dr Wasi Mohamad's Mental Health and Wellbeing Services LTD. Building 2 Charlesworth Court, Off Knights Way, Battlefield Enterprise Park, Shrewsbury, SY1 3AB. I almost guarantee you come out of there feeling better than you went in. It is a private clinic but it is only the cost of a really nice handbag. That was for you Claire. X I am sure there will be a huge fallout when this book is published but you know what? Bring it on. I hope that this book helps to rid the stigma which surrounds Mental illness and helps sufferers realise that they can come out the other side with a great future ahead of them. Please just hold on for dear life. You will get better.

I am going to think of all the amazing people who have Bi Polar including Sir Winston Churchill and I am hoping that one day I will embrace this illness as part of who I am. As Winston say's "I am ready to meet my maker. Whether my maker is prepared for the great ordeal of meeting me is another matter" and I think that applies to me too.

What I have to do now is find a way to make some money because like a baker, I need the dough.

A concerned young mother to be asks her midwife "what position will I be in for the birth?" The midwife replies "pretty much the same position at the time of conception really".

Junie Pritchard

I wish that I could meet Doctor Who and step into his tardiss, go back in time, to a time after my children were born but before I worked for Social Services. If that were possible I would never, ever have stepped foot in the place.

I am now spending my time knitting scarves for Dr Who's darlekks. It goes like this; knit 8, pearl 8, extermin 8. One then casts off. This is a technical term known by knitter's and nutter's alike.

When this has been done the scarf is then complete. And so is this book.

Please take especially good care of yourselves,

June.

Printed in Great Britain
by Amazon